ENDING
MEN'S VIOLENCE
AGAINST
THEIR PARTNERS

ENDING
MEN'S VIOLENCE
AGAINST
THEIR PARTNERS
One Road to Peace

RICHARD A. STORDEUR
RICHARD STILLE

SAGE Publications
International Educational and Professional Publisher
Newbury Park   London   New Delhi

For information address:

SAGE Publications, Inc.
2455 Teller Road
Newbury Park, California 91320

SAGE Publications Ltd.
6 Bonhill Street
London EC2A 4PU
United Kingdom

SAGE Publications India Pvt. Ltd.
M-32 Market
Greater Kailash I
New Delhi 110 048 India

Printed in the United States of America

Library of Congress Cataloging-in-Publication Data

Stordeur, Richard A.
    Ending men's violence against their partners : one road to peace /
Richard Stordeur and Richard Stille.
        p.   cm.
    Includes bibliographical references (p.   ).
    ISBN 0-8039-3499-8. — ISBN 0-8039-3500-5 (pbk.)
    1. Wife abuse — Prevention.   2. Abusive men — Counseling of.
I. Stille, Richard   II. Title.
HV6626.S76   1989
362.82'92 — dc20   89-27851
                                                                       CIP

94   15   14   13   12   11   10   9   8   7   6   5

CONTENTS

FOREWORD

Eleven years ago, I was writing a paper, "Domestic Violence: Issues in Designing and Implementing Programs for Male Batterers," for a panel I chaired in August 1978 at the meeting of the American Psychological Association in Toronto. This week I finished reading the publisher's draft of this book, *Ending Men's Violence Against Their Partners*. I was struck by all that has been accomplished in the interim and by all that is left to be done.

In 1978 there were only a handful of individuals who were intentionally developing intervention programs for men who batter. I had asked four people to be on that original APA panel; only two of us had actually counseled batterers. A few people here and there across the United States started programs. For the most part, we had no contact with each other, and there were no books on how to do this counseling. Our approaches evolved out of knowledge about domestic violence gained from the battered women's movement and a commitment to working directly with perpetrators of this abuse. Some of us tried well-respected individual, couples, or family counseling approaches for batterers, only to see these approaches fail over and over again. By 1978 we had left behind those inadequate theories and embarked on a variety of specialized programs for perpetrators of domestic violence.

These specialized programs attempted to overcome the weaknesses found in traditional individual, couples, or family approaches to this problem. The goal of the intervention became ending the batterer's violence rather than "curing" individual, marital, or family pathology. Holding the individual accountable for his battering became the hallmark of the specialized programs. A recognition of the victim's need for safety and self-determination replaced victim-blaming strategies. Counseling was provided to perpetrators in groups separate from victims. Psychoeducational approaches were developed and used. The violence is seen as the result of individual, family, and societal dynamics. Consequently, treatment had to focus on all the dimensions that influence perpetrators to batter. While there were differences in content, these were the commonalities of the specialized programs.

These programs brought us as therapists out of our offices into contact with law enforcement, criminal justice systems, victims' advocates, educators, religious institutions, and, of course, many more batterers. What we learned from those experiences we put into workshop presentations or brief articles. For the first time, we started to meet each other, to discuss differences, and to reflect collectively on our experiences, and the oral tradition of this field began. Intertwined with the oral tradition, a few treatment or intervention manuals were written in both Canada and the United States. Many of these original manuals are referenced in this volume. Programs multiplied in both countries, and research about perpetrators started to appear in professional journals. For the first time, books about treatment for those who batter women appeared on the market.

At the same time, the battered women's movement had successfully brought widespread attention in North America to the crippling effects of domestic violence. As attention to the problem increased, so did the number of ways to provide intervention for perpetrators. Discarded marital and family theories of domestic violence have become popular again, largely among those who have a professional attachment to those theories rather than experience with domestic violence. Sometimes these "couples" or "family" programs are cited as "new" techniques, without the historical perspective that they are the same old approaches that were used for years before the specialized programs were developed and then were rejected for being inadequate.

Unfortunately, victim blaming has once again become popular as we struggle with the demands of epidemic domestic violence. It seems easier to label victims of domestic violence as "participating in their own victimization," "enablers," or "codependents" than to acknowledge the power of one intimate's violence to shape the behavior and attitudes of another. Somehow, if we can find fault in the victim's behavior or in her family of origin, we do not have to accept the reality that she is like us and that we too are vulnerable to victimization. It seems easier to work with the victim's so-called problems than to hold the batterer accountable, to work at his rehabilitation, and to alter the social mores that foster his violence. Victim blaming may be easier, but that does not make it right.

The more we know about the problem, the more we understand how deeply embedded it is in the culture. While most people would say that they do not believe a man should kill his wife, many are reluctant to change the male models that set men up to desire power and control over others as a sign of their manliness. In a recent newspaper article headlined "Turning Out Wimps? Day Care Lacks the Male Influence" (*Seattle Times*, May 11, 1989; originally printed in the *Wall Street Journal*), it is clear that not being aggressive and violent toward others is viewed as being weak and unmanly. The article describes a man with 15 years of day-care experience promoting his "positive roughhousing gear" for preschoolers. The purpose of the pint-sized foam battering rams is to foster "power, bravery, courage, fortitude, strength, and stamina" by having the children hit each other with the foam tools while screaming, "Kill each other! Blow each other's heads off!" The proponent of the gear provides a simple message: "Female mollycoddling is turning America's tykes into wimps." He ignores the research findings that show that teaching children aggression only fosters aggression against others rather than providing ventilation for steamed-up children. The more children do it, the more they want to do it. The more men are violent, controlling of others, the more they want to do it. After all, the alternative is to be seen as a wimp.

A few pages later in the same edition of the newspaper, we see the logical extension of this male model of power: "Behind Closed Doors: Marriage Deteriorates, Woman Loses Life." An ex-marine (definitely not a wimp) shot his wife to death after years of domestic violence and then stole a plane from the Boston airport and buzzed the downtown area while shooting from the window of the plane. Social mores change slowly, and in the meantime more of us become victimized by the lust for power and control over others.

While *Ending Men's Violence Against Their Partners* focuses on counseling for men who are violent against their partners and not on all the social forces contributing to the problem, the counseling is based on a clear understanding of these roots of domestic violence. The authors provide detailed descriptions of assessment interviews, initial contacts, and the three stages of the treatment group process.

The book expertly steers the therapist new to this work through a maze of complex issues. For counselors well seasoned in working with batterers, it offers an insightful way to reflect on their own programs. *Ending Men's Violence Against Their Partners* provides just that: one way to assist those who are violent in becoming more peace-filled in their intimate relationships.

—Anne L. Ganley

PREFACE

Fifteen years ago there were virtually no counseling programs for assaultive men on this continent. Small, under-funded, obscure organizations pioneered these programs in the late 1970s as a response to the emerging awareness of the plight of battered women. The first half of the 1980s saw professional, mainstream social services beginning counseling services for wife abusers. By 1984 there were over two hundred programs in the United States and more than thirty in Canada.

Those of us who worked in these early programs had to learn from each other through personal, shared information, occasional journal articles, and conferences and workshops. Occasionally, books appeared on counseling wife assaulters. No single work described batterers' counseling in a detailed, thorough presentation.

We began this book a few years ago with this goal in mind. This book will instruct the counselor in particular clinical skills, strategies, and program content. It will present a group treatment program as the treatment of choice, but will also lead the reader through the preparatory stages of individual assessment and counseling.

There are limits to what we present in the book. We have developed a theoretical perspective through our work and the treatment we describe comes out of this perspective. Although we have briefly reviewed other approaches, it is beyond the scope of this book to describe them thoroughly. Should the reader wish to have a more complete knowledge of couples counseling with batterers, for instance, that knowledge will have to be acquired elsewhere.

In addition, the treatment approach described here addresses physical violence as its primary focus. Although we address other forms of abusive behavior, including psychological, emotional, and sexual abuse in relationships, treatment which would attempt to adequately address these issues is likely to be long-term. Our treatment approach starts men on the road to peace, it does not describe their journey to the end of the road.

The book is divided into four parts. The first part examines current theory and research in the area and identifies what we believe to be the most salient and essential factors in understanding the wife assaulter. The second part of the book examines preparatory work, including first contacts and assessment prior to entering the group program, and details crisis intervention work with batterers.

The third part of the book covers the group treatment program. We treat each activity to be accomplished in treatment as a module. The final part covers counselors' issues, examining the personal impact of this work on counselors and salient interpersonal issues with co-workers.

Our advice to the reader is to use this book as a practice guide, but to continue to read and consider the exciting new thoughts which emerge constantly in this field. One of the rewards of working in the field of domestic violence (and you will need rewards if you choose to work with violent men) is the sharing of ideas with some of the brightest and most exciting people in any clinical discipline.

We recognize that counselors working with violence come from a variety of professional and para-professional backgrounds and represent a variety of political viewpoints. Many counselors are sensitive to nuances of the terms "counselor," and "therapist." We treat them as synonyms, for both strive to systematically help others change. Neither implies psychopathology in our clients and should not be construed as a departure from our view that battering is primarily a social rather than psychological problem.

As with any major project, a great deal of encouragement, assistance, and support has been provided by colleagues and friends. We have been strongly influenced and informed by the Domestic Abuse Project of Minneapolis, Minnesota and the Domestic Abuse Intervention Project of Duluth, Minnesota both in the development of our own clinical approaches and in the writing of this book. The reader will find them referenced often throughout the book.

We wish to thank Daniel Sonkin and John Briere for encouraging us to write this book and for their continuing support through the pitfalls of writing and publishing. Cornelia Wicki and Marsha

Runtz have also provided us with immeasurable amounts of support and encouragement through the project.

Gloria Rixen, Anne Hartung, and Orvin Lommen of the Domestic Violence Treatment Program at North Central Human Services Center in Minot, North Dakota provided valuable editing comments and content suggestions in early drafts, as did Linda Grottelueschen of Women's Action Program in Minot. Lucy Berliner and Paula Pasquali have also given us valuable suggestions for parts of the book. Thank you to all. We would also like to thank our editor, Charles (Terry) Hendrix at Sage, as well as his assistant, Christine Smedley, for supporting the work and providing valuable assistance throughout the project.

We would like to express our appreciation to our colleagues in this field, as a group. They are too numerous to name individually, but their insight, courage, and dedication has both taught us and inspired us. Finally, we would like to thank the men who had the courage to ask for help and to begin that first step on the road to peace. We hope to see more of them as we travel down this road together.

PART I

THEORETICAL
PERSPECTIVES

1

PERSPECTIVES ON WIFE ASSAULT

Fifteen years ago, specialty counseling programs for men who assaulted their wives or partners were virtually nonexistent. There was little, if any, professional literature addressing the evaluation and treatment of batterers. Since the early 1970s, the women's movement had begun to identify the extent and impact of the problem on women in our culture and addressed the problem by working to provide safety and support for victims of male violence. As public attention to battered women increased, counseling programs for assaultive men gradually developed. Many of these programs had their origins in "nonprofessional" grass-roots men's organizations that were sympathetic to feminist concerns. Many developed in conjunction with shelter programs, while others began in more traditional mental health settings. Many of these organizations had a broader focus in their desire to change traditional male roles and to challenge male privilege.

As specialty services for wife abuse increased, more research was published and journal articles and the occasional book on counseling wife assaulters began to appear. Today there is an accessible body of literature reflecting current theory and practice in counseling batterers, although there is still very little research on outcome success (Sonkin, Martin, & Walker, 1985).

As in any scientific and clinical field, there is a great deal of controversy regarding the causes of men's violence toward women and the appropriate treatment to end that violence. There is debate as to what constitutes "violence" and how broadly or how narrowly one should approach the problem. This is an area where a professional cannot approach treatment without a theoretical perspective and some understanding of the research literature accompanying that and other perspectives. Given the widespread and pervasive effects of our culture's norms and socialization experiences, practitioners attempting to intervene in the field of wife assault without a theoretical understanding of the problem will be subject to their own acculturated biases, most particularly the implicit patriarchal view that colors every aspect of our society.

The purpose of this chapter is to provide an overview of the theoretical approaches to men's violence against their partners. First, we will look at definitions of wife assault and how extensive the problem is in our culture. Then, the major theoretical approaches that have been presented in the literature will be examined, with relevant critiques of each. Finally, we will present our perspective to enable the reader to better understand our clinical approach to the problem.

Our perspective represents our theoretical understanding derived from the literature, the thinking of others, and our own clinical experience. Although our experience tells us that it is the most effective approach to ending men's violence against their partners, we also are delighted when new ideas and conceptions of the problem are presented, and we strive constantly to keep our minds open to innovative thinking.

DEFINING WIFE OR PARTNER ASSAULT

Defining what the terms *wife assault, battering, abuse, violence, family violence,* and *domestic violence* mean has been a subject of controversy in the recent mental health and research literature. It is an important controversy, as terms can reflect implicit biases and can structure the ways in which people view reality. Terms also will carry differing definitions when they are used in different contexts. For instance, a legal definition of assault will likely differ from a research definition or from a clinical interpretation of a behavior. At times, terms like *violence, abuse,* and *aggression* are used interchangeably, easily confusing the public, novices to the field, and other professionals (Gelles, 1985).

Legal definitions of wife or partner abuse, in most cases, focus only on assaultive acts that lead to visible injury. Mental health professionals often use the word *abuse* to include a number of assaultive and nonassaultive, but injurious, acts perpetrated by adults toward other adults or by adults toward children. Gelles (1980) notes that many definitions of child and wife abuse include malnourishment, failure to thrive, sexual abuse, and marital rape. He also notes that, generally, there is a difference between violence and abuse as these terms are used in the literature. The term *violence* most often refers to all forms of physical aggression, while the term *abuse* refers to those physical and nonphysical acts that cause physical and emotional injury.

A number of writers in this field have objected to the terms *family violence* and *domestic violence* on the grounds that they obscure the fact that males are predominantly violent toward women and children (Bograd, 1988; Breines & Gordon, 1983; Dobash & Dobash, 1979; McGrath, 1979; Schechter, 1982). They see this terminology as implicitly blaming the victims as contributors or perpetrators of violence on a level equal to that of male batterers.

Although much has been written in the field of interpersonal violence, particularly in the last decade, relatively few definitions of the term *battering* exist. Existing definitions differ in terms of the variety, frequency, and severity of assaultive behavior. Some definitions focus solely on the physically assaultive act. An example of this is Deschner's (1984) definition of battering as "a series of physically injurious attacks on an intimate or family member that forms part of a repeated, habitual pattern" (p. 21). Walker (1979), on the other hand, defines a battered woman as one "who is repeatedly subjected to any forceful physical or psychological behavior by a man in order to coerce her to do something he wants her to do without any concern for her rights" (p. xv).

Some authors, such as Anne Ganley (1981b), do not distinguish among violence, abuse, and battering. She defines wife battering as "the assaultive behavior between adults in an intimate, sexual, theoretically peer, and usually cohabitating relationship" (p. 8). The strength of this definition is in specifying the behavior committed and its context. Although the definition suggests mutual assaults, Ganley clearly notes in her writing that she is describing male behavior. Also notable is the absence of repeated assaults as a criterion for use of the term.

Ganley (1981b) outlines four forms of battering: (1) physical, (2) sexual, (3) destruction of property and pets, and (4) psychological. Physical battering, the most obvious form, includes all assaults directed by the perpetrator against the victim's body. It includes a range of behavior from less severe acts, such as spitting, pinching, and slapping, to more severe assaults, including choking, punching, and stabbing. Sexual violence involves physical attacks on the victim's breasts or genitals, coerced sexual activity accompanied by threats of violence, or sexual assault or rape. Violence against objects or pets constitutes violence toward the person emotionally and also serves to remind the victim of the potential for violence against her. Psychological battering is carried out with emotional or psychological weapons and includes behaviors such as threats of violence, suicide threats, controlling sleeping and eating, threats to take or harm children, and forcing degrading behavior. Ganley differentiates psychological battering from emotional abuse, as the former is done within a climate of physical violence and terror. According to this view, an emotionally abusive behavior may be labeled psychological battering where there has been at least one incident of physical violence preceding it.

A number of writers have recently argued against the notion that wife assault should be defined by the act of physical assault alone. These writers propose that battering is one part of a continuum of behavior used to maintain power and control over women (Bograd, 1984, 1988; Pence, 1985; Pence & Shepard, 1988). Violence, in this context, is defined as any behavior that causes the victim to do something she does not wish to do, prevents her from doing what she wants to do, or makes her afraid (Adams, 1988b). By looking at the physical assault in isolation from the context of power, control, and male violence against women in our society, professionals may be diverted from the purpose of the act, focusing instead on individual explanations.

In this book, we describe a treatment program for men who have physically assaulted their female partners on at least one occasion. We agree with the formulation that battering is one act in a continuum of controlling and abusive behaviors whereby a male maintains power over his female partner in a relationship, and our clinical experience with men who batter confirms this dynamic. Although

Walker (1979) states that many women reported psychological abuse as the worst component of their victimization, we have defined battering as at least one incident of physical assault for the purpose of admission for treatment in our program. However, a broader definition of male violence toward spouses and partners, focusing on the continuum of abusive and controlling behavior of the batterer, is necessary to approach the treatment of these men effectively.

HOW EXTENSIVE IS WIFE OR PARTNER ASSAULT?

Estimates of the incidence of wife or partner assault in our culture vary considerably. The most conservative estimate suggests that 12% of all wives are physically abused by their mates each year (Straus, Gelles, & Steinmetz, 1980). Straus et al. (1980) estimate that one in six couples experiences at least one violent incident, while one in eight inflicts serious injury. Other studies have suggested that the incidence is as high as 50% (Straus, 1978) to 60% (Gelles, 1974; Walker, 1979). Thorman (1980) states that 37% of wives surveyed who applied for divorce gave physical abuse as one of the complaints. Although these figures vary, and although wife assault is likely to be an underreported behavior, it may be that at least one-half of all adult women in relationships have been or will be physically assaulted by their partners.

One method of looking at the severity of the problem is to examine how many men approve of using physical force in their intimate relationships. The National Commission on the Causes and Prevention of Violence reports that one in five husbands approves of slapping wives in some circumstances (cited in Bern & Bern, 1984). Stark and McEvoy (1970), in a national survey, report that 25% of males and 16% of females approved of a husband slapping his wife under certain circumstances. Briere (1987), sampling a normal population of male college students, found that 79% said that they would use physical violence against their wives or partners in at least one of a number of circumstances; 75% said they would use force if she had sex with another man, while 64.9% would use force if she told his friends that he was "sexually pathetic."

Batterers have been found to come from all socioeconomic backgrounds, occupations, races, and religions (Giles-Sims, 1983; Sonkin et al., 1985; Star, Clark, Goetz, & O'Hara, 1979; Straus et al.,

1980; Walker, 1979, 1984), although they appear to be overrepresented in the lower socioeconomic and unemployed group (Gaguin, 1978; Saunders, 1982; Straus et al., 1980).

Battering also appears to be associated with other violent behaviors, and is not likely to be isolated to assaulting one's partner or assaulting only the current partner. Gayford (1975), for example, reports that over one-half of all wife assaulters also batter their children. These findings are supported by Hilberman and Munson's (1978) report that one-third of the batterers in their sample beat their children. More recently, Coleman (1980) found that 12% of batterers abused their children and Sonkin et al. (1985) reported that 57% used physical punishment on their children.

Wife assaulters also tend to have assaulted in previous relationships and a significant percentage are violent outside the home. Coleman (1980) found that, of the 60% of her sample who were married previously, 40% had been violent in a previous relationship. A total of 30% of her sample were violent outside the home. Sonkin et al. (1985), with a sample of 42 men, found that 93% of the men were violent in a previous relationship and 45% were violent outside the home.

A high percentage of batterers also appear to assault their partners sexually (Sonkin et al., 1985; Thyfault, 1980; Walker, 1979). From their research, Sonkin et al. (1985) report that 59% of the battered women in their sample were forced to have sex with their partners against their will, while 49% reported that this had occurred more than once. Some 41% of their sample reported being forced or coerced into unusual sexual acts, which included being tied up, threatened with a gun, beaten, or intimidated.

Studies suggest that marital rape is closely associated with high levels of physical violence in a marriage (Frieze, 1983). In Russell's (1982) study of a random sample of women, 162 of 644 women reported being raped, beaten, or both raped and beaten by their husbands. When the number of marriages was considered (some had been married more than once), 37% of 175 violent marriages contained both rape and physical assault of wives.

There is also some evidence emerging that suggests that a significant proportion of men who assault their wives also sexually abuse their children (Russell, 1982; Walker, 1979). While there is little definitive research that assesses the incidence of marital rape and child sexual abuse in families where men batter their partners, clinical experience suggests these three acts often occur together (Frieze, 1983). Many battered women have also reported that their partners are avid consumers of pornography (Patai, 1982; Walker, 1979).

Some studies have reported that violence by women toward their male partners is as prevalent as violence by men toward their female partners (Gelles, 1974; Straus, 1978; Straus et al., 1980). Although this research has been used to argue that men are victimized socially and legally by the domestic violence movement (McNeely & Robinson-Simpson, 1987), the research has failed to take into account the differing contexts in which men or women might use violence (Pagelow, 1981). Saunders (1988) found that the most frequent motive for violence reported by the women he sampled was self-defense. Very few women reported initiating an assault.

THEORETICAL PERSPECTIVES

Wife assault has been a focus of research and theory for approximately twenty years. Across this period of time there have been a number of major theories proposed for what causes men to assault their partners. Research and clinical efforts directed at understanding and changing wife assaulters are guided by theoretical perspectives. Although perspectives tend to evolve over time and give way to new theories, the perspectives presented below are still used to develop research and clinical treatment programs.

Although we present our own perspective at the end of this chapter, we feel it is important for practitioners to be aware of other perspectives. Many of the perspectives presented here have apparently logical constructs that are tempting to accept. Without previous exposure to these ideas and an understanding of the problems identified with them, the counselor may be misled. This might result either in problems in providing therapy or in "reinventing the wheel." The main reason to critique the past is not simply to be critical using the advantage of hindsight, but to learn from others' efforts and move forward.

INDIVIDUAL PSYCHOPATHOLOGY

Traditional early theories of wife assault focused on the personalities or individual characteristics of either the abuser or the victim. This approach suggests that intrapsychic, psychological, or biological abnormalities in the individual cause men to be violent toward their partners. Theoreticians using this approach have suggested a number of possible psychological problems, including immature personalities, personality disorders, poor impulse control, low frustration tolerance, dependency, depression, developmental trauma leading to misogyny or other ego functioning problems, fear of intimacy and/or abandonment, jealousy, addiction, and other psychiatric illnesses (Deschner, 1984; Faulk, 1974, 1977; Lion, 1977; Oates, 1979; Schultz, 1960; Shainess, 1977; Snell, Rosenwald, & Robey, 1964; Symonds, 1979).

Biological theories have also been suggested. Money and Ehrhardt (1972) posit some influence of androgen on fetal development, while Elliot (1976) believes that an unknown (but underestimated) number of wife and child batterers experience explosive rage due to neurological and metabolic diseases.

Wives have also been implicated as having personality or psychological disorders that lead their male partners to assault them. Snell et al. (1964), examining twelve battered women and their assailants referred to psychiatrists by the courts, described the women as aggressive, masculine, dominant, sexually frigid, and/or masochistic. Though stating that battering is not the victim's fault, Shainess (1977) claims that "people pick mates responsive to their own (unrecognized) neurotic needs" (p. 115). Though she labels these women masochistic, she denies that they enjoy suffering. Instead, she uses the term to describe a state in which women suffering from low self-esteem fail to see the true nature of their role and therefore do not take action to end abusive relationships.

Some writers claim that serious empirical problems plague studies that explain wife assault in terms of individual pathology. Dutton (1983) believes many of these studies are tainted by (1) a tendency to generalize from psychiatric or prison populations to the population in general, (2) a failure to use large samples of wife batterers systematically, (3) the tendency to rely on data provided by the victim, and (4) failure to account for acute situational pressures in the battering relationships. In addition, few abusive men evidence diagnosed psychopathology (Maiuro, Cahn, Vitaliano, Wagner, & Zegree, 1988) and, of those who do, there is no consistent pattern of psychopathology for batterers (Bograd, 1984).

Theories based on individual psychopathology imply that violence is beyond the batterer's control, using descriptions such as "paroxysmal rage attacks" (Lion, 1977), "psychiatric abnormality" (Faulk, 1974), or "uncontrollable rage and primitive attack behaviors" (Deschner, McNeil, & Moore, 1986). These theoretical views tend to reinforce batterers' own defenses and denial, although most batterers can also see that their violence is deliberate in terms of its location, target, and severity (Ptacek, 1988). Clearly, the notion that wife abuse results from abnormal behavior tends to minimize or eliminate the notion of personal responsibility on the part of the batterer and obscures the societal context in which men abuse women. This approach also tends to give contradictory and nontherapeutic messages to men about their violence and how to end it (Adams, 1988b). Adams (1988b) suggests that using this approach shifts the focus away from the battering behavior as a primary treatment issue, viewing it as a symptom of a more diffuse, larger, intrapersonal problem.

FAMILY SYSTEMS THEORY

From the family systems perspective, violence is a relationship issue, with violence being one symptom of a disturbed or pathological relationship (Cook & Frantz-Cook, 1984; Elbow, 1977; Everstine & Everstine, 1983; Geller, 1982; Hanks & Rosenbaum, 1977; Hoffman, 1981; Neidig & Freidman, 1984; Symonds, 1979; Weitzman & Dreen, 1982). One of the basic premises of systems theory is that all parts of the system contribute to the maintenance of homeostasis, defined as the tendency of a system to maintain a dynamic equilibrium and to undertake operations to restore that equilibrium whenever it is threatened (Goldenberg & Goldenberg, 1985). The family system works continually to maintain this homeostasis, even when it is achieved through dysfunction. Thus all members of the family participate in the system and carry the responsibility for family dysfunction. In this context, battering is no longer simply the responsibility of the batterer, but a behavior that is maintained by the actions of all family or system members.

Family systems theory suggests that battering is the result of repetitive interactions between family members characterized by certain relationship structures or dynamics, and that it serves a functional role in maintaining the relationship (Bograd, 1984). In attempting to equalize the responsibility for the violence, proponents of family systems theory have implicitly or explicitly blamed the victim. It then becomes the victim's responsibility to change her behavior to stop the violence perpetrated against her. Often treatment success is defined as keeping the relationship together, rather than stopping the abuse (Adams, 1988b; Brygger & Edelson, 1987).

Bograd (1984) provides an excellent critique of the systemic approach from a feminist perspective. She states that systems theories are biased, in that they blame battered women for violence while excusing the abusive man. The seriousness of violence is underemphasized by viewing it as simply one of many system problems. Systems theories imply that women are responsible for controlling their husbands' feelings and actions, while ignoring the power differences between women and men, not only in marriage, but in our culture in general. Additionally, these theories imply disapproval of nontraditional allocations of power and status in relationships (Bograd, 1984).

Family systems theorists tend to advocate either family or marital therapy as the most appropriate intervention for domestic violence. When batterers and victims are seen together in family therapy, both minimize the violence in the relationship. Many battered women report that they were assaulted following couples therapy sessions (Adams, 1988b), and the fear of future violence will inhibit a woman talking about present or past violence (Ganley & Harris, 1978). Additionally, if a woman talks about the violent behavior of her partner, the therapy may focus on what she did to "provoke" him. If she reports ongoing violence or abusive behavior, she may be viewed by the therapist as "resistant."

SOCIOLOGICAL OR SOCIAL STRUCTURAL PERSPECTIVE

Sociological theories emerged, in part, in reaction against the traditional clinical approaches (Gelles, 1985). These theories view wife abuse as behavior resulting from factors within the social structure (Finkelhor, Gelles, Hotaling, & Straus, 1983; Gelles, 1979; Straus et al., 1980; Straus & Hotaling, 1980). Macoby and Jacklin (1974), for example, have suggested that social conditions mediate the expression of violence. In Gelles's (1979) "social structure" theory, family violence is seen as due either to structural stress producing frustration and violence or to socialization in the use of violence in the culture.

Sociological theorists have linked social structure to social learning (Ferguson & Rule, 1983; Feshbach, 1964). Gelles (1979), for instance, suggests that violence is a response to a particular structure or situational condition, such as unemployment or poverty, and, therefore, it is differentially distributed among different social classes. He also suggests that a person's experience with violence will result in a belief that it is acceptable; in effect, people will be more or less likely to use violence as a result of their individual learning histories.

Reseaᵢch supporting the hypothesis that violence is more prevalent in certain social groups has been criticized as being based on populations, such as prison inmates, in which members of disadvantaged classes are overrepresented (Bern & Bern, 1984; Stahly, 1978). Masamura (1979) has also noted various studies that indicate that different types of violence do not appear to covary with each other across societies.

There is increasing evidence that frustration from the environment and from societal factors leads to a higher incidence of violence in the family (Bern & Bern, 1984). However, the use of violence as one response to stress and frustration is most likely related to cultural norms surrounding the use of violence and individual learning. Straus (1976) believes that the high frequency of wife assault and the disproportionate frequency with which women are victims reflect Euro-American cultural norms that, in effect, make the marriage license a "hitting license." Indeed, Shotland and Straw (1976) found that 65% of males and females intervened in a staged assault when they believed the participants were strangers, while only 19% intervened if they thought the participants were married.

Straus (1976) believes that sexist attitudes and practices support the existence of wife battering for several reasons: (1) Men lacking in personal resources will use violence to buttress a position of superiority in the family, (2) sex-role differentiation and inequality produce antagonism between men and women, (3) women find it difficult to escape abusive marriages due to the lack of alternative roles for women and the consequent pressure to remain in the traditional role, and (4) the male-oriented criminal justice system makes it extremely difficult to secure legal protection from assault.

Although some of the sociological theorists mentioned above

have pointed to social norms and values that support the sexist structure of our culture, Bograd (1988) notes that a number of sociologists are not necessarily antifeminist, but "gender neutral." They see violence as a problem for both sexes, as in the research mentioned above that suggests that both sexes are equally violent.

The "violent culture" theory has been criticized as a diversion from the issue of violence against women in a patriarchal society (Bograd, 1988; Dobash & Dobash, 1979; Gondolf, 1985c; Schechter, 1982). Bograd (1988) argues that stress is not necessarily externally imposed on a family, but that it is part of the way in which heterosexual relationships are structured along lines of gender and power. In addition, these theories do not explain why some men are violent and others are not (Ganley & Harris, 1978), or why men primarily assault women.

Sociological theories appear to have contributed most to our understanding of the problem of wife assault when they have addressed the patriarchal nature of our society, the power differential between males and females, and the role of societal values, such as misogyny and the cultural view of masculinity, in normalizing violence. They offer less clarity when they view violent cultures and external stresses as causes of wife assault. Clearly, the notion of mediating or removing external stressors has limited value in ending men's violence toward women.

SOCIAL LEARNING AND COGNITIVE-BEHAVIORAL PERSPECTIVES

Bandura's (1973) social learning analysis is a hallmark in the study of aggression. Instead of assuming innate aggressive instincts or drives, Bandura regards aggression as learned behavior. One means of learning aggression is a modeling process, where informal observation of the behaviors of influential models, and of consequent rewards or punishments, provides an observer with either the inhibition or disinhibition for repeating these acts. Bandura and his colleagues have demonstrated that children model adult aggressive behavior, and will increase or decrease the modeled behavior in response to witnessing whether it is rewarded or punished (Bandura, 1965; Bandura, Ross, & Ross, 1963a, 1963b, 1963c).

Children also will report wanting to be like an aggressive adult when that adult is rewarded.

Bandura's theory has been used to support the notion that violent men learn to be violent as children by watching or experiencing the violence in their families of origin. This view is supported by a number of studies that have found that men who are violent have a high incidence of witnessing or experiencing violence as children (Carroll, 1977; Owens & Straus, 1975; Rosenbaum & O'Leary, 1981a, 1981b; Roy, 1977; Sonkin et al., 1985; Ulbrich & Huber, 1981).

In addition to violence learned in the family of origin, social learning theory also focuses on violence as learned and reinforced in the culture and through trial-and-error experiences (Ganley & Harris, 1978). Ganley (1981b) states that men who respond to stress with violence experience an almost immediate reduction in bodily tension and an increase in physiological arousal. This sudden transition from unpleasant tension to relaxation and a sense of physical well-being reinforces the tendency to use violence in the future as a tension-reduction mechanism.

Violence then is seen as a learned response to stress, from observing others and/or from trial-and-error experiences. Individual stressors can be either internal or external. Examples of internal stressors may be feelings of insecurity, feelings of inadequacy, or personality difficulties, while external stressors may include unemployment, illness, or interpersonal difficulties. In this model, violence is not caused by individual psychopathology or societal stress, but rather by the way in which certain men have learned to respond to these difficulties.

Once men have used violence, the reinforcement for violence increases the likelihood that it will be used again. The use of violence may then become cyclical. Lenore Walker (1979), based on her interviews with battered women, has proposed a model of wife assault termed the "cycle of violence," which follows a pattern of three distinct phases: tension building, the acute battering incident, and kindness and contrite, loving behavior. According to Walker, though the beginning of any intimate relationship may be characterized by bliss and caring, relationship demands invariably produce stress. As stress builds, the man begins a gradual process of escalation evidenced by increasingly aggressive behavior. In the tension-building phase (Phase I) a circular process occurs in which the man experiences the effects of stress, labels those effects as anger, escalates in his anger, behaves aggressively to achieve catharsis, and returns to a state of equilibrium to face again the effects of stress. The cathartic value of aggression tends to be short term, and the process tends to increase the stress and anger experienced by the batterer.

When anger is eventually expressed through physical violence, the acute battering incident (Phase II) occurs. In comparison to Phase I, it usually is a relatively short phase, lasting anywhere from a few seconds to a few hours. Although there may be instances of physical abuse during Phase I, they are usually less severe than the acute battering of Phase II. The tension reduction accomplished by violence brings about relaxation and signals the transition to Phase III.

Phase III is characterized by the man's kind, affectionate, and attentive behavior toward the woman. He may realize the wrong he has done and is likely to panic at the thought of losing his partner. Kindness, gift giving, and promises to change are designed to persuade her to stay in the relationship. As the cycle is repeated many times in a relationship, Phase III may be either truncated or entirely absent. Phase III then leads back to Phase I, as the effects of stress again result in the man's gradual escalation. If the relationship ends, he is likely to reproduce this cycle in his next relationship.

Cognitive factors have also been hypothesized to play a part in the expression of violence. Novaco (1975) reviewed several studies that demonstrate that the magnitude of an aggressive response is related to the perceived aggressive intent of the opponent, justification for aggression, self-esteem, and awareness of anger level. Behavior has also been demonstrated to be contingent on statements people make to themselves (Meichenbaum, 1977). Ellis (1977) proposes that rage always is preceded by absolutist, irrational demands related to a person's desire to have his or her own way. Examples of unrealistic demands include self-statements such as "She should have listened," "She should never do that," or "She should obey me."

Hauck (1974) has used these ideas to produce a six-stage model of irrational self-statements that lead to anger:

(1) I want something.
(2) I didn't get it and I am frustrated.
(3) It is awful and terrible not to get what I want.

(4) You shouldn't frustrate me! I must have my own way!

(5) You're bad for frustrating me.

(6) Bad people should be punished.

Social learning and cognitive behavioral theories suggest that, since violence is a learned behavior, batterers can change as a result of "unlearning" the behavior or learning new behavior (Adams, 1988a; Edelson, Miller, & Stone, 1983; Ganley, 1981b; Sonkin & Durphy, 1982). Treatment tends to focus on skills and deficits, rather than on individual pathologies or relationship dynamics (Ganley & Harris, 1978). In psychoeducational treatment programs, violent behavior tends to be the focus of treatment, and violent men are generally seen either individually or in groups (Adams, 1988b).

Social learning theory has been criticized for taking too narrow a view of men's abusive behavior and not addressing the function of that behavior in maintaining power and control over women by individual men and by men as a class (Adams, 1988a, 1988b; Gondolf, 1985a, 1985c; Pence, 1985; Pence & Shepard, 1988). Adams (1988b) notes that psychoeducational programs vary in how explicitly they address abuses of power or the sexist expectations of abusive men. A number of treatment programs with a social learning perspective focus only on anger control, ignoring a wide range of other abusive and controlling behaviors (Gondolf & Russell, 1986).

FEMINIST AND/OR SOCIOPOLITICAL PERSPECTIVES

A feminist approach to the assault of women by their male husbands and/or partners focuses on the sociopolitical context of male power and control in society. This view defines violence in a broader context as one of the methods by which men oppress and subjugate women. Wife assault is thought to be sanctioned by the society and maintained by political, social, and economic factors within our society (Gondolf, 1985a, 1985c). According to Bograd (1984), "violence (such as rape or battering) is the most overt and visible form of control wielded by men as a class over women" (p. 559).

Feminist theorists seek to understand and explain why men, as a class, use physical force against women and how this serves a function in a particular society, rather than why a particular man uses violence against a particular woman (Bograd, 1988; Chapman &

Gates, 1978; Dobash & Dobash, 1979; Martin, 1976; Pagelow, 1981; Pence & Shepard, 1988; Russell, 1982; Schechter, 1982; Walker, 1979, 1984). In this perspective, individual men are not only trained and reinforced to be violent against women, but the patriarchal social structure and men in general are rewarded by women being restricted and limited by their fear of men's violence (Bograd, 1988). Wife battering will continue until the sexist society that maintains it is challenged and changes, even if individual men cease their violence toward their partners.

From a feminist perspective, two statements are fundamental: (1) No woman deserves to be beaten, and (2) men are solely responsible for their actions (Bograd, 1984). Bograd (1984) emphasizes four points within this perspective: (1) There is a distinction between the verbal expression of anger and physical assault, (2) men and women can control their behavior, (3) men and women have a right to physical safety, and (4) blaming the victim shifts attention from the patriarchal context of battering.

Although generally skeptical of the effectiveness of changing individual men as a means to end violence against women, most feminist theorists do support working with and teaching men to be nonviolent. From a feminist perspective, work with men who batter must also be accompanied by efforts to increase both social and legal consequences for batterers (Adams, 1988b; Pence, 1985; Pence & Shepard, 1988). Practitioners from this perspective are likely to focus on skills deficits of individual batterers, although they also educate and challenge batterers regarding their sexist expectations and their controlling behaviors (Adams, 1988b; Adams & McCormick, 1982; Brygger & Edelson, 1987; Currie, 1983; Paymar & Pence, 1985; Pence & Shepard, 1988).

OUR PERSPECTIVE

We live in a society where resources, power, privileges, rewards, and justice are distributed unequally. In addition to the unequal distribution of power and wealth by race and age, there is an overall inequality by gender. People live in hierarchies defined by race, age, and gender. In an analogy to the notion of fractals in physics, this structure is reflected in every aspect of organizations or systems in our culture. Within the broader context of society, men have more power than women, and adults have more power than children.

Within the individual, our culture values those traits it defines as masculine over those it defines as feminine. This is not the result of some reality that what is male is, in fact, somehow better than what is female. Rather, given the general physical superiority of males, males have been able to subjugate females through violence or threat of violence, and have thus been able to define what is valuable and what is not.

In our culture, this hierarchical organizing principle operates in families. Though each member of a family may hold some power, as family systems theorists propose, when the accounting is done it is the adult male who emerges as the most powerful family member. Although there have been major changes in our society in this century, the family as an institution and a concept has never totally escaped its historical roots. The Latin root of the word *family* is *familia*, a term referring to the slaves belonging to an individual. This concept includes the assumption that men owned their wives and children as they owned slaves and other property, and could deal with them as they pleased.

As repulsive as the notion of slavery may be in our culture, the notion that men own their wives and their children still survives in some form. For instance, when a man and woman marry, it is still common practice that she take her husband's name and give that name to her children. Even when children are sexually or physically abused, the courts are still reluctant to remove parental "rights."

In an intimate heterosexual relationship, the assumption of ownership will lead a man to assume that he has certain rights concerning his "property." He may assume that he has the right to make all decisions concerning domestic matters. He may control all the financial resources. He may assume that he has the right to determine whom his wife may see, where she may go, if she may work, and when she may do things. He may assume the right to sexual access whenever he wants it. He may also assume that he has the right to punish his wife if she does not comply with his wishes or meet his expectations. In a patriarchal society such as ours, men hold the belief that "a man's home is his castle."

When men assault their partners, this assumption of ownership and the right to control and dominate is readily apparent when outsiders intervene. In our first contacts with men who have been arrested for assaulting their partners, we frequently notice that their response to arrest is shock and outrage. They do not believe that anyone in our society has the right to interfere in "domestic matters."

This belief is also reflected by the society at large in its reluctance to intervene when a man assaults his partner. It has been only in the past ten years, and through the incredible efforts of such pioneers as Ellen Pence in Duluth, Minnesota, that police in some communities have developed policies requiring their officers to arrest batterers. Prior to this, assault laws that in theory should have been applicable to wife assault were rarely enforced. In addition, medical and social welfare personnel, who often see the effects of men's violence toward their partners, have done little to assist the victims or to attempt to intervene to end the violence.

Indeed, the victim is often blamed for the violence she receives, and multiple bureaucratic roadblocks prevent her from leaving her violent partner. For example, the 60- to 90-day wait for financial assistance for a woman or her children in most communities often dictates a woman's need to return to a violent relationship in order to feed and shelter her children. We have seen women who have been beaten and raped to such an extent that they were dissociative and in shock. When their partners subsequently raped or beat their children, these women were blamed by professionals for not doing something to protect them. Often their children are taken away from them, and they may be charged by the criminal justice system as equally responsible for their children's victimization.

Physical assault is only one method by which men gain and maintain power and control over women. Our society compartmentalizes different acts into discrete categories. While services provided by community agencies may need to be specialized (such as sexual assault treatment, child sexual assault treatment, wife assault treatment and shelters, child abuse services, "family" services, and specialized crime investigation units), this compartmentalization carries the risk of overlooking the reality of the function these separate acts have as a way of degrading and subjugating women as individuals and as a class.

We maintain that there is a continuum of violence against women in our society that includes sexist and degrading language, pornography, wife assault, child sexual assault, rape, sexual mutilation, resource deprivation, and murder. From this perspective, wife assault is seen as one behavior on a continuum of behaviors that serve the purpose of maintaining the power and domination of a patriarchal society.

Wife assault is seen neither as a result of the intrapersonal problems of an individual male nor as a result of the dysfunctional dynamics of a particular relationship. Indeed, the norms of our culture permeate the attitudes of all males in a pathological manner and set dysfunctional standards for all heterosexual relationships. We discard the notion that social class, defined by economic level or race, has any causal relationship to wife assault. The reality defined by the dominant group in any culture (white males, in our culture) is carried by all members of the culture (Schaef, 1981). From our perspective, the causative influence of social class is the differentiation of power by gender.

When interpersonal or intrapersonal characteristics of wife assaulters are examined, in order to differentiate wife assaulters from men who do not physically assault their wives, one must keep in mind a number of important factors. First, the importance of these characteristics is most likely to be in the extent to which they are present, rather than in their presence itself. All men may display certain characteristics to some degree, while batterers may display them to an extreme. For instance, while clinicians report a strong need to dominate and control as characteristic of assaultive men (Elbow, 1977; Ganley & Harris, 1978; Symonds, 1979; Weitzman & Dreen, 1982), men in our culture, in general, tend to attempt to control and dominate women to some degree.

In addition, many of the characteristics demonstrated by these men may be a result of their violence rather than a cause of it. Low self-esteem, for instance, may be an internal response to the knowledge that the man has used violence against the person he depends upon for caring and support. Finally, while it is important to address characteristics that may increase the probability of a man using physical violence to control his partner, changing these factors does not necessarily address the wide range of behaviors that men use to control their partners. Focusing on interpersonal characteristics alone minimizes or ignores sexist expectations and assumptions that include power and control as a primary theme.

Our perspective, as is evident from what we have said above, is a profeminist one. However, we also believe that the social learning and cognitive-behavioral perspectives have much to offer, both in treatment and in understanding wife assaulters. From our perspective, ending men's violence toward their partners involves addressing the violence on multiple levels.

Sexist attitudes and expectations must be confronted on both individual and societal levels. Men are solely responsible for their violence toward women, and there must be clear societal and legal consequences for this violence. Individual men must be confronted, not only on their physical violence, but on the whole range of controlling and dominating behaviors they employ against women.

Individual men who attempt to end their violence also need nonviolent and nonabusive skills and attitudes to replace the ones we are challenging them to give up. Understanding and addressing the characteristics of assaultive men that increase the probability for continued violence is essential. We need to give individual men tools to assist them on their road to peace.

Given that our patriarchal society will not change overnight and that men in our society who are reaping the rewards of violence will resist relinquishing their domination, men who attempt to give up their violence will be faced with covert and overt pressures from other men to come back in line with the attitude of masculine superiority. We need to "inoculate" these men against this pressure by helping them to see it for what it is. Although it may seem logically absurd that we should need to reward men for their nonviolence, men need to be convinced of the personal and societal benefits of empathy, of not objectifying women, of intimacy based on equality, and of relinquishing their abusive power if we are going to be effective in the long run.

2

CHARACTERISTICS OF MEN WHO BATTER

As stated in Chapter 1, the roots of domestic violence are not to be found in looking at the psychopathology of wife assaulters. Indeed, a review of the traits of men who batter that have been identified in the clinical and research literature may appear to read like a shopping list of negative attributes. Many of these traits may apply to people who have never been physically violent in their relationships. For each individual batterer, some traits mentioned here are likely to be present, although the clinician may find batterers who appear to possess none of them.

The individual characteristics of batterers mentioned in this chapter are not presented in order to give the impression that wife assaulters are necessarily a discrete group of men. As mentioned in the previous chapter, a continuum model of male behavior that suggests that batterers are more similar to other males than different from them reflects our experience and theoretical perspective.

Overall, the characteristics presented in this chapter identify deviations from the "norm" that appear to maximize the potential for violence in intimate relationships and allow the batterer to justify its reoccurrence. Some of the characteristics may "set the stage" for wife assault to occur, such as family history, overidentification with the stereotypic male role, perceptual distortion of situations, and jealousy and controlling behaviors. Others may identify cognitive responses to the violence, such as minimization, denial, and projection. Some traits will identify longer-term emotional and personal results, such as depression and low self-esteem.

Some proposed typologies of batterers will be reviewed, although we find very little clinical benefit from these classifications and feel that they can confuse or obscure the direction of clinical practice. The central issue in the treatment of wife assaulters is ending the violence; the defining characteristic of wife assaulters is that they have physically assaulted their partners. Treatment is aimed at the act of violence itself and the concurrent controlling and abusive behaviors that are associated with violence toward women. However, addressing and confronting individual traits within treatment increases the likelihood that men will remain nonviolent.

The characteristics reviewed here have been divided into six groups: (1) skills deficits, (2) defenses, (3) personal traits, (4) situational characteristics, (5) historical factors, and (6) attitudes. A short summary of typologies of batterers follows the review of these traits.

SKILLS DEFICITS

A number of authors have identified a lack of intrapersonal and interpersonal skills as characteristic of wife assaulters (Browning, 1983; Foy, Eisler, & Pinkston, 1975; Ganley & Harris, 1978; Goode, 1971; O'Brien, 1971; Rimm, Hill, Brown, & Stuart, 1974). This lack of skills may be due to a number of factors. Assaulters may have had little opportunity to learn such skills in their families of origin, their male socialization may not have provided them with appropriate learning, and they may have learned to devalue and shun such skills in response to the pressure they perceive to be masculine. The lack of these skills provides them with few alternatives to conflict management or expression of feelings other than anger and violence.

Identification of Emotions

Men who assault their partners tend to be unable to recognize or acknowledge the emotions they feel, other than anger (Bernard &

Bernard, 1984; Ganley & Harris, 1978; LaViolette, Barnett, & Miller, 1984; Margolin, John, & Gleberman, 1988). They may see many of these feelings, such as sadness, fear, or embarrassment, as unacceptable for them as men. Avoidance of emotion also results in their being slow to recognize stress or frustration, allowing it to build until they feel that their anger is out of control (Ferraro, 1984).

This learned inability to recognize or express a wide variety of emotions and the tendency to experience and express them as anger or rage has been termed the "male emotional funnel." When men are in situations where they feel sadness, loss, or embarrassment, or where others do not meet their expectations and they feel rejected, abandoned, inadequate, jealous, or afraid, their fear or lack of familiarity with these emotions causes them to label their feelings as anger (Saunders, 1982). In their attempt to maintain control, they often detach or attempt to ignore this experience of anger, which then funnels into rage.

As these men attempt to suppress and deny the existence of their anger, they often appear to react passively to situations. When they finally respond with rage and aggression, others see this as impulsive and unpredictable. Indeed, as a result of the success of their avoidance, suppression, and repression, most batterers have no conscious awareness of their original, primary emotional response, such as sadness or rejection, or of the process by which that primary emotion was transformed into rage.

Perceptual Distortion

Men who assault their partners tend to distort situations cognitively and emotionally to fit their own perceptions of the world and their expectations of themselves and others. They often misperceive neutral communications as threatening or insulting to them, fueling their anger and rage. They tend to perceive others as hostile and rejecting (Bernard & Bernard, 1984). In a study of conflictual discussions among couples, Margolin et al. (1988) found that physically abusive husbands reported feeling more attacked, more fear, and more sadness than nonassaultive husbands, leading to more anger, more physical arousal, and more overt negative behaviors.

This distortion is commonly observed in batterers' reports of interactions with their spouses and others. If a supervisor is having a bad day and is not friendly to him, such a man may assume that the supervisor is angry with him and may do something to hurt him; he subsequently feels threatened, and then angry. If his partner is fifteen minutes late, he assumes she is having an affair and is going to leave him; he then feels abandoned, rejected, and angry. Battered women report feeling that there is nothing they can say or do, as the most neutral situations and statements are distorted by batterers into threats, criticisms, or rejections.

The cognitive processes that mediate this distortion were discussed in Chapter 1. Ferguson and Rule (1983) hypothesize that the perception or misperception of harm by another will increase anger. Whether or not this anger is expressed as aggression is a function of a person's values, his perception of social disapproval, and the likelihood of retaliation by the other person.

Communication Skills

Wife assaulters have been described as having difficulty expressing verbally what they think, feel, and want (Ganley & Harris, 1978), and as being nonassertive both in their families and in the outside world (Browning, 1983; Ganley & Harris, 1978; Rosenbaum & O'Leary, 1981b; Saunders, 1982; Sonkin, Martin, & Walker, 1985). Ganley and Harris (1978) note that assaultive men appear to be poor listeners, are unable to communicate directly, and confuse assertiveness with aggression. Although many batterers may have good verbal skills in some areas, such as manipulation, they tend not to use these skills in expressing their feelings assertively.

Sonkin et al. (1985) hypothesize that this lack of assertive ability may be linked to a fear of abandonment and individuation. In other words, when a person says no, he or she risks incurring the anger of the other person and possible rejection. It is also likely that avoidance and suppression of primary feelings, which shields these feelings from conscious awareness, precludes their expression.

For batterers to learn the appropriate, nonviolent expression of feelings and desires, in place of aggression, requires intervention at a number of levels. First, accurate identification of primary feelings is necessary. Batterers also must learn to reframe and reinterpret their cognitive and emotional distortions. Finally, they must learn new, assertive, nonaggressive, and nonmanipulative skills in interpersonal communication.

DEFENSES

Psychological defense mechanisms tend to serve two main purposes: to hide the reality of one's behavior from oneself and from others. Most batterers use some form of the defense mechanisms of minimization, denial, and projection of blame onto others or their circumstances. Using these defenses allows them to avoid responsibility for their behavior and to obscure the reality of what they have done. A full, nonminimized acceptance of their behavior and their responsibility for it risks evoking a deep well of shame, embarrassment, and guilt. Given that their behavior is illegal and often disapproved of socially, they also may see it as in their best interest to minimize, deny, and project blame (Sonkin et al., 1985).

This pattern of defending oneself can be seen with other issues besides violence. Men often deny or minimize to themselves and others the significance of important events or emotions that have profound effects on their lives (Davidson, 1978; Ganley, 1981b; Pagelow, 1981). In their lives outside of a relationship, denial and projection of blame can add to their feelings of distrust, hostile intentions, and persecution by others. If men are going to take responsibility for their abusive behavior, they must be directly confronted on their defensive distortion of their actions.

Minimization

Wife assaulters minimize the frequency, intensity, severity, and consequences of their violence (Adams & Penn, 1981; Bernard & Bernard, 1984; Dutton, 1986; Saunders, 1982). Often men will make statements such as "All I did was push her away," "It hasn't happened that often," "She wasn't hurt that bad," or "She'll be okay, she'll forget about it."

Although these men tend to minimize their own behavior, they also exaggerate and overpersonalize the behavior of others. Batterers tend to see their wives as being as violent as they are when women attempt to defend themselves. Their punches are not all that bad, while their partners' words to them are experienced as devastating.

Denial

Denial by men who assault their partners can take many forms, ranging from outright denial of violence to denial of intention to denial of responsibility. The most common excuse offered by batterers is some form of "loss of control" (Adams & Penn, 1981; Coleman, 1980; Dutton, 1986; Ptacek, 1988). Men say they "flipped out," didn't know what was happening, or were intoxicated and couldn't help themselves.

For example, Ptacek (1988) interviewed twelve men who had assaulted their wives to examine how they framed excuses and justifications. He found that batterers used more excuses than justifications, although they tended often to excuse themselves first and then to offer justifications, in an internally inconsistent fashion. Ptacek found that 94% of his sample offered the excuse of alcohol, frustration, and/or loss of control. One-third said their violence was the result of using alcohol or drugs. In countering these excuses, Ptacek cites Gelles's (1974) data showing that drunken behavior is learned, and Bandura's (1973) work that points out that aggression is only one response to frustration.

In addition to loss of control and intoxication, batterers often ascribe their behavior to confusion (things were crazy, I didn't know what I was doing) or lack of intention (I didn't mean to), or simply deny it (she's lying) (Adams & Penn, 1981). They also deny the internal, emotional injuries they cause, such as fear, humiliation, degradation, and assault on the partner's identity (Ptacek, 1988).

Projection of Blame and Externalization

A common defense used by assaultive men is to blame their wives or circumstances for their violence (Adams & Penn, 1981; Bernard & Bernard, 1984; Coleman, 1980; Dutton, 1986; Elbow, 1977; Ptacek, 1988). Often men blame their partners' verbal "aggression" as being the cause of their battering (Coleman, 1980; Ptacek, 1988). Most men believe that both partners carry some responsibility, although many blame their partners entirely (Coleman, 1980).

Blaming their partners often reflects the unreasonable expectations wife assaulters have of wives and of relationships. They say that their wives or partners are not good mothers or good housekeepers, or that they are frigid or flirtatious. Batterers' own feelings of jealousy and dependency require that their partners isolate themselves from others, and when their partners violate this condition in some way, they are blamed for their husbands' assaultive responses.

When men report that their partners "provoked" them, either verbally or by their behavior, they are suggesting that there is a "proper" way for a woman to respond or act with the man with whom she is involved. When she does not act in that way, he has the right to force her to comply with his wishes, using violence if necessary (Ptacek, 1988).

Clinicians report that batterers have a tendency to feel that everything was caused by the outside world (Ganley & Harris, 1978), presenting themselves as victims of circumstances beyond their control. When a man claims that he was violent as a result of the stress he is under, because he is unemployed, because he came from a bad family, or whatever, this is another way of projecting the blame for his behavior onto others or circumstances.

Clinicians, especially males, should be very careful not to collude with violent men in their rationalization, minimization, and denial. The early clinical literature on batterers suggests that these excuses were accepted as true, with clinicians using the same terms batterers used, such as "loss of control," or blaming victims in the same way that batterers did (Ptacek, 1988). Men are solely responsible for their violence, and the variety of ways in which they are violent (in the home, with their wives, behind closed doors, often hitting without leaving visible marks) demonstrates that they have a great deal of control over their assaultive behavior.

INDIVIDUAL TRAITS OR PERSONALITY CHARACTERISTICS

The personality traits generally cited in the literature as associated with wife assaulters tend to focus on a central theme. This theme suggests that assaultive men may have feelings of inadequacy and low self-worth, become very dependent in relationships, and their dependency is reflected in jealousy and extreme controlling behaviors. They may display depression, although it is often situational, a result of experiencing the consequences of their abusive and violent behavior. They can be very charming and appear loving at times, suggesting a kind of "Jekyll and Hyde" personality (Bernard & Bernard, 1984).

Although many batterers are likely to present with some of the personality characteristics mentioned below, few will be seen as disturbed enough to be classified as mentally ill. Clinical studies suggest that 10% or less of the population of assaultive men are clinically "disturbed" (Browning, 1983; Coleman, 1980; Gondolf, 1985a, 1985b; Straus, Gelles, & Steinmetz, 1980). Often this disturbance is labeled as sadistic (Gondolf, 1985a) or as severe depression or suicidal behavior generally related to separations from their partners (Coleman, 1980).

The traits of batterers reviewed below do not constitute an exhaustive list, and some characteristics might arguably be grouped in other categories. For instance, isolation may be seen as a personal trait of batterers. However, we review it under the section on situational characteristics. The reader is cautioned not to assume that because a client assaults his partner, he will inevitably demonstrate these characteristics. Our clinical experience suggests, however, that most wife assaulters will present with some of these dynamics.

Dependency, Jealousy, and/or Controlling Behaviors

Wife assaulters have been characterized as being extremely dependent on their partners (Bernard & Bernard, 1984; Browning, 1983; Coleman, 1980; Elbow, 1977; Faulk, 1977; Ganley, 1981b; Ganley & Harris, 1978; Hilberman & Munson, 1978; Maiuro, Cahn, Vitaliano, Wagner, & Zegree, 1988; Saunders, 1982; Sonkin et al., 1985; Symonds, 1979; Walker, 1979). This dependency tends to create emotional conflicts for the batterer, as he is likely to fear real intimacy. In this sense, he has an extreme, childlike need of his partner, while at the same time he denies having this need. This may lead him to devalue his partner and to feel anger toward her, since she represents the thing he hates about himself.

This ambivalence creates a "push-pull" emotional conflict, with the batterer feeling fear and panic that he will be abandoned and concurrently feeling the need to run away or distance himself from the relationship. We see this in our clients' conflicting statements, such as "If she leaves me I'm going to kill her," and "I don't need this, I'll just leave and find someone else."

This overwhelming "neediness" is unlikely to be met by any person. In a narcissistic fashion, the batterer demands that his partner validate his overadequate image of himself. Any criticisms are felt as rejections. If his partner makes any autonomous moves, the batterer may become violent, homicidal, or even suicidal in an attempt to prevent what he sees as abandonment.

In order to reduce his feelings of anxiety about abandonment, the batterer is extremely jealous and controlling. Since batterers are oversocialized in a stereotypic masculine role, they feel the right to control their partners, children, and anyone else with less perceived power or status. Violence is only one act in a repertoire of controlling behaviors.

Extreme jealousy appears to be a common characteristic of these men (Bernard & Bernard, 1984; Ganley & Harris, 1978; Maiuro et al., 1988; Martin, 1976; Roy, 1982; Saunders, 1982). Of the women interviewed by Hilberman and Munson (1978), 95% reported that their husbands were extremely jealous. Similar findings are reported by Gayford (1975), Roy (1977), and Rounsaville (1978). This jealousy may at times be so severe that the men may become significantly depressed and clinically paranoid (Elbow, 1977; Maiuro et al., 1988; Makman, 1978; Saunders, 1982).

A batterer's jealousy often extends jealousy of other men to include friends, family, or his own children. A batterer will often follow his partner, keep track of the mileage on the car or refuse his partner use of the car, phone his partner at work and home to check up on her, or refuse to let his partner leave the house without him. Often batterers will try to destroy relationships between their partners and family, friends, or their children, and they may assault their partners' children, parents, or friends, both male and female, as a result of their jealousy.

Batterers report that they become enraged when their partners argue with them, do not clean the house to their expectations, and/or do not predict their wishes or needs perfectly (not having dinner ready when they are hungry, not having the shirt they want to wear cleaned). If their children act out in public, their partners and their children may be beaten. They assume the right to make decisions about their partners' lives, such as whom the partners see, whether they work or go to school, or how they dress.

Jealousy is only one form of the extensive control batterers attempt to exercise over others. This control is an extreme of the traits to which most men are conditioned, including possessiveness and domination over women (Gondolf, 1985b, 1985c; Saunders, 1982). The batterer's need to control and dominate has been reported in a number of clinical studies (Elbow, 1977; Ganley & Harris, 1978; Gondolf, 1985b, 1985c; Maiuro et al., 1988; Martin, 1976; Symonds, 1979; Weitzman & Dreen, 1982).

Traditional male sex-role socialization places strong emphasis on men being in control in all aspects of their lives, and batterers tend to overidentify with these dysfunctional and stereotypic masculine values and expectations (Gondolf, 1985c). They hold high expectations of their own abilities to regulate their feelings and behaviors and are often described as rigid. Their patriarchal belief system grants them the privilege and power to enforce their expectations on their partners, using violence if necessary (Gondolf, 1985c).

Alcohol and/or Drug Abuse

Traditional beliefs about men who batter often include the assumption that alcohol or drug use causes men to assault their wives. Although many studies indicate a high association between battering and alcohol or drug abuse (Bernard & Bernard, 1984; Ganley & Harris, 1978; Gelles, 1974; Hanks & Rosenbaum, 1977; Roy, 1982; Schuerger & Reigle, 1988; Zacker & Bard, 1977), battering also occurs when substance use is not involved (Ganley & Harris, 1978; Gondolf, 1985c; Roy, 1977).

In a review of the previous literature, Fitch and Papantonio (1983) found that more than one-half of batterers interviewed abused alcohol and more than one-third abused drugs. In Sonkin et al.'s (1985) study of wife assaulters, 62% had used alcohol during their last assault, 43% had been violent both with and without alcohol, and an equal number (29%) had been violent either only with alcohol use or only without alcohol use; 46% scored on testing as having a chemical abuse problem. Gondolf (1985b) found that the majority of men who were assessed on entry into treatment were not abusers of drugs or alcohol.

Experience in working with men who batter suggests that the relationship between battering and chemicals is complex. Chemically dependent batterers often enter chemical dependency treatment programs expecting that abstinence will solve their problems with violence. In most cases, these men continue to batter after success-ful treatment (Ganley, 1981b). Batterers also admit that they some-times use alcohol in some situations in order to batter. Not only does the alcohol provide a disinhibiting influence (Frank & Houghton, 1982), but after the incident these men can blame their abusive behavior on the alcohol. Battering may be related to alcohol in terms of motivation, as well: The use of alcohol and battering may both be attempts to gain a feeling of power (Browning, 1983; McClelland, 1975).

Sonkin et al. (1985) report that men who are predisposed to vio-lence are more likely to be violent when using drugs or alcohol. In addition, when men batter while under the influence of chemicals, they are more likely to cause more serious injuries (Browne, 1986; Coleman, 1980; Sonkin, 1987). Obviously, the presence of alcohol and drugs increases the lethality of a violent situation and needs to be confronted directly in treatment.

Depression

Studies have reported that depression is a characteristic of assaultive men (Ganley & Harris, 1978; Sonkin et al., 1985). Most of the men studied, however, were in treatment programs as a result of their violence, and it is not clear whether depression is a normal characteristic of batterers or a result of the failure of their violence to control others. Some studies have suggested that depression covaries with anger and hostility, while not specifying whether one is causal to the other (Maiuro et al., 1988; Moreno, Fuhrman, Brown, & Allred, 1987).

Our clinical experience suggests that the depression we see in assaultive men tends to be related to the remorse they present on en-tering treatment (Coleman, 1980), or to separation or the threat of losing the person on whom they are dependent. When batterers manage to convince their partners to return to the relationship, the depression appears to lift quickly. When experiencing this panic, however, these men may be suicidal (Ganley & Harris, 1978; Sonkin et al., 1985). Coleman (1980) found that, of the less than 10% of batterers who attempted suicide in her sample, all did so in response to separations.

Low Self-Esteem

Research studies and clinical reports indicate that many wife assaulters have low self-esteem, low ego strength, and a feeling of inadequacy (Ball, 1977; Coleman, 1980; Maiuro et al., 1988; Waldo, 1987; Walker, 1979). Sonkin et al. (1985) suggest that low self-esteem may be a result of childhood experiences and of batterers' unrealistic expectations of their behavior and achievements. Additionally, Saunders (1982) suggests that lack of self-esteem and a sense of inadequacy may be partly responsible for the feelings of dependency, jealousy, and possessiveness noted in assaultive men.

Other researchers argue for a different role of self-esteem in affecting batterers' behavior. Goldstein and Rosenbaum (1985), for example, found that batterers scored lower on a measure of self-esteem and perceived more situations as damaging to their self-esteem. They suggest, however, that low self-esteem is not necessarily etiologically related to assaulting one's partner, but rather that assaulting one's partner lowers self-esteem.

Our clinical experience suggests that both these arguments have value. Overall, a sense that one is not all right, not enough, or not good enough does seem to be related to using violence against others. We see men who present as overly confident of themselves and their abilities, yet on further examination their sense of inadequacy becomes apparent. Low self-esteem does appear to be related to batterers' dependency and their need to control. On the other hand, their violent behavior increases their already diminished sense of themselves, leading them into a downward spiral of dysfunction.

"Jekyll and Hyde" Characteristics

Bernard and Bernard (1984) have reported that the men they have seen for treatment initially seemed socially and interpersonally skilled, amiable, and capable of effective communication. Later, after they had been in treatment, they were found to be almost exactly the opposite. Bernard and Bernard (1984) called this the "Jekyll and Hyde" presentation of batterers. Others have reported that these men do not typically appear powerful and threatening, but rather ineffectual and pathetic (Finkelhor, 1985; Maiuro et al., 1988).

Wife assaulters are often described by clinicians and by their partners as charming and lovable (Ganley & Harris, 1978). Certainly, most violent men are not violent all the time, and one of the reasons a battered woman may stay in a relationship is the hope that this charming, loving side of her partner's personality may "win out" over the violent, abusive side. Indeed, batterers can have positive, loving, and caring characteristics. However, our clinical experience suggests that this charming side is often one of the methods by which batterers convince women to be involved with them and manipulate them to stay after a violent incident. At times, this charm almost appears to be a parody of true affection, and often reflects a traditional, stereotypic notion of romance, rather than intimacy.

SITUATIONAL CHARACTERISTICS

Situational characteristics are those factors in the environment that might be more or less likely to increase the probability of an assault by a man who has some proclivity to abuse his partner. Isolation is often a "self-imposed" situation, although this is not always the case. None of the factors discussed below causes wife assault. In fact, many batterers are not isolated, unemployed, or under undue amounts of external stress. These factors may also emerge as a result of the violence and the batterer's controlling behaviors.

Isolation

The isolation commonly reported by wife assaulters is often psychological and emotional, as well as social. They tend to be distrustful of others, afraid of close, intimate relationships, and unable to share their emotions, other than anger and rage. They often confuse sexuality with affection or even courtesy, resulting in an inability to have female friends and not allowing their partners to have any contact with men. Their stereotypic sex-role indoctrination prohibits them from emotional contact with other men, which they often see as homosexual behavior.

In addition to feeling isolated themselves, batterers often isolate their partners and their children. In part, this is due to their dependency, control, and jealousy. However, isolation also serves the purpose of minimizing outside interference in their violent behavior. Even when wife assaulters report having many contacts and acquaintances in the community, their relationships tend to be superficial (Ganley, 1981b).

The isolation these men feel and create increases their dependency on their partners. Their partners may be their only personal contacts, even though these contacts may lack any real intimacy. Without their relationships with their partners, these men would feel totally isolated and alone in the world.

Stress

The presence of stress, both internal and external, has been associated with battering (Ganley & Harris, 1978). These men have learned to respond to stress with attempts to control others and with violence. When a batterer experiences stress—usually as frustration, helplessness, and anger—and strikes out in response to these emotions, his stress has been temporarily reduced and he may experience a physiological "high." His violence, often resulting in the immobility of the victim, allows him temporarily to regain complete control of a stressful or personally threatening situation. As a result, he has received a powerful positive reinforcement for his use of violence, which increases the likelihood that he will use it again (Sonkin et al., 1985).

Although we identified what we consider to be the primary cause of violence in the previous chapter, we consider stress to play a major role in the behavior of batterers. Stress is an effect of our dysfunctional patriarchal society and the heterosexual relationships commonly defined by its values. Additionally, the characteristics we describe in this chapter are also stressors for the men who possess them. Although battering cannot be explained by the presence of stress, stress is a salient characteristic of most wife assaulters. As mentioned in Chapter 1, focusing on stress reduction, while having useful short-term benefits in stopping violence, is not likely to be a long-term solution.

Status Inconsistency or Unemployment

Wife assault has been found to be associated with unemployment (Fitch & Papantonio, 1983; Gaguin, 1978; Lewis, 1987; Straus et al., 1980). This may be due to a number of factors: Loss of income may increase the batterer's stress, lack of employment may be seen as a failure to live up to his status expectations (Hornung, McCullough, & Sugimoto, 1981; O'Brien, 1971), or lack of a job may increase the time spent at home, increasing the opportunity for violence. In addition, Prescott and Letko (1977) report that batterers are more likely to be dissatisfied with their work.

In addition to unemployment, a difference in skills or status between a batterer and his partner may cause a batterer to use violence to demonstrate his ultimate power over her (Allen & Straus, 1980). Rounsaville (1978) found that the majority of battered women studied possessed job skills and/or education superior to that of their assaulters. His partner's superior skills are likely to threaten a batterer's ability to control her and to make her dependent on him to meet the financial needs of the family.

CHILDHOOD HISTORY OF VIOLENCE IN THE FAMILY

A number of studies have suggested that men who batter are more likely to have witnessed or experienced violence in their families of origin (Coleman, 1980; Fagan, Stewart, & Hansen, 1983; Rosenbaum & O'Leary, 1981a; San Francisco Family Violence Project, 1982; Schuerger & Reigle, 1988; Star, 1983; Straus et al., 1980). Estimates of the proportion of abusive men who come from violent family backgrounds have ranged from 50% (Sonkin et al., 1985) to 75-80% (Fitch & Papantonio, 1983; Waldo, 1987). Roy's (1982) survey of 4,000 cases of spouse abuse in New York revealed that 80% of these abusers came from violent homes.

By witnessing or experiencing violence as a child, the batterer learns through modeling that this is an appropriate way to deal with feelings. He also has little opportunity to learn other, more appropriate skills. In addition, the experience of violence in the family of origin is emotionally damaging and may leave the batterer with a generally higher level of anger and hostility. Sonkin et al. (1985) have shown that batterers who were physically or sexually abused as children experienced more anger than batterers who were not abused.

Stacey and Shupe (1983) question the role of childhood abuse in battering. In most studies the percentages obtained were not compared against control groups. If one-half of all heterosexual relationships contain some violence, it may be that close to half of all children have witnessed or experienced violence in their homes.

Browning (1983) found no difference in the histories of child abuse or violence in family of origin between batterers and nonbatterers. Briere (1987) also found no correlation between self-reported likelihood of using violence against a spouse and a family history of violence.

Our clinical experience suggests that enough men report a history of family violence that it does appear to be a variable. On the other hand, we have seen men who report no history of violence in their childhoods; experiencing violence as a child does not necessarily predict that a man will batter. As with other characteristics, these are important issues to explore in treatment. However, they can also be used by batterers as justifications and rationalizations to avoid taking responsibility for their assaultive behavior.

ATTITUDES

Although much has been written about the attitudes batterers have about marriage, sex roles, and women, little research has been done in this area. Most clinical descriptions of batterers suggest that they overidentify with the stereotypic masculine role and that they believe that men should be strong, dominant, superior, and successful (Bernard & Bernard, 1984; Coleman, 1980). In addition, they may have attitudes that justify the use of physical force against the ones they love (Saunders, 1982).

Briere (1987), sampling normal male college students, found a correlation between endorsement of the use of force against wives and negative attitudes toward women, attitudes supporting wife abuse, and attitudes supporting interpersonal violence. In addition, Saunders (1982) suggests that if a man believes that the use of violence is acceptable, he may be less likely to internalize controls that would inhibit violence.

Our clinical experience with assaultive men suggests that many of them do have a set of stereotypic attitudes and beliefs related to what men are supposed to be like and how women should be subservient to men. They also appear to have a callous attitude toward others' pain and suffering. Through learning and subsequently living with such dysfunctional attitudes, they appear to have never developed any sense of real empathy for others.

TYPOLOGIES

A number of writers have attempted to categorize wife abusers into types or categories. Elbow (1977), for instance, divides abusers into "controllers," "defenders," "approval seekers," and "incorporators." Faulk (1974) proposes five types of batterers based on interviews with 23 men awaiting trial on criminal charges for assaulting their wives: "dependent and passive," "dependent and suspicious," "violent and bullying," "successful and domineering," and "stable and normally affectionate."

Deschner (1984) suggests that batterers fall into one of eight categories: (1) social chaos/deprivation type, (2) child-parent type, (3) obsessive-compulsive type, (4) abnormal response to crying and loud complaining type, (5) specific scapegoat type, (6) pathologically jealous type, (7) mental illness type, and (8) mental disturbance type. A weakness in Deschner's typology is that she relies heavily on typologies of child abusers. Although there may be dynamics that are similar between child abuse and wife assault, there are also differences.

As mentioned at the beginning of this chapter, we have found little or no use for these typologies in clinical practice. Typologies tend to obscure the similarities batterers share and distract from assessment of individual differences among these men. We have not found any distinct "groups" of batterer types that would easily categorize the men we see.

SUMMARY

In this chapter we have reviewed the research and clinical findings on the characteristics of men who assault their wives. We have also attempted to share our own clinical observations of the men we have worked with. When one views these characteristics from an overall perspective, a picture of violent men emerges that we feel supports our perspective on battering.

This view suggests a portrait of a man who has been socialized in a patriarchal system and has overidentified with that system's beliefs, leading him to restrict his behaviors to those prescribed by the stereotypic masculine image.

His stereotypic sex-role training has provided him with few skills in intimate communication and he has learned to avoid and suppress his emotions. He is psychologically isolated, and his failure to live up to his rigid expectations have left him with low self-esteem. He may have seen his mother assaulted when he was a child, or he may have been beaten himself, leaving him feeling hurt, angry, and inadequate. He may have learned from this violence that the way to deal with his frustrations is to act out his anger.

Given his psychological isolation, he needs someone else to fill the void in his life. The only way he can allow himself to be intimate with another is through a heterosexual relationship. As this is his only other human contact in the world, he is extremely dependent on and jealous about his partner, and needs to control every move she makes to keep her from abandoning him. He believes that, as a man, he has the right to do this. At the same time, his stereotypic masculine training suggests that he should not depend on anyone, and he hates his partner for his own dependency. His need for power and control may also be acted out in drinking or using drugs.

Under internal or external stress, this man batters his partner. Violence helps him to regain control of a threatening situation, but he then feels panic that she may leave him. He also may detest his own behavior, but, through minimization, denial, or projection, he avoids looking at it. If his partner leaves him, he will become depressed and possibly suicidal or homicidal. If she does not, his violence has worked and he will use it again to gain control over her.

Although this picture is somewhat oversimplified and certainly does not fit every batterer, some component of these traits has been present in almost every man we have seen for batterers' treatment. In order for men to change, we must challenge their sexist beliefs and attitudes, demand that they give up their controlling and violent behaviors, confront their defenses and insist they take full responsibility for their violence, and teach them to identify and express their emotions appropriately.

3

TREATMENT PERSPECTIVES

The theoretical perspectives reviewed in Chapter 1 have given rise to a number of treatment modalities for men who assault their partners. Many of these modalities include areas that are addressed in common, but differ by how much each area is emphasized and the theoretical base from which the battering is approached (Brennan, 1985). Treatment of batterers has involved individual therapy, marital and family therapy and couples' groups, anger control groups, psychoeducational and psychotherapeutic groups, and coordinated programs involving group treatment and community intervention.

In reviewing theoretical perspectives and batterers' characteristics, we have already made a number of statements regarding the problems with both individual and marital/couples therapy as applied to wife assaulters. When men are seen individually and intrapsychic issues are addressed, counselors are more likely to overlook or lose sight of both societal and patriarchal dynamics and power and control issues. Mental health professionals may subtly and overtly impart their own sexist and patriarchal views to their clients by supporting explanations that are biased against women, supporting social structures that oppress women, and using stereotypic feminine traits as models of mental health for women (Bograd, 1984).

By its nature, individual therapy tends to be a supportive environment. In effect, counselors may end up colluding with batterers and supporting their justifications and continued use of power. Correcting intrapsychic problems is not likely to decrease the violence if the batterer is still being rewarded for his behavior and continues to gain compliance from his partner through his violence (Adams, 1988b; Adams & McCormick, 1982; Rosenbaum, 1986).

Marital or couples therapy and family therapy, derived from a family systems perspective, equalizes the responsibility for the violence between the batterer and his partner (Adams, 1988b). As mentioned in earlier chapters, this treatment approach does not address the violent behavior of the batterer as the main problem, but rather the interactions between the couple, which are seen to lead to violence. We view this treatment modality as abusive to women, sexist in nature, not effective in stopping men's violence, and dangerous for battered women.

At times, most treatment programs will see men individually, especially if they are in crisis, and some will see the couple together after extensive and successful group treatment aimed at ending the violence. We feel, however, that these approaches should never be used in directly and initially addressing men's violence toward their partners.

The most common form of treatment with batterers is the psychoeducational or psychotherapeutic group approach (Roberts, 1984). These programs also tend to differ from each other in what areas they emphasize most and in their theoretical base. Although some programs have had informal or clinical evaluations of their success rates, no formal comparative studies have been reported that suggest which form of treatment is most successful (Sonkin, Martin, & Walker, 1985).

Some psychotherapy group approaches focus solely on anger control, while others may use some forms of anger control within their programs. In this chapter, we will review anger control techniques and address the issue of using these techniques in isolation. We will review psychoeducational and psychotherapeutic models. Finally, we will look at the issue of using educational and therapeutic models in coordination with other community interventions.

We have chosen to focus our efforts throughout this book on treatment provision, since we feel that the subject could not be covered adequately in less space. While the treatment approach presented in this book would be described as a psychoeducational and a psychotherapeutic group approach, we stress the importance of coordinating treatment efforts with structural interventions to alter our society's covert and overt support of violence against women. Helping individual men to end their violence toward their partners, while essential in the struggle to end violence toward women in our society, can be a "finger in the dike" effort without a major change in our society's patriarchal and oppressive attitudes and behaviors toward women.

ANGER CONTROL TECHNIQUES

Essentially behavioral and cognitive-behavioral interventions, anger management and control techniques have been an integral part of most group approaches to treatment since the development of batterers' treatment programs. Ganley and Harris (1978) list the identification of anger (and other feelings) and increased ability to manage anger as two of seven primary treatment objectives for batterers. Sonkin et al. (1985) identify the development of stress-reduction skills, visual imagery, self-hypnosis, progressive relaxation, and other stress-reduction techniques as one of fourteen primary goals of treatment.

Some authors have recently argued against the use of anger control treatment for men who batter (Gondolf & Russell, 1986). Gondolf (1985a, 1985c) states that a variety of anger control programs have emerged without an empirical data base to support them. Other writers have questioned the importance of anger as a problem for wife assaulters, suggesting that rigid sex-role attitudes and expectations and the need for dominance and control are more closely related to their violent behavior (Dobash & Dobash, 1979; Maiuro, Cahn, Vitaliano, Wagner, & Zegree, 1988; Schechter, 1982).

Although these arguments appear to be valid, the issue may be more one of how much one focuses on anger control, the message that may be imparted to men about why they are violent, and what treatment success means, than of the use of anger control itself. Our experience is that anger control is one of the tools men can use to stop their physical violence immediately. It imparts the message that they can control their violence, thus implying to them that they are, in fact, responsible for their behavior. On the other hand, it is only one component of a treatment program that must focus on power and control issues and on male socialization to violence against women.

Anger control has focused on three main areas: (1) relaxation and stress reduction, (2) accurate identification of emotions and cognitive restructuring, and (3) interpersonal skills development. In this section, we will essentially focus on a review of these areas. More detailed presentations of these issues can be found in the descriptions of the treatment modules.

Relaxation Training

Relaxation training has been used in a number of treatment programs described in the literature (e.g., Deschner, McNeil, & Moore, 1986; Edelson, 1984; Ganley, 1981b; Sonkin et al., 1985). Edelson (1984) describes relaxation training as learning the ability to identify and relax increasing body tension. A relaxed state is seen as incompatible with an angry, agitated state or with an anxious state (Wolpe, 1973). If a person can relax, she or he can perform more easily and effectively in stress-inducing situations (Edelson, 1984).

Most relaxation training programs are based either on Jacobson's (1938) progressive relaxation method or on some form of guided imagery or self-hypnosis. In using Jacobson's progressive relaxation method, the client first purposely tenses muscles in particular parts of the body and then relaxes these muscles naturally due to the tension applied. The client is led through each muscle group in the body (hand, forearm, neck, and so on) until a state of total relaxation is achieved. This helps clients not only to learn how to relax, but also to identify feelings of tension and relaxation.

Guided imagery or self-hypnosis usually involves the counselor taking clients through verbal relaxation suggestions and then using imagery (usually visual scenes) to deepen the sense of peace, comfort, and relaxation. The clients are then trained to do this with their own internal scripts in situations outside of counseling.

Relaxation training as a form of anger control is usually most effective when combined with other interventions, such as cognitive restructuring (Novaco, 1975) or time-outs (removing oneself from a stressful situation). Although a useful component of a program, our program tends to devote only a limited amount of time to it.

Identification of Emotions and Cognitive Restructuring

Lack of ability to know what one is feeling, a rigid set of sex-role stereotypic expectations of self and others, faulty styles of thinking, and distortion of events were identified as common characteristics of batterers in the previous chapter. Anger and violence are seen as resulting from rigid beliefs and expectations, mixed with the batterer's needs and dependency, that contribute to the distortion of neutral events into apparently threatening situations. Cognitive restructuring involves teaching self-monitoring and identification of feelings, challenging the irrational beliefs of the client, teaching the client to challenge irrational beliefs on his or her own, and teaching the client to replace distorted patterns of thinking with more appropriate internal dialogues (Edelson, 1984).

One of the ways in which batterers' treatment uses cognitive restructuring is through education on identification of feelings and the cycle of violence and through self-monitoring with diaries called "anger logs." In addition to assisting the batterer to reinterpret his anger as a more primary emotion, identification of feelings directly confronts his expectations of himself and others. Learning about the cycle of violence connects his distortions to the escalation of his anger and his subsequent violence, and helps him to identify the long-term consequences of his behavior. In general, cognitive restructuring helps the batterer to analyze his thinking patterns and interrupt and alter them. Self-monitoring with an anger log generalizes this intervention from the therapy setting to the environment. In addition to direct confrontation, role play, and education on cognitive restructuring, we also use covert sensitization as a means of self-monitoring and behavioral interruption.

Interpersonal Skills Training

In addition to supplying men with tools to remain nonviolent, interpersonal skills training functions as an anger control method by teaching men how to resolve conflicts without the use of coercion and violence. Interpersonal skills usually involve conflict management, the development of empathy, and assertive, noncoercive, and nonmanipulative communications.

Edelson (1984) has identified eight procedures to be used in a specific sequence in interpersonal skills training:

(1) Identify the interpersonal situations that are most difficult for an individual.
(2) Identify the "critical moment," the point at which a person may have acted differently to alter the outcome.
(3) Examine all the possible choices in the situation and choose the one most likely to enhance the chances of a positive outcome.
(4) Model the interaction for the client.
(5) Role-play the interaction with the client.
(6) Provide feedback on the client's communication.
(7) Rehearse the situation with the client.
(8) Contract with the client to use the new skills practiced in a situation.

Using this model, Edelson (1984) suggests that the client should learn to identify and state the parameters of a problem, be able to identify and express his feelings and state his partner's point of view, and be able to offer solutions and negotiate a final compromise. If the stress becomes too high in a situation, he should be able to remove himself by taking a time-out.

The use of the anger funnel model, mentioned in the previous chapter and described in the treatment modules, is one of the primary tools in teaching identification of feelings. By combining this model with the behavioral techniques mentioned above in preparing the anger log, training can be generalized from therapy to interpersonal encounters.

In addition to the anger control techniques mentioned above, we also use aerobic exercise as a stress-reduction technique. This generally includes walking, running, or cycling. We discourage violent or competitive exercises as ways to reduce stress, and absolutely prohibit exercises that mimic violence, such as chopping wood.

Some therapists have suggested that physical aggression toward an object or verbal aggression can help to control anger and violence. We disagree. Physical aggression toward an object serves to maintain the reinforcement value of violence. The belief that verbal aggression relieves stress and thus reduces the likelihood that physical aggression will be used has not been confirmed by research (Adams, 1988b; Berkowitz, 1973; Straus, 1974; Tavris, 1982). Verbal aggression is another form of violence that can be used by these men to control and dominate. Encouraging verbal aggression on the grounds of expressing oneself honestly and relieving stress simply justifies this form of violence (Pence, 1985).

As mentioned above, anger control techniques are part of a larger, more comprehensive treatment program. Used by themselves, they tend not to be successful as a long-term intervention aimed at ending the abusive use of power associated with violence. The potential for a return to violence is significant as long as the use of power and control continues.

PSYCHOEDUCATIONAL GROUP INTERVENTIONS

As of 1985, Gondolf (1985c) reported that approximately 150 treatment programs dealing directly with batterers had been developed. Some of the more well-known programs include the Domestic Abuse Project of Minneapolis, the Domestic Abuse Intervention Project of Duluth, Minnesota, RAVEN of St. Louis, EMERGE of Boston, and AMEND of Denver. Since 1985, new programs have continued to develop, both at a grass-roots community level and in more traditional mental health settings. The majority of these programs are psychoeducational group interventions.

Psychoeducational group treatment programs are not what would normally be categorized as traditional psychotherapy groups, although many group treatment programs using this model contain some psychotherapy components. Their central focus, however, is to educate the batterer about his violence and to attempt to have him accept responsibility for his violence and understand how his violence damages his family and himself (Bern & Bern, 1984).

These programs tend to differ in terms of which skills are emphasized and how much emphasis is placed on educating men regarding male power and control issues (Adams, 1988b; Pence & Shepard, 1988). Skills emphasized have included systematic relaxation training (Edelson, Miller, & Stone, 1983; Ganley, 1981a; Purdy & Nickle, 1981; Sonkin & Durphy, 1982; Sonkin et al., 1985), assertiveness (Lange & Jakubowski, 1976; Sonkin & Durphy, 1982), cognitive restructuring (Edelson et al., 1983; Brygger & Edelson, 1987; Sonkin et al., 1985), and education on male socialization to oppress women (Adams, 1988b; Brygger & Edelson, 1987; Pence & Shepard, 1988).

Although most programs contain some training in social skills, a number of authors have pointed out that this training should take place only after a nonnegotiable abstinence from violence has been achieved (Adams, 1988b; Gondolf, 1985c). Ganley (1981b) has listed seven commonalities in effective treatment programs:

(1) a clear and consistent primary goal of ending the violence
(2) a focus on the batterer taking responsibility for his behavior
(3) the use of confrontation
(4) the use of a psychoeducational approach
(5) a structured format
(6) the use of a directive approach by the counselor
(7) the use of groups

Most programs use either a small group approach (Edelson, 1984) or education groups separate from therapy groups (Pence & Shepard, 1988). The use of groups in this setting is a much more effective and powerful approach than seeing the men individually. Men are exposed to a variety of feedback in group and are reinforced by other men who are trying to change (Edelson, 1984). Groups are especially effective in an educational setting, where material can be shared efficiently and the group can be used to stimulate men's thinking about the material through such procedures as brainstorming and directive feedback. Skills training can proceed more effectively when several men participate in modeling and role-playing situations. Groups are also effective in decreasing men's isolation and in helping them develop interpersonal support systems (Sonkin et al., 1985).

Most group programs are time limited, with a group of men starting the group together and finishing together. They use a structured format, with material and objectives to be covered sequentially. The length of the group programs reported have ranged from 6 sessions (Frank & Houghton, 1982) to 32 sessions (Brygger & Edelson, 1987). Many of the programs are coordinated with battered women's support groups, although generally one-half or more of the men participate without their partners (Brygger & Edelson, 1987). Gondolf (1985c) reports that approximately one-third of the men who enter the RAVEN program drop out before completing treatment.

A number of these programs, such as EMERGE in Boston and RAVEN in St. Louis, are self-help groups. Although EMERGE and

RAVEN are supervised by mental health professionals, other self-help programs have been criticized for providing a setting where men may reinforce each other in their sexist attitudes and violent behavior (Gondolf, 1985c).

Psychoeducational programs have been criticized by feminists when their interventions are primarily aimed at stress reduction and interpersonal skills training, and power and control issues are ignored or minimized (Adams, 1988b). Groups that ignore these issues may collude with the men in their sexist attitudes and defenses. Group leaders who identify with some aspects of "men's liberation" may impart a notion that the men are victims, rather than focusing on their victimizing (Gondolf, 1985c).

Two model programs that address these issues are the Domestic Abuse Project of Minneapolis and the Domestic Abuse Intervention Project of Duluth. Although their pioneering community coordinating efforts will be discussed in the next section, a brief highlight of their treatment programs can serve as a model for a feminist psychoeducational program.

The Domestic Abuse Project was developed in Minneapolis in 1979 (Brygger & Edelson, 1987). It uses a multisystem intervention approach by providing safety to women and children, treating men, supporting and empowering women, and working at changing social institutions. The men's treatment program is a group program that meets for 2½ hours twice a week for 16 weeks. The program first addresses issues of safety through the development of Control Plans and teaching men about cues to violence and anger escalation.

Early sessions focus on power and control issues by examining violence as a way of controlling women, analyzing violent incidents, and discussing issues related to aggression and hostility. Relaxation and skills training are also provided. Later sessions focus on group process and individual problems, as well as addressing male socialization, sexual abuse, parenting, and family of origin issues (Brygger & Edelson, 1987). Brygger and Edelson (1987) report that two of three men who complete the program are nonviolent six months after completion.

The Domestic Abuse Intervention Project (DAIP) was founded in Duluth in 1979 as a model project and has since been replicated in more than twenty Minnesota communities (Pence & Shepard, 1988). It was developed as a community intervention approach to domestic violence, of which the men's program was only one part. The central focus of the program is addressing the social acceptance of male violence and the use of violence to control and dominate women (Paymar & Pence, 1985; Pence & Shepard, 1988).

The program is divided into counseling groups supervised by DAIP and education classes run by DAIP. The men in the program contract for 26 weeks, including 2 orientation sessions. Of the men in the program, 80% attend 12 weeks of group and 12 weeks of education; 20% attend 24 weeks of education. The counseling groups focus on anger management, stress reduction, and conflict resolution. While the counseling groups introduce the concept of power and control, the education programs emphasize it. In addition to the use of time-outs and anger logs in the counseling groups, DAIP also uses "control logs" for men to monitor their controlling behaviors (Pence & Shepard, 1988).

Our perspective on wife assault emphasizes the critical significance of patriarchy in our society, male socialization in dominance and control over women and children, and the sanctioning of the use of violence as a tool to enforce this dominance as the root of men's violence toward their partners. Although we see the need for individual skills training and addressing individual issues with men who batter, we also believe that psychoeducational treatment programs must address these core issues if they are to be effective. As vital as these issues are, men are unlikely to change their abusive behavior solely as the result of education. Therefore, batterers' programs need to address the problem on multiple levels.

COORDINATED COMMUNITY INTERVENTIONS

Batterers' treatment programs vary in how much they may be coordinated with battered women's services and whether they are part of a larger, community-based intervention to end men's violence against their partners. Men's programs run in isolation are not as likely to be effective as are coordinated programs. Without open lines of communication to other services, they run the risk of becoming isolated, closed systems that are vulnerable to the socialization pressures of our culture and to the inherent male socialization of the (usually male) group leaders. Gondolf (1985c) suggests that coordination with, if not direction by, women's services should be a fundamental stipulation of providing services for men.

Any program that addresses men's violence against their partners must be nonsexist in nature (Bern & Bern, 1984). Although most men who choose to work with wife assaulters may view themselves as relatively nonsexist or as feminists, the pervasive nature of male sex-role socialization is often not easily apparent in its sometimes subtle expression. Men can collude with other men in unrecognized, covert ways, supporting their male expectations, stereotypes, and dominating behaviors. Due to sex-role socialization, men often use violent or aggressive language in dealing with problems, subtly reinforcing aggression in male clients. Constant communication and monitoring of these behaviors on the part of batterers' counselors by women who work with victims or by women cofacilitators can help men to work more effectively with their clients and to improve their own lives.

When batterers' programs are separate organizations, they need to be careful that they do not compete with women's services for funding or power (Gondolf, 1985c). However, Gondolf (1985c) also believes that men's programs may benefit from some separation from women's shelters and from being distinct organizations. Men should take primary responsibility for ending men's violence against women, and women should not be responsible for changing men. On the other hand, male socialization often leads men to respond negatively when they feel their power and autonomy, as well as their good intentions, are challenged. Although ostensibly coordinated with women's services, some men's programs have balked when challenged on issues of colluding with clients or subtly reinforcing male stereotypes. In order to challenge batterers to give up their power and control over their partners, men's counselors need to identify and challenge themselves on their own power and control issues, particularly in their relationships with women's programs.

In addition to coordinating batterers' treatment services with women's services, these programs will be most effective when they are part of a community response to men's violence against their partners. One of the fundamental principles inherent in a community response is that domestic violence is illegal and that there should be criminal justice consequences for wife assault. In order to implement such a response, men's and women's services need to be involved in a community change effort that involves many agencies, including the police, prosecutors, judges, educators, medical services, and mental health services.

As mentioned above, a pioneer effort at community intervention in domestic violence has been the Domestic Abuse Intervention Project in Duluth, Minnesota. Begun with a grant in 1979, the program enlisted the cooperation of the police department, prosecuting attorneys, and judges to respond to domestic violence as a crime. A mandated arrest policy was established whereby an officer was required to make an arrest when there were visible injuries that were inflicted within the previous four hours by an individual cohabiting with the victim. The judges removed domestic assault from the bond schedule, resulting in the batterer remaining in custody until arraignment. During this period, the victim is visited in her home by advocates from the women's services program and the batterer is visited in jail by a volunteer from the men's program. First offenders are routinely sentenced, upon being found guilty, to either time in jail and a fine or suspension of sentence if the offender participates in and completes the treatment program.

In addition to increasing the arrests for domestic violence in Duluth, positive results regarding nonviolence following treatment have been reported (Novak & Galaway, 1983). Police injuries incurred while responding to domestic violence situations also dropped significantly (Pence, 1985).

Since the inception of the Duluth project, other cities have developed their own proarrest policies and court-mandated treatment programs, including Minneapolis, Seattle, Denver, San Francisco, and Atlanta (Adams, 1988b; Brygger & Edelson, 1987; Ganley, 1981a; Paymar & Pence, 1985; Pence & Shepard, 1988; Star, 1983). In a survey of 44 batterers' treatment groups, Roberts (1984) reports that 48% had a strong referral program with the courts, while 23% had minimal or no court coordination.

The development of lines of communication to community agencies, usually male dominated, can be time-consuming and frustrating. One person in a key position who resists change can sabotage most of a community effort. The slow and tedious process of educating and convincing people to change often seems overwhelming and fruitless.

At times, treating the immediate and individual suffering from men's violence against their partners can drain and divert energy from attempts to change our patriarchal society (Gondolf, 1985a,

1985c). The importance of this work, however, cannot be emphasized enough. Without increasing social and legal sanctions against
wife assault, and without changes in our society's patriarchal sanctioning of men's domination and control of women, our treatment
programs will have only a minimal effect in ending men's violence
against their partners.

PART II

INDIVIDUAL CONTACTS

4

FIRST CONTACTS

If we were to assign priorities to the different components of the helping process in terms of how essential each is to doing a good job, we would put first contacts or beginnings near the top of the list. Though this is true of most counseling models, our experiences with batterers lead us to highlight this stage of our relationships with these men. A first contact is a foundation for the man's relationships with both therapist and program. In view of an abuser's fluctuating motivation and his psychological defenses, the soundness of this foundation seems especially important. We believe that the quality of a first contact with an abuser is a major factor in determining what follows.

The topic of beginnings is reminiscent of a beginner's course in counseling skills. Novice counselors take little for granted in first sessions; on-the-job training requires concentration. With perseverance and talent, the counselor learns those skills that are appropriate to the beginning phase of the helping process. Nevertheless, as counselors become more experienced, consciousness of the importance of beginnings recedes into the background. They develop a routine first-contact style. Counselors' interests then gravitate to the latest exciting advancements in techniques employed in what is often referred to as the "middle phase" of helping.

While this is understandable, it can be helpful to go back to the basics to review what might have been learned and forgotten. When a review of those basics is concerned with the beginning phase of helping, one remembers how absolutely pivotal this phase is in terms of its power to facilitate or hinder what follows. The premise of this chapter, then, is that the success or failure of an assaultive man to follow through with counseling beyond a first contact depends, in large part, on the nature of that first contact with the therapist.

This chapter examines beginnings. Batterers on the road to peace have a difficult journey. Those who stumble at the start may abandon the road. Counselors will be better guides if they know the men who start the journey. With this in mind, we present a discussion of what propels men to seek help and the counseling skills that are helpful in nurturing this motivation. To help illustrate first-contact issues and skills, we will present and discuss extensive dialogue from a first-contact session.

CLIENT PRESENTATION

Despite the frightening label, a batterer is not very different from people with other problems. Like others, he has various stressors creating tension. He may handle some well and others not so well; like other people, he sometimes feels overwhelmed by life. He is different from others in an important way; he has learned that striking out against another relieves stress, helps him to feel powerful, masculine, and in control. Most important, then, is that at least one of his coping mechanisms is extremely destructive and hurtful to others.

At various points in his life, a man who has a problem with violence will experience extreme distress. We think this distress is inextricably connected to this particular problem. This is not to say that other maladaptive coping mechanisms (e.g., chemical abuse) are not connected to the distress. However, we believe that the consequences of using violence extend into every dimension of his life. While the effects on victims are well known, his violence also always returns to haunt him. It destroys his intimate relationships, feeds his shame, breeds secrecy, and obliterates self-respect.

A batterer in distress may become so infused with helplessness and hopelessness that he feels compelled to get help. If he sees a professional, he may or may not disclose his problem with violence.

When this problem remains a secret, we believe counseling will have minimal value; symptoms may be relieved but the problem will persist. Additionally, a dangerous man will continue his lethal behavior. Consequently, we recommend standardized screening for violence in all counselors' first contacts with any client. The sooner this aspect of a violent man's life can be identified, the sooner he can receive appropriate help.

The Man's Motivation

In looking at first contacts, a discussion of the motivating factors propelling a man to seek help is useful. What motivates him to reach out? One obvious answer is that he realizes he has a problem with violence and is convinced that he cannot deal with it on his own. Though some men do arrive at this conclusion and voluntarily identify battering as the problem, motivation for seeking help is usually more complex.

It has been stated that men who batter their partners

(1) minimize or deny the seriousness of their behavior (Davidson, 1978; Ganley, 1981b; Law Enforcement Assistance Administration, 1981; Pagelow, 1981);

(2) externalize responsibility for the violence to situations and other people (Ganley, 1981b; Law Enforcement Assistance Administration, 1981; Star, 1980; Walker, 1979);

(3) need to control and dominate people, particularly their partners (Ganley, 1981b); and

(4) isolate their victims and keep a shroud of secrecy over the abuse (Walker, 1979).

It is also claimed that wife abuse is an expression of the man's domination of a woman (Dobash & Dobash, 1979; Martin, 1981), and that men believe this power to dominate is necessary. If we accept as true both the characteristic behaviors and the power motive, we are left with an interesting question: Why would a batterer begin to abandon his defenses and relinquish power by seeking help for his violence? The question is even more compelling in light of the ways in which violence has been functional for him in the relationship. Violence against a partner can be viewed as a means to an end. As a tool, it is instrumental in achieving goals. Violent behavior is reinforced by some of these consequences:

(1) It ensures that the man "wins" disputes.
(2) It provides immediate relief from the unpleasant effects of high stress levels.
(3) It maintains the status quo in the relationship.
(4) It often ensures that the woman will not leave him, and thereby guarantees that the relationship will continue.

We have noticed that a man's decision to get help is the result of new, self-defeating consequences of abuse. Whereas violence was once reinforced by the rewards it produced, it may begin to generate aversive consequences or punishment for the man. In our experience, most men step forward after some very significant, unusual, and aversive events have occurred. Very often, these events include one or more of the following:

(1) His partner is threatening to leave him. One way to prevent her leaving is to get help. On occasion, the woman may specify professional help as a condition of her staying.
(2) His partner has actually left him. Again, "voluntarily" getting help or following through with her demand that he get help is one way to preserve the relationship.
(3) Following his violence, he is in the "honeymoon stage" or the stage of "kindness and contrite, loving behavior" of the cycle of violence (Walker, 1979). At this point, his reluctance to see violence as a problem may be reduced and he may act on his promises to change his behavior. Guilt may be a motivator.
(4) A new event or element surfaces that totally alters his perspective on his behavior. For example, for the first time, his behavior may have resulted in severe bodily harm to the woman, or his violence may have extended to his children. Realizing the impact of his behavior on others may weaken his minimization and denial.
(5) The authorities have intervened and have ordered him to seek help.

In the above situations, the man may be direct with a therapist in his disclosure of abuse. However, abuse may also be revealed indirectly. A man may seek help for a matter ostensibly unrelated to violence. In the course of exploring another problem area with a therapist, violence against women and/or children may emerge. A few examples follow:

(1) Couples counseling may be sought by a couple because of a deteriorating relationship.
(2) Family counseling may be utilized when "acting-out" children are seen as identified patients.
(3) Medical help may be sought for stress-related disorders.
(4) Mental health hospital emergency departments or crisis hotlines may be contacted by a man experiencing a crisis.
(5) Life-threatening situations with the potential for suicide or homicide may involve police and other emergency services.
(6) The courts may order a man into counseling because of his history of violence outside the home.

Whether the man is seeking help directly or indirectly, there is usually some degree of pain and distress propelling him to look for solutions outside his typical problem-solving abilities and support systems. A useful way of looking at motivation for seeking help is in terms of its external or internal locus. External motivators can be seen as pressures having their source outside the man. Court-mandated counseling, demands by the partner to seek counseling, threats of family dissolution, and pressure by child protection authorities are all examples of external motivators. Internal motivators have their source within the man. They may be feelings and thoughts about the abuse that are somewhat independent of external pressures. Fear that violence will escalate to murderous proportions, the realization that current behavior is a reenactment of his own father's behavior, and concern about the effects of violence on his children are all examples of internal motivators that may be sufficient to kindle a desire for help.

It is difficult to classify motivation to seek help as purely external or purely internal. We have noticed that men who ask for professional help because of their violence are, initially, more powerfully motivated by external factors. For most there is the threat of some loss—loss of relationship, family, personal liberty, and so on. Counselors should remember the universality of this threat when they categorize clients in terms of motivation. For example, therapists often accentuate differences between court-mandated and non-court-mandated clients. Though there are differences between the two groups, we think the influence of external motivators on all abusers makes the traditional voluntary/involuntary categorization scheme less clinically relevant than it appears.

Ambivalence About Change

Usually, by the time a man sees a counselor, he is haunted by ambivalence. The negative side of this ambivalence retards growth and change. It may be founded in fear. Fear of losing power over his partner, of a diminished masculinity, or of her gaining power over him are common. A man who does not know how to respond constructively to conflict is frightened by what he sees as his only alternative—passivity. Consequently, he chooses to walk the well-worn path of violence and abuse. Like water, he follows the path of least resistance in his response to stress and conflict. Also on the negative side, shame may influence a man against seeking help or following through with a specialized counseling program after a first contact with a therapist. A man may fear being punished if the true extent of his behavior is known by others. His avoidance of talking honestly about his violence requires skill and sensitivity from counselors.

There is a positive side to this ambivalence. We believe most abusers, at a deep level, have moral qualms about their behavior. This sense is there despite initial pretense that everything is fine. In our experience, most abusive men who voluntarily progress to the point of seeing a counselor have at least an ill-defined but persistent conviction that something is terribly wrong in their lives. Overtly, they may protest that it is their partners' fault or that it is a relationship problem. However, if conversations with a counselor can proceed to the point where a man is asked, "How do you feel about the way you handle conflicts with your partner?" self-doubt or outright self-contempt usually surfaces.

Again on the positive side, while violence once "worked" for him, it may be bringing fewer rewards than it once did. It may even be producing negative or aversive consequences of some kind. The best thing that can happen to an abuser and those he hurts is that his violence becomes increasingly self-defeating. This can jar him into seeing the tragic costs of his behavior toward others and toward himself, and can nurture the motivation to change.

Circumstances and Client Presentation

Men who abuse their partners may be roughly divided into groups according to the circumstances motivating them to seek help. With each group, we have noticed certain common behaviors that seem related to the circumstances motivating them to seek counseling. We discuss five variations in client presentation so the reader may know what to expect in first contacts.

(1) Mandated men responding with compliance. It is usually criminal justice authorities who order men to seek help. However, in some locales, child protection agencies may pressure men to get help with the threat of denying access to their children. In either case, the effect is similar. Fear of loss is a powerful motivator. In one situation, there is potential loss of freedom through incarceration; in the other, there is potential loss of family.

Many mandated men behave with compliance in a first contact in the hope that the therapist will submit a favorable report to authorities. Often, a compliant man behaves in a manner suggesting that his violence is not an issue for him. His immediate agenda is to placate. If he is able to attain control over the first session, he may demonstrate this by avoiding discussion of his violence, and by attempting to influence the counselor to like him. A compliant man may also present issues in a way that suggests he is a victim of a vindictive or unstable partner who has deceived authorities.

(2) Mandated men responding with belligerence. A hostile stance in a first contact may communicate a variety of messages. It may be a man's way of expressing fear. Fear of confusing circumstances and an uncertain outcome, fear of having the full extent of his violence exposed, and fear of losing his family are all examples of vulnerabilities protected by open belligerence. Because of this fear, hostility toward the therapist may be a method of controlling the session and the counselor and thereby reducing the fearfulness of the situation. If we accept that an abuser needs to feel in control of people and situations, this behavior makes sense.

Belligerent behavior may serve another, more obvious function. Many men are angry and indignant about their involvement with the criminal justice or child protection systems. They believe the state has no business interfering in "family matters." Venting these feelings at people in positions of obvious power is risky. In contrast to probation workers, judges, and child protection workers, the counselor may be regarded as a safe target for suppressed anger.

We have noticed that some men ordered into counseling fluctuate between belligerent and compliant behavior. If they discover that their attempts to control the counselor through compliance do not work, they might attempt to exert control through belligerence.

(3) Men who are charged with court appearance pending. A man who has been charged with assault but has yet to face the court process may understand that it is in his best interests to enroll quickly in a counseling program. Very often a defense attorney advises the man in this regard. During his first session with the therapist, he may appear eager to please but preoccupied with having the counselor write a letter to aid his defense. Alternatively, he can be distant and uninvolved when talking about violence but suddenly responsive to any discussion of his legal predicament.

(4) Men with partners in shelters. Occasionally, a man will arrive at a batterer's counseling program shortly after his partner has fled to a shelter. He may be referred by emergency or crisis services, or by the shelter itself. Having entered the phase in the cycle of violence (Walker, 1979) known as "kindness and contrite, loving behavior," which often follows abuse, he feels sorry and makes promises never to do it again. His idea of help at this time is to find an ally in his effort to convince his partner to come home. A counselor normally experiences a clash of agendas with such a man. The man wants "action," perhaps in the form of a phone call to the shelter; the counselor wants the man to look at himself and his behavior.

(5) The "aware" or "feminist" man. Though rare, counselors will occasionally meet an abuser who presents himself as a liberated or aware man. He identifies himself as a member of a consciousness-raising group or a men's organization. He speaks well on topics such as sex roles, feelings, and parenting. In a similar vein, a counselor might meet an abuser who seems aware of the issues of oppression, and speaks in a politically correct manner. Being liberal, he may voice support for liberal and feminist concerns, strive to appear well read, and launch a discussion of sophisticated issues.

We see at least two possible ways of regarding this man. This type of presentation may simply be the man's way of "establishing credentials" with the counselor. In this case, it is fairly innocuous. With minimal prodding, the session can turn to the central problem. Second, a man who identifies strongly with egalitarian beliefs and movements is in an untenable position; his behavior is radically at odds with his beliefs. Retreating to intellectualism may be a defense against looking at his abuse.

These presentations, fluctuating motivation, and ambivalence often make for difficult first-contact sessions. The remainder of this chapter will explore elements of a constructive counselor response.

COUNSELOR PRESENTATION

Skillfulness and Technique

Of course, counselors beginning to work with abusers will be concerned about particular skills helpful with this population. Some of the major ones will be discussed in this section. We believe that, in preparing to start this work, particular counseling techniques must be based in awareness of some broader issues. Traditionally, this awareness has been distinguished from technique. However, our definition of the term *skilled* embraces more than particular techniques. To us, the skilled family violence therapist's technique is rooted in and informed by attitudes, beliefs, and perspectives on the problem and intervention. Attitudes about wife assault, responsibility, gender roles, therapist role, and program mandate, to name a few, give a grounding for the employment of technique. Though these elements of skillfulness are not examined in this chapter, we urge the reader to consider seriously those portions of previous chapters touching on these and the final chapter on counselors' issues prior to starting a group. While we are not sufficiently arrogant to expect all readers to agree with our position, we hope that our statement of the issues will be thought-provoking.

Therapist Responsibility

Two basic outcomes are possible in a first contact. On the one hand, the man may persistently cling to his defenses, deny that a problem with violence exists, and leave the encounter having learned little. In such an instance, it is possible that he may harden himself against the prospect of ever again seeking help. On the other hand, he may risk lowering his defenses, entertain the notion that he has a problem, and be willing to return to see the counselor or willingly accept an appropriate referral.

Counselors may have learned in their training that clients must accept responsibility for their behavior. This belief is often most helpful in those situations where, despite all attempts on the part of the counselor to be helpful, a client is simply not receptive. Counselors can relieve themselves of a responsibility that belongs to the client. While there is considerable wisdom in this stance, we contend that the most effective therapists are able to approach a client and his problems in a manner that facilitates client receptivity. While ultimate responsibility belongs to the client, the therapist has some responsibility to invite the client to change. Metaphorically speaking, the counselor tries to open the door or clear the path for change. Because this population is so defended against the issues of responsibility and the need for change, the counselor needs the skills that will help clients see themselves and their behavior clearly.

If the task of a counselor in a first contact can be summarized in one phrase, it might be this: to become an ally of that part of the man that gravitates toward change. Using another metaphor, ambivalence is like an old-fashioned balance scale. On one side are fear, shame, bravado, pride, and so on—all threatening to isolate the man from things that can help him change and grow. On the other side of the scale are knowledge of wrongful behavior and desires for a better life, better relationships, and self-respect. The counselor's job is to nurture everything on the latter side—to tip the balance of the scale and thereby help the man onto the difficult road to peace.

In opening the door to change, we believe there are specific, indispensable techniques or skills that must be employed. These are not new counseling skills. All trained counselors have learned them. However, if the counselor is to do effective work with batterers, they are skills that should be honed to the point of excellence.

Talking About Violence in Behavioral Terms

Perpetrators of violence often minimize the seriousness of their behavior (Ganley, 1981b). This will be evident in a man's choice of language. Counselors will hear about "little fights" or "lovers' quarrels" or "giving her a little tap," and so on. Such language disguises full-fledged, injurious assaults as insignificant events. Obviously, to determine the true nature of a man's problem for the counselor and for himself, more appropriate language is needed.

Most readers would probably agree that a lovers' quarrel resulting in the woman getting a black eye could be described as an assault, battering, or violence. The client, on the other hand, is not at all accustomed to using these terms to describe his behavior. Instead, he uses terms that minimize these actions. Like most people, he associates the word *batterer* with a stereotypical image—a huge, threatening, alcohol-abusing, frightening thug. When a counselor uses such terms to describe the man or his behavior, the client is likely to respond defensively. These labels create barriers between client and therapist at the worst possible time. Rather than setting up barriers, a first-contact session is a time to conceive a trusting relationship. Rather than using inflammatory labels, it is beneficial to use descriptive language that is concrete and not open to interpretation. For instance, the meanings of such words as *slap, punch, kick, push,* and *spit* are quite obvious, in contrast to the term *violence.* A man either did or did not slap his partner. In contrast, endless debates can occur if the counselor tries to make a man accept the term *violence* before he is ready to do so. For most abusers, this is a significant conceptual leap.

Another advantage to using behavioral description is that it provides the counselor with a quick means to gauge the life-threatening potential of a man's violence. For instance, violence with weapons is more severe than violence without. Given the potential for homicide, it is essential to determine a client's lethality rating as soon as possible.

After speaking with the client about the specific behaviors in which he engages, the counselor can begin discussing the label that best describes the problem. At this early point in the counseling relationship, the term *violence* may be acceptable to the abuser. The counselor might approach this naming of the behavior by asking the man if, in light of his own behavioral description, he thinks he might have a problem with violence.

The therapist's ability to talk openly and specifically about violent acts is beneficial for another reason. If the man is feeling ashamed, he may look for rejection by the counselor. If the counselor approaches violence by using the term *batterer* in an accusing, angry tone, the man may deduce that he is going to be punished for his behavior. The therapist can then expect him to be defensive and secretive. Equally unhelpful is an approach suggesting extraordinary personal discomfort with the man and his behavior. For instance, the counselor may use euphemisms or "pussyfoot" when it is necessary to talk about detailed violence. The counselor will essentially communicate this message: "Though I have to talk to you about your violence, I am uncomfortable and afraid." The effect of this message is unfortunate. If this is the batterer's first attempt to talk openly about his violence, it may well be his last. He may conclude that if a professional therapist cannot listen to him without being horrified, perhaps nobody can.

The best approach is to seek a factual account of the violence while avoiding inflammatory terms and euphemisms. In our experience, most abusers are visibly relieved to discover they can talk openly about behavior they have hidden for so long.

Communicating a Value Statement About the Violence

While personal judgments about the man are not helpful, it is important that he hear a judgment about his behavior. Making this statement can be a delicate matter; the therapist does not want to alienate the man. The statement should not be harsh or punitive, and it need not be lengthy. A simple declaration revealing the counselor's opinion of hitting or hurting others is usually sufficient.

The timing of this message in a first contact and the context in which it is delivered are important. We often find it helpful to deliver this message almost in the same breath with an empathic or supportive statement. The pairing of the two messages essentially says: I am here to support you, and I understand your difficulties and struggles. I also want you to know that I think it is wrong to hit or otherwise hurt another person. It is important for you to know that it is wrong, but it is equally important for you to know that I am here to help you.

Balancing Confrontation with Support and Empathy

When an assaultive man minimizes or externalizes responsibility for his violence (Ganley, 1981b), the counselor must confront these distortions firmly but respectfully. At times, a man clings tenaciously to these defenses, presenting a considerable challenge to a counselor. This task can be particularly challenging for a counselor who is just beginning to work with offenders.

Many counselors learn the skills of their profession from schools or from other counselors who subscribe to a humanistic philosophy. When this philosophy informs practice, certain beliefs about clients and certain counseling techniques are emphasized. Some familiar examples of these are as follows:

(1) Be empathic; pay special attention to emotions and help the client explore how he feels about things.
(2) Trust that the client will be truthful.
(3) Trust the client to define the problem adequately in his own terms.
(4) Trust the client to arrive at adequate solutions to his problem. Out of respect for the client, be nondirective.

While there is wisdom underlying these statements, we believe over-emphasis on them in counselor training can create professionals who are ill equipped to work well with offenders.

When we began this work, we discovered that we needed to develop a greater ability to be confrontive. We needed to become more vigilant listeners. We needed to listen more closely to what the client was saying to identify defensiveness and rationalization. When we identified these, we needed to choose consciously which perceptions or statements to confront. Above all, we went through a major struggle in learning to be comfortable with what initially seemed to be combative, even mean, behavior.

A prerequisite of developing confrontive skills was the ability to distance ourselves from what the client told us. The use of the verb *distance* in this context should not be taken to imply a lack of warmth, but an ability to stand back from the content of the counselor-client interaction and observe the process. The therapist should be able to examine what the man says critically for minimization, externalization, and self-serving rationalization. This often enables the therapist to know that a man's most sincere convictions about his behavior are fundamentally incorrect.

Of course, counseling sessions that consist only of confrontation are not helpful in a first contact. While confrontation can serve as a mirror in which the man sees the truth of his situation as another sees it, this activity by itself can be brutal. To preserve and nurture the counseling relationship, a counselor must balance confrontation with supportive and empathic responses. Empathy in this context involves the ability to understand the man's experience of his world as if the therapist were "standing in his shoes." It involves the ability to understand how it feels to perceive the world in this way. Equally important is the therapist's ability to tell the man that he knows how difficult things are for him.

Confrontation alone, of course, cannot nurture a constructive relationship. And the overuse of empathic skills with an assaultive man interferes with correcting faulty beliefs about himself and the world. What is needed is a balance between the two, or an interweaving of the two into a productive response to a violent man.

Confronting Judiciously

In a first contact, a man will often respond argumentatively to the counselor. He will present a wide variety of situations and issues as a blatant challenge. Those issues imply a range of possible discussions, from simple to highly complex and sophisticated. At this early point, the therapist must recognize those issues that are currently within the client's grasp and those that will not be until later. The counselor must exercise discretion concerning what to address at the moment and what to leave for another time.

For example, when a man says that he has no choice other than to strike out when he is angry, the counselor should recognize that the man is capable of understanding the idea of leaving the situation before deciding to hit. Conceptually, this solution is relatively simple. If, however, the man loudly proclaims that he has a "right to rule the roost," the therapist might correctly decide that addressing this sexist notion at the moment is unwise. This complex issue would be better addressed once the man is enrolled in group counseling. If the counselor does decide to debate the issue of men's rights, he or she might lose credibility and fracture the tenuous relationship; abusers have fled from counselors for less serious reasons. From the man's perspective, the counselor's ideas about relationships would sound as credible as someone arguing that the world is flat.

Alternatively, the counselor may assess a man as able to begin to struggle with his "rule the roost" philosophy from a practical perspective. While avoiding a debate on the man's right to rule, the counselor can invite the man to examine the daily costs of controlling others. Having never thought of it in these terms, the man may begin to see how his expectations and beliefs get him into trouble. Again, the decision to follow this tack in a first contact requires practiced discretion.

We often respond to some clients' issues by consciously deciding not to respond. Recognizing the pitfalls, we will sidestep certain issues. One way to do this is to acknowledge what the man says, but immediately return the focus to a more workable, previously mentioned issue such as violence. Another way is to give recognition to feelings a man has about that issue but avoid openly disagreeing with his stance.

Ability to Control the Interview

Because counseling offenders involves dealing with well-developed defenses, a therapist should maintain control over the interview. This is crucial when a man appears to be avoiding the issue of violence by controlling the session and the counselor. A man can do this in a number of ways. Talking at length about superfluous issues, complaining about his partner, changing the subject, directing hostility at the therapist, incessant questioning, and many other strategies can be effective in structuring the interview on his terms. If these strategies are successful, the session typically becomes mired in issues that are tangential or unrelated to abuse. When the session ends, the therapist feels frustrated or even mildly victimized. The only accomplishment was the man's successful avoidance.

Being aware of attempts to control while they are occurring is a prerequisite of stopping them. Therapists should be aware in advance of the objectives of a first session (discussed below). With these in mind, they can identify false trails or red herrings almost immediately. Upon finding one, counselors should acknowledge the issue and refocus the session respectfully but firmly.

Judiciousness in Talking About Feelings

Because men who assault their partners are often unfamiliar with emotions other than anger (Ganley, 1981b), a counselor who insists that a man identify his feelings during a first contact is often seeking the impossible. Most assaultive men respond to questions concerning how they feel about this or that by reporting anger or frustration. Concentration on a broad range of feeling labels at this early stage is usually not productive.

Nevertheless, the man's emotional limitations should not stop the counselor from empathizing through reflecting feelings. For example, responses such as "That must have been very disappointing for you" or "Did you feel put down when she said that?" are ways to strengthen the counseling relationship without demanding that the man be emotionally fluent.

Ability to Adopt Several Roles

As will be seen in later discussions on group counseling with this population, a counselor may alternate among several roles in working with assaultive men. In the group context in particular, a therapist often finds it necessary to move rapidly from one role to another. Perhaps the two most frequent of these roles are *teacher* and *counselor.*

The role of teacher is essential to this work to the extent that a program adopts a learning perspective on wife assault. If the therapist accepts that abusive behavior is learned and sets out to help men learn more appropriate behavior, teaching new skills will be a major aspect of counseling. Hence the ability to help a varied collection of men understand relatively sophisticated concepts and skills is necessary. The role of counselor is essential because men are not in a classroom learning only about things external to themselves. In much of what occurs, they are the subject. They are encouraged to risk revealing themselves to other men and to counselors. Furthermore, the group's purpose is to create personal change. Personal sensitivity and counseling skills are needed to facilitate this process.

Another common role is that of *enforcer.* Helping assaultive men requires the ability to set limits, enforce rules, and follow through with consequences. We sometimes make unpopular decisions. We inform authorities of certain behavior; we warn victims of danger; we demand compliance with program requirements; we sometimes expel men from the program. The therapist needs a tolerance for being disliked or being the object of intense anger.

Counseling Objectives

During a first contact, the counselor will realize that the abuser has a variety of needs. Indeed, the list of issues presented by some men seems overwhelming. We believe that when abusive behavior comes to light, it ought to be the focus of a first-contact session when not displaced by emergency issues. We strive to reach three objectives in the first session:

(1) The man must recognize that his behavior is violent or abusive. Only if there is some agreement on this can there later be meaningful counseling to replace violence with nonviolence.
(2) The man must recognize that his violence or abuse is a problem in and of itself. (It is possible to recognize violence without regarding it as a problem.)
(3) The man must accept some measure of personal responsibility for stopping his violence. If there is no such acceptance, then he can continue to blame other people and situations for his behavior.

While reaching all three objectives is essential prior to a man entering group counseling, the degree to which each is actually attained varies from one man to another. In reality, no client achieves these objectives totally in the beginning phases of counseling. Such basic misperceptions about himself and others do not die quickly. They resurface at various points in counseling. What is important at this stage is that the man begin redefining his problem in terms of the three objectives above.

MAKING CONTACT

We will enliven the discussion of first contacts by presenting an example of a counselor's first contact with an assaultive man. The dialogue presented below is an example of a man approaching a therapist, asking for help in convincing his wife to come home. Though there may be several constructive responses to this request, one effective approach is suggested here.

This simulated encounter between a male counselor and an assaultive man is compressed for training purposes into a 25-minute session. The counselor has made considerable accomplishments in this encounter. In a real situation, it would require an hour or more to make the same headway. We have interrupted the encounter periodically to discuss what has transpired.

JIM: Yah, I was told to contact you guys, but I'm not really sure why. The police left this card with me right after they took my wife away. I'm not sure what you can do for me. But, uh, I guess it wouldn't hurt to talk to someone.

COUNSELOR: The police were at your place?

J : Yah, they came last night. My wife called them. I'm not sure why. She's never done that before. But they took her away somewhere. Some kind of women's shelter. I don't know where that is. Do you know where that is?

C: There is a women's shelter here in the city, but I'd like to know more about what happened. You say the police came and took your wife away, and they took her to a women's shelter. What happened before that?

J : Look, I'd really just like to find out where she is so I can talk to her.

C: Well, I'm willing to be helpful if I can, but I do need to know some of the details. You look a bit upset.

This man entered the counselor's office with a short agenda. His aim was to discover the location of the local battered women's shelter. If he were given this information, he likely would have attempted to contact his partner and persuade her to return. In being "helpful," the counselor could have provided that information and considered the job finished. Had that been the result, there would have been a lost opportunity to examine the broader problem—his abuse. Additionally, he would have unwittingly helped the man harass the woman at a time when she needed peace and protection.

Fortunately, the counselor refused to accept the man's agenda. Instead, he prodded, looking for information as a way to engage the man. In trying to understand the background of this situation, the therapist is asking for very concrete information. He balanced his questioning by recognizing that the man had powerful feelings about something.

J : Okay. Just before that, we had a fight. We've had fights before. I hit her. She hits me. We've had arguments and sometimes it gets pretty heavy. She's given me a black eye and I've given her a black eye. We've always been able to handle it. But this time the police were called in.

C: She called the police?

J : Yah, she said before that she was going to do that. She's made lots of threats like that. This time she called. I could have called the police too. She hit me.

C: So she called the police because of what? Can you tell me exactly what happened there?

J : Well, we were at dinner, and the kids were making a racket as usual. I'd had a long day and I like things quiet when I'm eating dinner. I like to have a peaceful moment or two when I come home. That's a man's right, isn't it? To have some quiet and get a little attention. I don't get it at work. So they're yelling and screaming, and I'm telling them to be quiet. And I do discipline them if they get out of hand. I told one of the kids to go to bed. Then she started butting her nose in again. And it just went from there.

C: What do you mean, "butting her nose in again"?

J : Well, she doesn't like my disciplining the kids. She interferes, interrupts.

C: What happened then?

J : Uh. Just let me make this clear. I'm not saying that it's not her business what happens with the kids. But in our home it's my right to discipline the kids. When I'm home, I take care of discipline. When I'm home, I run that home! She's interfered before when I wanted to spank them. So this time she interfered again. It just went from there. I can't remember who shoved who first, but I hit her a couple of times. She ran off to the bedroom and called the police from the bedroom phone.

C: You hit her? How did you hit her?

J : I punched her. In the face somewhere.

C: Was she injured?

J : I think I blackened her eye. I'm not sure. It didn't show up yet. But that's not the first time that's happened. What I don't understand is why she felt like she had to call the police because this has happened before. Like I said, she hits me too! It's not like I just come home and start punching her around!

C: Jim, you sound pretty angry about all this.

J : Sure I'm angry about this! I don't understand what's different about this time. I'm angry that she's gone! I'm angry that the kids are gone! I'm all by myself. What am I going to do? I'm not going to go on as if nothing happened.

Fortunately, Jim is fairly verbal. In many first contacts, the counselor has to be more active in seeking information. However, Jim is not too unusual in this respect against the broad spectrum of men who batter. In this example, the counselor only has to ask brief questions. Perhaps because of the recency of the assault and its surprise outcome, Jim is ready to talk.

While gradually disclosing the details of what occurred, Jim states that his partner also hit him. One possible reason for Jim's saying this is that he feels ashamed about his behavior. Not wanting to be seen by others (and by himself) as the ogre in this family, Jim paints a picture of mutual violence in which both parties are equally responsible. Although this version of the facts may be comforting for him, it is our experience that most men making this claim are minimizing the seriousness of the situation by externalizing responsibility.

Even if Jim's situation is one of those relatively rare instances of "mutual spousal abuse," it is irrelevant at this particular moment. We believe it would be more appropriate to explore this issue in a formal assessment session. The focus now ought to be on the way Jim handles conflict. For this reason, the counselor merely takes note of his viewpoint. He does not demand evidence of mutuality nor does he argue with Jim, because both tacks would diffuse the focus on Jim's problem. Furthermore, sidestepping Jim's issue at this moment avoids unnecessarily stressing a fledgling counseling relationship.

Jim's description of events at the dinner table goes further than suggesting mutual responsibility. It indicates that he feels victimized by his family. He says that his rights as a man have been violated and invites the counselor to join him in this belief. The counselor could have agreed with him and thereby helped blur the issue of Jim's responsibility; or the counselor could have disagreed and entered into a long discussion about men's rights. Instead, he wisely sidestepped the issue and asked for more information about the events. In particular, he asked for a more concrete description of how Jim hit his wife. Being a rather general term, *hit* could have meant a slap, a push, or a punch. It could have involved the use of objects or his hand. It may or may not have caused an injury. The therapist has wisely established the exact behavior under examination in this session. He has also conveyed that plain, concrete talk about violence is permissible.

While getting information, the counselor is also careful to pay attention to the Jim's feelings. He does this at various points by asking or by reflecting what seems apparent. In doing this, he conveys that his search for information does not overshadow his concern for Jim.

C: So the fact that your wife and kids are gone is a real surprise to you.

J : Well, of course it's a surprise.

C: How about the police? What did they do?

J : The police actually took me down to the station. They charged me. I've never heard of that happening before. Then they let me go. But I can't understand how they can lay a charge against a man for being in a fight with his wife. What goes on inside our home is not their business! Like I said, she hits me sometimes too. Am I supposed to lay charges against her too? How can you run a family this way, if people are laying charges each time they touch each other? I'm supposed to appear in court because of this too. How's that going to look when we appear in court together?

C: So you were charged. Jim, it sounds like you broke the law.

J : Broke the law?

C: What were you charged with?

J : [agitated and angry] I was charged with assaulting my wife. And that doesn't make sense. I mean, my father was never charged with assaulting my mother, and they hit each other too. They fought. I know that goes on in lots of places. What if all these people were going through the courts and being charged? Where would the real criminals be going?

C: Jim, it sounds like that's going to be happening now that police are laying charges when there are assault cases in the family. I think what you're saying is that, before this time, men were breaking the law in the family and were not charged. Now, the laws that have been on the books for years are starting to be enforced. Sounds like this is a shock for you.

J : It's a surprise to me and it would be a surprise to a lot of other men I know too. Being charged for bringing a little order into the home. That's all I was trying to do.

C: Jim, it's sounding to me like you're wanting me to take your side in this. You want me to side with you and say that hitting her was okay, and that the police shouldn't have been called.

J : I'm not asking you to take my side. I'm not someone who says hitting people is okay. I think it's right to discipline the kids. That's okay, and I would expect you to agree with me about that. I'm not asking you to excuse the fight that went on. What makes me mad is that I don't see it as my fault, and that it was both of us fighting—fighting each other. I'm not asking you to come to my side. I'm just saying that common sense says ... [pauses, flustered] this would upset you too!

In expressing disbelief that the authorities could come into his home and interfere in a "fight" between a husband and wife, Jim is like many men who batter. Relatively sudden changes in law enforcement have caught many abusers unaware. The disbelief and shock are usually genuine. What is important about the counselor's response is that he takes a moment to educate Jim about the difference between illegality and enforcement. Jim should be made aware that assaults in the family have long been illegal.

Also of interest at several points in this dialogue is Jim's use of the passive voice. He talks about "the fight that went on," or how things "happened." Jim's use of the passive voice functions to distance him from his violence. It excludes any implication of personal responsibility for the events. It conveys the impression of outside forces creating and drawing him into a whirlwind of activity.

Jim seeks agreement from the counselor on a number of issues in this dialogue. At times it sounds like an expectation; occasionally it is almost a demand. He has a strong need for an ally to agree that he is truly a victimized man. There is a subtle dynamic operating here because Jim is speaking with a man. He expects another male to support him in his traditional notions of men's roles and men's rights. From Jim's perspective, any man should understand that a man has a right to discipline his children, a right to peace and quiet, a right to rule his home.

While not all counselors would agree with us, we believe a therapist should definitely not support an assaultive man in his beliefs about male privilege. Offering this type of support, even if only to strengthen the counseling relationship, indirectly supports the man's violence. If one accepts that many men batter to reinforce their power over women (i.e., a male right), support for male privilege is support for the reality that gives birth to violence. The counselor has acted wisely in not supporting Jim in these beliefs. He has also correctly judged that Jim is not ready to be challenged thoroughly on his sexist beliefs. A more appropriate and potentially more productive place for addressing this is in group counseling sessions.

C: Jim, aren't you assuming that what goes on in your family necessarily goes on in my family? Aren't you saying that violence in the family necessarily goes on in every family? Maybe it doesn't.

J: Well it goes on in my family. I wouldn't call it violence.

C: What would you call it?

J: It's fighting. Husbands and wives have fights. You see it everywhere. You see it on TV and in the cartoons. My father and mother fought and I think their father and mother fought. Guys I work with have fights at home. They talk about it all the time—about disciplining their wives.

Some even beat their wives. But I'm not like that. Some of it's pretty sick. Some of it's really violent. I'm not like that.

C: Jim, because you think it happens everywhere, and it probably does happen in a lot of families, does that make it right? Does that make it something that's good?

J: [pauses] Well, I don't like fighting. So I don't think it's good that people fight.

C: "Fighting" is kind of a general term. You said that you probably gave her a black eye and that this has happened before. And that's something you're not willing to call "violence"?

J: [pauses] Well, it's violence. But so is her pushing me. I mean, if you want to call that violence . . . maybe it was a little extreme . . . that's like telling me that spanking my kid is violence.

C: Maybe it is, Jim. But what I'm chiefly concerned about now is what you call what you did to your wife. What you call a punch in the face that gives her a black eye. You call that "fighting," but you don't call that "violence."

J: I didn't intend to give her a black eye.

C: You didn't intend to, but you did it.

J: Well, you've got to understand that when this stuff happens, I don't plan out a fight. I don't say to myself, "Now I'm going to punch her." It just happens. I get really angry. She gets in the way, or she does something wrong, and suddenly we're fighting. I agree, it isn't good to punch someone in the eye, but I can't stop it once it starts. I don't have control over that.

C: Jim, I can understand from what you're saying so far that this is a real shock for you. That something that seems to be a usual occurrence has just happened. You've taken a shot at your wife and she's got a black eye. But something different happened this time. She called the police. She wanted protection. And you've found yourself charged with assault. But at the same time you're asking me to agree that what you did was not violence. Now I know that you're angry and I know you feel mystified, deserted, and confused by all this. That's understandable. But at the same time, I want to draw a line. Jim, I think that kind of behavior, the hitting of any human being, is wrong. It bothers me that you're using other people's violence toward you to justify your violence toward them.

Jim is defending his actions by citing the prevalence of violence in the family and by alluding to social endorsement for violence. In this sense, Jim's defenses are quite sophisticated. Fortunately, the counselor reminds him that it doesn't happen everywhere. Furthermore, even if it is common, the crucial question still remains: Is it right? The counselor answers this question firmly but gently by saying he believes hitting is wrong. Jim feels compelled to agree.

A crucial question for Jim emerges in this section: Can his behavior be labeled "violence"? In this dialogue, one is never sure if Jim has fully accepted that his behavior is violence. It seems unavoidable that he make this conclusion, but his agreement seems half-hearted and tentative. This is not unusual in a first contact. What is important is that he begin to entertain the idea. If counseling is successful, he will grow increasingly certain that his behavior is a problem in future individual and group sessions.

Jim also attempts to excuse himself by saying he did not intend to give his partner a black eye. While the bruise may not have been intended, the violence most certainly was. However, at this moment, the counselor avoids an argument about whether or not Jim makes decisions to be violent. That fact that men are in control and make decisions about violence is addressed in detail in group counseling. What is important for Jim to acknowledge at this point is that he did it and that he could have chosen not to do it by walking away.

J : Well, I can only take so much. How long would you stand there and take whatever's happening? She calls me down. Sometimes she won't listen to me. She dismisses me. I can only take so much. I agree with you, that ideally we shouldn't be fighting with each other. There shouldn't be hitting going on. But where do you draw the line? I can't stand there and take it!

C: Are you saying that you get pushed to the point where it feels like you lose control? That you have no other choice?

J : Yah, that's right. I get there somehow. I'm not crazy! I don't just hit people. I get pushed. When I come home at the end of the day, I want things to go right. I got enough trouble at work. She knows that! We've talked about that hundreds of times. She knows I don't want her interfering with what I do.

C: I can understand that at times you feel pushed. It's fairly normal that arguments happen in every relationship. Where I want to draw the line is where you say, "I get pushed to the point where I have no choice but to hit." I don't believe that's true. I think you have other choices. But you're choosing to hit.

J : [pauses] Well, I know what some of those other choices are. I can leave, but then how am I going to look if I run away? Men don't run away from fights.

C: Would it be running away? Or would it simply be going away to cool off? Can you see it that way?

J : I've done that. A few times. It's not like every time we argue, I hit.
C: Jim, I'll bet when you did it before that you stopped yourself from hitting.

Jim is trying to convince the counselor that he has no choice but to strike out when his partner behaves in a certain way. Essentially, he invokes what we call the "myth of the breaking point": A man can endure only so much before he has to explode with violence. While it may be difficult for Jim at this point to accept that he makes decisions in the midst of violence, he is probably capable of understanding that he can leave the situation prior to hitting. Jim's initial response to the idea of leaving the argument is to equate it with cowardice. He believes it is not masculine to walk away from fights. The counselor responds to this by reframing the act of leaving as a strong, decisive measure of self-control.

J : [pauses] It worked, but it's hard to do that because when you're there and she's saying things to you and I'm saying things back, and the kids are around . . . And what are the kids going to think? If we're having a fight and I leave, the kids are going to think their father's a coward. It has stopped me from hitting but it's not easy to do.
C: Jim, I've talked with a lot of men who've hit their wives, and many of those men grew up in families where there was violence. When those men were kids, they saw their fathers hit their mothers, or they themselves were hit. You're saying it would be a poor example to your kids if you walked away. Maybe it would be a good example. Maybe if your kids see you hit your wife, they're going to grow up the same way. They're going to learn that the way to solve conflict is that you hit.
J : [looking thoughtful] My dad hit my mom, and I didn't like it.
C: Okay, so there was violence in your family.
J : [pausing and seeming sad] Well, there was. Yah, they fought. And sometimes it was pretty bad. And he drank, and he'd come home sometimes, and they'd get into awful fights. And I'd hide under the covers or my brother and I would huddle together and try to drown out the noise. It was scary. But I don't think that goes on in our home. I don't think our kids are scared by it.
C: Jim, if you were scared by it in your family, don't you think your kids are scared by it too? Because you're telling me how it felt for you as a little kid to be in that kind of situation. And you're telling me that you have almost the same kinds of things happening at home now.
J : [pauses, then speaking softly] Yah, they might be scared.
C: Jim, you look a little sad.
J : [pauses] I never thought of that part before. My kids mean a lot to me.

C: I'm glad that they are important to you. Let's get back to you, though. Do you still think this fighting or hitting isn't violence? Especially after remembering what it was like to be a kid where that happened?

J : Well, like I said, it is violence. But what about her hitting me? You'd have to say that she's violent too, wouldn't you?

C: Jim, I've never met her. I don't know her. I'm going to be neutral about her right now. But are you worried that I'll take her side in this if you admit that hitting is violence?

J : Yah, that's right. You know she's not so pure either.

C: Jim, I don't want to take anybody's side when it comes to marriage conflicts. What I can do is to help you look at the way you handle those conflicts. You sort of admit that you handle them with violence. Is the way you handle those conflicts a problem for you?

J : Well, sure it's a problem. But what am I supposed to do about it?

The counselor has an interesting response to Jim's fear that his children will think he is a coward. Earlier in this contact, Jim mentioned that violence occurred in his family when he was growing up. The counselor did not respond to it then. At this moment, however, the counselor decides to help Jim better realize how violence is affecting his children. Jim notes that his children are an audience to the violence and believes that they will look on him with disdain if he is not "masculine" and powerful. Jim is helped to see a more likely effect through being asked to remember what it felt like as a child in a home where there was violence. In effect, he is helped to have some empathy for the children. He begins to see that his children are probably a reluctant audience and that his behavior scares them.

At this early point, it is usually easier to elicit concern for the children as secondary victims than it is to help a man feel empathy for his partner. It is difficult to distort the reality of children's vulnerability. With partners, however, there is a great irony; many men feel victimized by their partners. They see them as powerful people who make their lives difficult. A man will likely have difficulty feeling empathy for someone to whom he attributes so much power.

Additional First-Contact Tasks

As this dialogue ended, Jim took a major step. He admitted more convincingly that he was violent and that violence was a problem for him. Some men can make this admission and walk away. They resist ongoing counseling and believe that they can somehow make it on their own. They may be on their best behavior for months or even years. In cases where violence is truly an isolated incident, it is possible that they will not repeat it. On the other hand, if violence is an established response to high stress levels and alternative nonviolent responses have not been learned, it is likely that violence will be used again. In these latter cases, men are trapped in the cycle of violence (Walker, 1979).

Men who replicate the cycle may deny its reality by convincing themselves they will never do it again. In attempting to prevent such self-deception in a first contact, we will explain the cycle to the man. Although Walker (1979) emphasizes the woman's experience of the cycle, we try to make it personally relevant by stressing the man's experience of it. The explanation is brief, but special emphasis is given to the third stage, in which promises of good behavior and apologies abound.

Explaining the cycle of violence to a man is an attempt to sell the idea of ongoing counseling. Essentially, it is a prediction of failure in his attempts to solve his problem on his own. It does not, however, communicate an ultimate pessimism. It conveys a reminder to the man, who may go on his own and fail, that somebody knowledgeable is still there ready to help at a later time. For other men, hearing a therapist describe their actual life experience enhances the counselor's and the program's credibility and may influence them to return. From another, more strategic point of view, explaining the cycle to a highly resistant man is "prescribing the symptom." A man who would otherwise leave with no aid may leave with a firm resolve to prove the counselor wrong. The rationale here is that some limited positive impact is better than none.

We advise that, before terminating a first contact, the therapist should equip the man with a simple anger control tool. We use a control plan, a tool developed in great detail during our groups but useful in rudimentary form at this early stage. There are at least two reasons for doing this. The first stems from the worry that, because of fluctuating motivation, the man will not enroll in abuser counseling. Providing him with at least one tool in rudimentary form at this stage is better than providing nothing. A second reason is that he might be violent between the first contact and a second session. Despite even a high level of motivation, a man who batters is dangerous; he could hurt or kill his partner before subsequent counseling sessions. We hold that the counselor is responsible for beginning to teach nonviolence immediately.

A final task is to make a contract with the man, specifying what each party will do next. The contract may simply be an explicit agreement on the time of a second appointment, or it could be an agreement that the man will contact a specialty counseling service. It can also specify what the counselor will do, such as contacting the agency to which the man has been referred to facilitate the transfer. In cases where the therapist is worried about the man not following through, an agreement that the counselor will contact the man for follow-up is also appropriate.

CONCLUDING REMARKS

We regard this phase of helping as pivotal in counseling batterers. There are special elements to batterers' presentations at the point of first contact with a therapist. We have emphasized the necessity of addressing these presentations by concentrating on those counseling skills especially relevant to the needs of abusers at this stage. While emphasizing the counselor's responsibility to maximize effectiveness at this crucial point, it would be unrealistic and perhaps unfair to forget the other side. Men who batter their partners have a greater responsibility to do what is necessary to change themselves. The best counselor in this field will make no headway with a man who is not ready to accept a large measure of responsibility for changing his behavior.

Some batterers are so entrenched in blaming, minimizing, and distorting reality that it takes something approaching catastrophe to force both the disintegration of old patterns and the learning of new ones. Often the culminating effect of old behavior patterns is a crisis. The assaultive man in crisis is the subject of the next chapter, which explores crises and how counselors can respond to these personal disasters.

5

CRISIS INTERVENTION

When an individual is faced with any personal problem and feels an urgent need to deal with psychological pain and tension, finding a solution takes on high priority. In most instances some kind of solution is found, discomfort ebbs, and the problem is gone. In everyday situations, most people rarely turn to counselors to resolve the difficulties. The lifeline, that imaginary thread extending from birth to death, is full of small bumps that irritate and aggravate but are easily handled. Then there are the larger hills and valleys—the more memorable stressors. In those situations, coping mechanisms and supportive elements may be either absent or inadequate for the task at hand. The person may feel forced to reach out to resources not normally utilized. It is at this point that counselors, social workers, and other therapists may be contacted to help solve a problem and bring relief.

Yet high levels of pain and confusion do not guarantee that an individual will seek outside help. People often manage to generate very creative solutions to their problems without professional help. At other times it is possible to muddle through a stressful period until the situation somehow changes and some sense of resolution occurs. In this last situation, some methods of coping may be functional in the short term but maladaptive in terms of their power to prevent recurrence of the problem.

Most readers experienced in providing brief therapy or crisis intervention will recognize that this is a common perspective embodied in crisis theory (Golan, 1978). It is certain that all people, at various points in their lives, will lose their equilibrium (or balance) and plunge into a state of disequilibrium (or crisis). Each time this happens, the distress will propel them to do a number of things to re-establish equilibrium and a sense of well-being.

Men who assault their partners are no different in these respects from people with other kinds of problems. A man who has a problem with violence will experience distress at some point in his life that is directly or indirectly related to his abusiveness. This distress may be so pronounced that a genuine crisis develops. Therapists in batterers' counseling programs can expect to deal with men in crisis at any point from intake to termination.

Because thorough coverage of crisis intervention would require an entire book, we are limiting this chapter to a brief discussion of major crisis intervention concepts. We have two major goals. The first is to examine how crisis, a universal phenomenon, is experienced and expressed by one group of people. The second is to discuss how the therapist can respond to abusive men in crisis.

In all wife assault cases, a crisis has life-threatening potential. Death, always a threatening specter in the background of family violence counseling, too often becomes reality. For this reason, counselors working closely with abusers or victims always know of the potential for injury or death from suicide or homicide. We believe that counselors are better equipped to prevent these tragedies if they possess well-developed crisis intervention skills.

CRISIS THEORY

In summarizing what is known about crisis, Golan (1978) notes that crises are normal events occurring at various points in a person's life. A crisis does not imply psychopathology or mental illness. Instead, it is one possible result of a disruption in an individual's homeostatic balance that can usually be traced to a hazardous event. This hazardous event leaves a person in a vulnerable state. If the problem continues unresolved and the vulnerable state continues, tension continues to rise and new, emergency methods of coping are employed. If these methods do not bring satisfaction, a precipitating factor may occur that throws the person into a state of disequilibrium. The person then has reached the state of active crisis.

Though many technical definitions of crisis exist, Caplan's (1961) definition is often quoted: A crisis is occurring "when a person faces an obstacle to important life goals that is, for a time, insurmountable through the utilization of customary methods of problem solving" (p. 18). When a crisis occurs, the individual demonstrates a series of predictable reactions (Caplan, 1964). At first, psychological and physical turmoil occur. This include aimless activity or immobilization and disturbances in body functions, mood, mental content, and intellectual functioning. Following this, or concurrent with it, is painful preoccupation with events leading to the crisis. Finally, there is a period of gradual readjustment as the person adapts to the new situation.

Stress and the person's response to stress figure predominantly in understanding the crisis model. Each individual responds differently to each stressor and has a finite capacity for tolerating stress. Caplan (1961) maintains that the state of the ego is one important aspect of mental health. In assessing that state, three main areas should be considered: (1) the ability of the individual to withstand stress and anxiety and to maintain ego equilibrium, (2) the degree of reality recognized and faced in solving problems, and (3) the repertoire of effective coping mechanisms available for maintaining balance.

FACTORS IN CRISIS ASSESSMENT

Identifying Stressors

Stress is a fact of the human condition. Depending on one's perspective at any point on the lifeline, it presents stimulating challenge, puzzles, or problems and suffering. Some stressors bring on powerful feelings of dislocation and discomfort and create a demand for readjustment. Holmes and Rahe (1967) developed the Social Readjustment Rating Scale, which can be used to evaluate the stress potential of common events (see Figure 1). One can expect to face most of these events in the course of a normal life. In the figure, we have placed an asterisk next to those stressors that are commonly experienced by men who batter prior to or during violence-related counseling. Of the 43 events listed, up to 14 frequently create ten-

Rank	Life Event	Mean Value
1	Death of spouse	100
* 2	Divorce	73
* 3	Marital separation	65
* 4	Jail term	63
5	Death of a close family member	63
6	Personal injury or illness	53
7	Marriage	50
8	Fired at work	47
* 9	Marital reconciliation	45
10	Retirement	45
11	Change in health of family member	44
12	Pregnancy	40
*13	Sex difficulties	39
14	Gain of new family member	39
15	Business readjustment	39
*16	Change in financial state	38
17	Death of close friend	37
18	Change to different line of work	36
*19	Change in number of arguments with spouse	35
20	Mortgage over $10,000	31
21	Foreclosure of mortgage or loan	30
22	Change in responsibilities at work	29
23	Son or daughter leaving home	29
*24	Trouble with in-laws	29
25	Outstanding personal achievement	28
26	Wife begin or stop work	26
27	Begin or end school	26
*28	Change in living conditions	25
*29	Revision of personal habits	24
30	Trouble with boss	23
31	Change in work hours or conditions	20
*32	Change in residence	20
33	Change in schools	20
34	Change in recreation	19
35	Change in church activities	19
*36	Change in social activities	18
37	Mortgage or loan less than $10,000	17
*38	Change in sleeping habits	16
*39	Change in number of family get-togethers	15
40	Change in eating habits	15
41	Vacation	13
42	Christmas	12
43	Minor violations of the law	11

SOURCE: Reprinted with permission from *Journal of Psychosomatic Research*, Vol 11, p. 216, Thomas H. Holmes and Richard H. Rahe, "The Social Readjustment Rating Scale." Copyright © 1967, Pergamon Press, Inc.

Figure 1. Social Readjustment Rating Scale

sion for these men. Of the 9 events rated most stressful by Holmes and Rahe, 4 are commonly encountered by therapists in their work with abusers. If we were to administer the scale as part of the intake process, we would expect abusers to have significantly higher scores than are found in the general male population.

Some researchers and therapists hold that stress is one key factor in explaining wife abuse (e.g., Ganley, 1981b; Straus, Gelles, & Steinmetz, 1980). Men who abuse their partners do so as a learned response to stress. Hence one helpful counseling strategy is to help a man learn how to deal with stressful events constructively and peaceably. In fact, many specialized programs recognize this and teach various stress-reduction techniques. However, reeducation does not occur immediately. It is usually a medium- to long-term objective. In the period between first contact and the time when new skills are consolidated, there is a precarious period during which a man is often enduring the effects of several powerful stressors but is poorly equipped to handle them without being abusive to others or himself. Though there is always some risk of tragedy with those who have learned to handle stress by being abusive, the period described here may constitute the time of highest risk for personal crisis, suicide, and homicide. A more detailed look at the most common stressors will help emphasize the need for counselor vigilance.

(1) Separation or divorce. Frequently, it is separation initiated by the woman that finally propels the man to seek help. A relationship that provided the man with stability for years is suddenly fractured, leaving him alone. While this is an intense stressor for anyone, its intensity for the abuser can be magnified by his possessiveness and his need to control and dominate a woman. The painfulness of separation often results in the man developing tunnel vision concerning the relationship. All his energy and concentration are focused solely on reconciliation. This preoccupation often seems like an obsession. In such cases, a man may hold total success or total failure as a human being as stakes in the battle to convince his partner to return.

(2) Arrest and detention. Where assaults have come to the attention of the authorities, arrest for assault and temporary detention are jarring, especially for a man with no such prior experience. Having what he perceives to be a family matter become a matter of public record may result in his feeling humiliated and exposed.

(3) Fear of the legal process. Whether civil or criminal, the legal process is often protracted and wearisome. Additionally, its expense

adds financial pressure. Many men are confused by the legal process, do not understand the hurried explanations given by their lawyers, and become convinced that nobody is protecting their interests. In family law proceedings, fear over devastating outcomes is common. Legal separation and divorce proceedings dealing with support payments and child custody can bewilder the average person. In custody disputes, court-initiated family assessments can exert considerable pressure.

(4) Worries about incarceration. Though the use of incarceration as a penalty for domestic assault varies by locale, batterers commonly worry about being jailed. Again, this worry may be especially pronounced for a man who is unfamiliar with the criminal justice system. Some men begin to think of spending years in jail. Some may have also been told that prisoners convicted of wife assault are regarded by fellow prisoners as little better than child molesters. Consequently, some develop the added fear of being assaulted or killed while in jail.

(5) Involvement of child protection authorities. In some cases, child protection workers are called upon to investigate reports of child abuse. The man may fear permanent loss of access to his children, criminal proceedings, and jail. Social workers investigating abuse may be highly confrontive, ask very pointed questions, and appear skeptical of the answers. Regardless of which parent is accused of abuse, there is enormous stigma for the entire family. If a man has been abusive and is denying it, keeping up the facade of the perfect parent takes a toll.

(6) Coping with living alone. Separation and divorce may induce shock and anxiety, and create a deep sense of loss. Additionally, this loss creates new trials. Where a relationship was organized traditionally, with a division of labor according to sex roles, the man may be faced with learning new tasks. Doing the laundry, shopping for food, cooking, cleaning, sewing, and other tasks previously done by the woman and taken for granted now fall on his shoulders.

(7) Disrupted social network. The man's social network can also undergo tremendous change. Where socializing typically occurs between couples, friendships can become strained or otherwise destabilized when a couple separates. If the issue of violence emerges, loyalties may be strained and friends may feel awkward and embarrassed. The man may be actively isolated by friends for his behavior or may isolate himself due to feelings of guilt. This dis-

ruption of social networks may also include a change in the man's relationship with in-laws. If he was liked by his partner's family and they then learn that he was abusive, they may become hostile and rejecting. The loss, or change of what was comfortable and familiar, can lead to feeling uncertain and alone.

(8) Financial problems. Many men will experience financial burden. For example, soaring legal fees, fines, the cost of a second residence, therapist fees, and absence from work may be more than can be accommodated by a single paycheck.

(9) Demand for change in group counseling. Ironically, membership in a batterers' group can be an additional source of stress. In this setting, the abuser is held accountable for his behavior. He must recount his violence in detail in the presence of others. He also must come to grips with deep feelings of guilt and shame elicited by this recollection. He is pressured to devise methods of avoiding violence and must report back to the group on his success or failure. When he attempts to rationalize his behavior or distort reality, counselors and group members confront him.

(10) Loss of old behavior. As a man is successful in changing his behavior, he must deal with a sense of loss. Through giving up controlling, abusive behavior, he is giving up power and his customary outlet for the effects of stress. To some men this surrender is perceived as sacrificing masculinity. As familiar ways of relating to others disappear, new skills being learned feel awkward and artificial. Essentially, this is grief.

Response to Stressors

It is difficult to perceive these stressors in a positive light. Most of these are sufficiently aversive experiences to result in crises for most people. In assessing their impact on an assaultive man, the counselor should know how the man perceives the various stressors and how he is attempting to cope with them. Both factors will have a direct bearing on the likelihood of his entering a state of active crisis. They will also directly affect his ability to resolve the crisis without resorting to violence.

The behavioral characteristics of men who batter cited by some writers can be a helpful reference point in assessing a man's response to various stressors (e.g., see Ganley, 1981b). Essentially, those characteristics are maladaptive ways of viewing and relating to

himself, his partner, and others. A man who embodies those characteristics to a great degree may have less resilience or adaptability in a
crisis.

One element of concern is the man's dependency on his partner.
A high level of dependency aggravated by lack of a support network
outside his relationship will result in an interpersonal vacuum if she
leaves him. His dependency on his partner, which leads to posses-
sive, controlling acts, is threatened. A man who is emotionally and
psychologically isolated from others will likely see the separation in
drastic terms. He often responds by saying, "I can't live without
her." Though others may sense exaggeration, from his perspective it
is true. When despairing enough, there is a fine line between "I
can't" and "I refuse" to live without her. While the first may be a
plea, the second is a threat. The distinction is so important that the
counselor conducting crisis assessment must attempt to know which
stance reflects his current state of mind.

Equally serious is the statement arising from the man's possessiveness. This is sometimes expressed as, "She can't leave me!"
There are at least three possible beliefs underlying this statement.
The first emphasizes his understanding that the true motivation for
leaving is that she wants to do something to him, rather than assert
her right to safety. Consequently, he feels victimized. The second belief is that his partner has no right to leave him. In this situation, her
leaving is seen as morally wrong. Sometimes he denies the reality of
separation; it is unimaginable that he could ever lose her. Through
denial, he perceives the separation as a temporary condition soon to
be remedied by persuasion or force.

Another problem for the assaultive man stems from the habit of
minimizing or denying serious situations. When severe stressors
occur, he behaves in a way that suggests they have little impact on
him. In denying the gravity of the situation, he also ignores or sup-
presses a normal emotional response. When emotions are suppressed, there is no regular outlet for them. Instead, the intensity of
these emotions accumulates until there is an explosion. This would
not be so serious if the emotional explosion consisted of crying or
other nonlethal expressions of pain. The so-called soft emotions,
however, are often perceived as feminine and not permissible for a
man. Too often, the explosion is one of abusive, and sometimes lethal, anger.

An ideal solution in breaking the sequence of denial, suppression, and explosion would be for the man to utilize a counselor or members of his counseling group for support. In this setting he could cope with the stress by verbalizing his pain in a safe atmosphere before he reached the explosive stage. This solution is difficult to implement because of interfering requirements of the male sex role. According to that role, an adequate man is independent. He is essentially strong and is a loner who needs nothing from others.

The tendency to externalize responsibility is also cause for concern. In everyday life the man experiences people and situations acting on him, while he merely reacts to them. This is often experienced as powerlessness and habitually expressed through passivity. During periods of high stress, externalization may be so exaggerated that it resembles paranoid thinking. The man may be convinced that everyone and every situation conspires against him. In this situation, he feels like an impotent victim. The risk involved in a crisis is that, after a long period of passivity, he may become aggressive. Aggression is more likely to be directed at somebody he sees as a persecutor, such as his partner. However, a man with a history of violence outside the relationship may lash out more randomly; occasionally, he may react against strangers having nothing to do with his situation but who happen to be there.

Elements of General Crisis Assessment

Crisis theory is concerned with a state of imbalance (or disequilibrium) occurring due to recent events in a person's life. A state of crisis can usually be attributed to a recent, identifiable, precipitating event in a person's life (Aguilera & Messick, 1978). Consequently, the focus of crisis assessment is on the immediate problem. It is an activity that is oriented to the present or the very immediate past. While elements of the client's history that illuminate the current situation are noted, they are not explored in depth.

Assessment in this context denotes a process of gathering information and reaching firm or tentative conclusions about the client's situation through talking with him and, perhaps, with others who are familiar with his situation or background. Assessment is a highly exploratory activity. Though other tasks must be addressed in a first crisis counseling session, assessment is one of the major goals. Several categories of information are needed for the therapist to understand the situation. The following list summarizes those areas:

(1) What is prompting him to seek help now? What has happened? Is there some key recent event responsible for this crisis?

(2) In what ways is he trying to solve this crisis? Of his attempts, what is working and what is not?

(3) How was he functioning prior to being in crisis?

(4) How is he functioning now?

(5) If anything like this has happened before, how did he try to handle it?

(6) As a general indicator of coping skills, how has he handled other crises?

(7) What are his personal strengths?

(8) What supportive systems and people are available?

(9) As an indicator of problems to be tackled first, which problems are causing him the most distress at the moment?

(10) In the short and long term, how life threatening is this crisis?

(11) What obstacles are there to solving the crisis?

Assessing Lethality

Because assaultive men often deal with stress through expressing anger and aggression, lethality is a central element of crisis assessment. Lethality in this context is of two kinds: danger to others and danger to self. We believe any man who batters must be considered dangerous. Habitualized violent responses to stress increase the chance that any person with such a history will kill somebody. Since a wife abuser usually restricts his violence to his partner, she is the logical target for homicidal impulses. Her life is always in more danger than that of a woman who is not involved with an abuser. When he is in crisis, the danger to her increases accordingly.

While therapists in this area must recognize that they work daily with lethal people, blanket statements about the lethality of an entire population do not help differentiate degrees of lethality. Some abusers are more lethal than others. Counselors who routinely assess abusers (especially those in crisis) for danger potential are in a better position to avert tragedy.

Factors in Assessing Homicidal and Suicidal Lethality

In gauging the risk of homicide or suicide, the following factors should be examined:

(1) Of all danger signals, we attach greatest importance to a

man's stated intention to kill himself or someone else. Clients who state this intention should be believed.

(2) In the assessment of homicidal lethality, the man's prior history of violence is highly relevant. Previous patterns of violence may forecast the shape of future violence. How life threatening has his violence been? Does he typically use weapons? What kinds of weapons have been used? What kinds of situations have been triggers for his most severe abuse? How do those situations compare to his present situation? Has he ever killed before?

(3) In the assessment of suicidal lethality, the man's prior history of suicidal behavior is highly relevant. Is there a pattern in his choice of methods for suicide attempts? How lethal are the methods of those attempts? What kinds of situations have been triggers for suicide attempts? How do those situations resemble his current situation?

(4) Outside of the domestic realm, has the man been in situations where the use of violence has been normalized? For example, does he have combat experience in the military? Has he been a bouncer or a police officer? Those who have lived in an environment where violence is legitimized and rewarded are more familiar with violence and may be less inhibited about using it.

(5) Does he have a specific plan concerning his intention to kill others or himself? When will he do it? Does he have a specific method or weapon in mind? What is the likelihood of that method resulting in death? If he intends to use a weapon, does he have one or does he have a plan to obtain one? Generally, a man with a specified plan is well on the road to carrying it through.

(6) To what degree is he hopeful or hopeless about the future? Can he see any alternatives to killing? Can he imagine his life getting better? Can he find a reason not to kill? A man without hope may not fear suicide or the personal consequences of homicide.

(7) Is there evidence of psychiatric disturbance? Are there pronounced disorders in his thinking? Does he harbor strange beliefs or delusions?

(8) Does the man have any support systems or supportive others with whom he feels a connection and who may be valuable when it comes to exploring alternatives to violence?

(9) Is he depressed? If so, how depressed is he? Has the level of depression changed? Periodic monitoring with an instrument such as the Beck Depression Inventory (Beck, Rush, Shaw, & Emery,

1978) may be useful. Because severe depression may leave the person with little energy to carry out a plan, therapists should be especially watchful when depression wanes. During this period, when higher energy levels are restored, a man may find the initiative to follow through with his plan.

(10) Has the man made final arrangements? Is he giving away his possessions, making out a will, or otherwise taking care of unfinished business? In particular, does he seem to be suddenly and inexplicably at peace with himself and others, as if a huge burden of indecision has been removed or a major struggle is over? Has his behavior suddenly changed? For instance, is he withdrawn or does he appear not to care about himself and his situation?

(11) Does the man's anger seem to be directed at himself or outside himself? The former may suggest suicide while the latter may suggest violence toward others.

(12) To what extent does he want actual death to be the result? If he could be shown an alternative, would he choose it? With homicidal threats, does he lay more emphasis on his desire to punish, to show he is powerful, or to actually kill? With suicidal threats, is it a desire to rest, to sleep, to punish somebody, or to actually end his life?

(13) Because it decreases inhibitions, alcohol or drug use increases the lethality of these situations. Because the combination of the two can have unforeseen deadly effects, overdoses intended as a plea for help can produce death. Moreover, Browne (1986) suggests that batterers using these substances may inflict more severe injuries than if they were not under the influence.

CRISIS RESPONSE

Goals of Crisis Intervention

Rapoport (1970) suggests six operational goals for crisis intervention that are organized in two tiers. The minimal requirements are as follows:

(1) Provide symptom relief.
(2) Restore the person's level of functioning to a precrisis level.
(3) Establish understanding of events precipitating the crisis.

(4) Identify remedial actions the client can take or those that are available through community resources.

Though not always possible, where there is opportunity, crisis intervention should also aim to do the following:

(5) Help the client understand the connection between current stresses and previous life experiences.
(6) Facilitate new perceptions, thoughts, and feelings as well as develop better coping responses.

Special Considerations in Responding to Batterers

For the most part, the goals of crisis intervention are the same for every population and every problem area encountered. Though there are minor variations, the basic methods of responding to individuals are more similar than dissimilar. Those methods are, after all, primarily a response to and a remedy for the state of crisis. They are applicable to crises stemming from premature birth, terminal illness, substance abuse, adolescence, and domestic violence. Though presentation of a detailed model of crisis intervention is beyond the scope of this book, we can discuss those elements of crisis response that take on particular importance in crisis intervention with assaultive men.

First we consider the emotional aspect of a crisis and how the therapist works with this. A skilled therapist recognizes the importance of attending to feelings in a crisis. Acknowledging the client's feelings and helping him explore them facilitates rapid development of a trusting therapeutic relationship. Additionally, a counselor encourages ventilation of feelings as a way of lessening the client's burden. Counselors should remember that an abuser is unfamiliar with and frightened of strong feelings. This may compound his difficulties in a crisis because strong emotions are inescapable. If he attempts to suppress them, they simply accumulate. The danger, of course, is that they may accumulate to the point where he can no longer manage them and there is risk of violent explosion.

In helping the man deal with powerful emotions, the therapist should strive to maintain a certain balance between two extremes. On the one hand, the emotional aspect of a crisis cannot be ignored by proceeding to a highly rational mode of problem solving. A man who is highly charged with emotion is unable to do this well. On the other hand, a therapist who emphasizes the emotional aspect of the man's situation, persists in attempting to elicit ventilation of feelings, and assumes an emotional fluency that simply is not present risks overwhelming and alienating the man. The balance between the two is found through observing the man's reactions and through eliciting feedback from the man about the helpfulness of the intervention. The point of balance will be unique to each man, because the ability to operate in the emotional realm varies from one person to another.

Counselors who discover this balance point have a second major task in helping with emotions. Emotional arousal needs to be labeled appropriately. If the man mistakenly labels a range of emotions as anger, and expresses these through aggression, he needs help to recognize what feelings are really at the root. For example, one of us worked with a man who came to group stating he had been in a rage all week. Immediately prior to group, he attacked two strangers on the street. He stated they did nothing to trigger his anger. Part of the intervention helped him understand that he was angry because his child custody court case seemed to be turning in his partner's favor. With careful probing from the counselor, he tearfully admitted that he was feeling fearful, powerless, and hopeless about the outcome. In the following session he reported diminished anger and an increase in the other feelings.

We urge counselors to be cautious in the emotional arena with batterers. In particular, encouraging anger ventilation for a batterer in crisis is not helpful. One result of this is that it will help maintain the thoughts generating the anger. For instance, if a man is angry because his partner has left him, his anger is escalated by particular thoughts about this event: She's doing this to punish me. This is immoral. I'll show her who's boss! Anger facilitation will interfere with attempts to change this dangerous line of thinking. A second thing it will do is reinforce the man's tendency to express arousal inappropriately as anger. Finally, though anger ventilation will provide some measure of relief, that relief is likely to be short term. To avoid these problems, we recommend that ventilationist aspects of a crisis intervention be governed by a cognitive approach in which anger is acknowledged but redefined as feelings that are less likely to promote aggression.

A second area needing special attention is the man's isolation. During a crisis, supportive people are needed more than ever. If the man perceives his needfulness as weakness, he will have difficulty accepting support. This could be expressed through denial of the problem and refusal of support. Very often, the man's anger or otherwise scary behavior will frighten potentially supportive people and drive them away.

In counseling a man in crisis, we often spend much time on convincing him of the need for support. In particular, we help him recognize the self-defeating consequences of self-imposed isolation. However, insight into this issue is not enough. When resources and supportive people are identified, further work is needed to assure that the man will take responsibility for getting support. This is often accomplished through verbal contracts that specify who he will contact, when he will do it, how many times he will contact them in a given period, emergency services he will access in the late hours, and so on.

The question of who will support the man becomes important when this concerns the man's partner. If he has relied exclusively on her support in the past, he may turn to her again with this need. Therapists should be aware that this expectation can be a heavy burden for his partner at the best of times. When considering the history of violence in the relationship and the instability of relationships when a man has entered batterers' counseling, his expectation of support may be unrealistic. If his partner is involved in battered women's counseling, his demands for support may well conflict with her needs. Since many counseling approaches with women encourage regaining independence and learning self-care, his dependency will threaten her struggle for self-determination. It can also interfere with smooth separation, legal restraining orders, and any plan she has devised to protect herself by ceasing contact with him. Furthermore, if she is accessing her anger about the abuse, his competing demand for nurturance is not only patently unfair, it creates a dangerous situation; if his vulnerability and dependency encounter anger instead of nurturance, he may choose to express his hurt through violence.

This is a complicated issue, the specifics of which will differ from one couple to another. As a general guideline, we agree with Ganley (1981b) when she states that one objective on the road to nonviolence is for the man to decrease his dependency on his partner. The best plan, then, is uniform discouragement of this dependency on her and encouragement of reliance on others. One method of redistributing the supportive role and reducing dependency on one person is to structure supports for the man within the counseling group. This can be achieved as soon as a group begins to reach the stage where mutual aid is a norm. When it is apparent in the group that a member is in crisis, specific verbal contracts can be arranged for several members to spend time with the man between meetings.

Because crises usually concern negative events, the man in crisis naturally faces despair. A crisis occurring during the beginning and middle stages of group counseling, a time when he is challenged to try new behaviors, can be particularly taxing. The therapist can assist the despairing man by putting his struggle in perspective. The man may need to hear from the counselor that difficulties with new skills are normal, that every man experiences failure and success, and that crisis is common. It is important that this be communicated in a way and at a time when the man will not perceive it as discounting his pain or as empty reassurance. It is a message that must be accompanied by empathy.

Beyond normalizing the crisis, it can be tremendously helpful to balance the preoccupation with negative factors by giving rewards for struggle and achievement. For instance, a man should be reminded that, of all the thousands of men who hurt their partners, he is one of the few to step forward and struggle for change. The therapist can also share perceptions of specific positive aspects of the man's personality or of his role in the group. Even seemingly negative aspects, when reframed, can provide rewards. During one of our groups, when helping a batterer in crisis, we told him that his skepticism of our knowledge and authority in the group helped us to be better teachers and counselors. While this is amusing, it was also true. The effect was profound. Having never before heard his obstinacy recognized as fulfilling any useful function, this man was touched and delighted. Interestingly, and perhaps predictably, he rapidly became a more productive group member.

Finally, anger control techniques are essential components of crisis intervention with batterers. While this book has not yet explored these in any detail, the basic tool known as a Control Plan (detailed in Chapter 8) will be most easily utilized by a man in crisis. In barest outline, a Control Plan is a set of preselected nonabusive alternatives to violence. The man is required to institute this plan when he detects signs of arousal that typically precede anger and violence. Because a crisis involves such rapid and unpredictable emotional swings, a well-developed Control Plan or other basic anger control tool is a minimal requirement. A man's use of such a tool can increase his sense of competency.

Responding to Lethal Threats

A man who is contemplating suicide or homicide may keep these thoughts to himself. One reason for this is that, initially, such thoughts may be fleeting and the feelings accompanying them may still be weak. Another reason may be that the cultural taboo surrounding suicide makes him feel awkward or ashamed. During our assessments, it is our policy to ask all new clients about suicidal thoughts. At any time after assessment, we ask any abuser who is under considerable stress if he has any thoughts about hurting himself or others. Unfortunately, many situations become volatile so quickly that a therapist may be faced with overt, sometimes dramatic threats. In these cases the primary response should be to accept the threat at face value. Additionally, the therapist should openly acknowledge to the man that he accepts the threat for what it is. In this way, the man will know he is being listened to and taken seriously.

Of course, a threat to kill may also be a disguised plea for help from someone who does not know how to ask for it directly. A more complete message underlying the threat might be, "I want you to know that I am in so much pain that I don't know what to do with it. I am afraid that I will deal with it by killing someone. Please help me not to kill!" Interpreting a threat as a dire need for help is often correct. Someone who has resolved to kill does not usually warn somebody who will be dedicated to stopping him. When he does warn, he is doing it for a reason. Hence his motive to kill is mixed with other motives. The man's decision to warn is often evidence of ambivalence. On the negative side, one part of him wants to do violence. On the positive side, another part wants to avoid it. It is as if the two parts of him are at war. If intervention can be summed up in a sentence, it is this: The counselor's task is to become an ally of the part that wants to avoid violence. In other words, the therapist tries to tip the balance in favor of nonviolence.

In practice, tipping the balance involves a number of strategies. It means helping the man see the negative consequences of killing. It means highlighting the number of nonviolent alternatives and stressing their positive consequences. It means helping the client ventilate powerful feelings in a safe environment such as the counseling session, rather than having them accumulate to an explosive level. In particular, it involves helping him recognize and express feelings such as frustration, inadequacy, rejection, and sadness for what they are instead of transforming these into anger and rage.

If a threat is a disguised plea for help, the element of danger is not removed. If a man does not feel helped in this situation he may choose to follow through with his plan despite intervention. A counselor can maximize his or her helpfulness by determining what the man needs. Though this may involve sifting through what is attainable and what is not, a plan of action on which both parties can settle is more likely to motivate the man than one devised by a therapist who forces certain alternatives.

We do not entirely rule out forcing an intervention on a client. Where it is apparent that other interventions have failed or we are faced with a sudden emergency situation, we will consider measures that remove control from the client. In these instances, evidence that inaction will result in severe injury or loss of life justifies taking unusual preventive measures such as moving for involuntary hospitalization or revoking probation. Thankfully, situations calling for these drastic solutions are rare.

Unfortunately, some counselors mistakenly dismiss threats as "manipulative tactics." Too often this phrase is used to convey the therapist's irritation with a difficult client. The therapist may see the man as playing games or attempting to get the upper hand in a power struggle. While manipulation sometimes is a factor in such a threat, the stakes are high enough that this interpretation should not be the chief consideration in formulating a response.

Beyond specific techniques or skills, there is one important (if somewhat nebulous) factor influencing a client's threats to kill. Though counselors may underestimate it in daily practice, we believe that the quality of the counseling relationship is a powerful force at this juncture. If the man trusts the therapist, senses caring, and feels understood, the therapist will be more important to him than if these factors were not present. In the former case, he is more likely to be influenced by the intervention. In these dangerous situations, we readily personalize our messages. For instance, "I don't want you to hurt her or yourself," or "I care about you and don't

want you to die," said truthfully and with conviction, can work won-
ders. A client on the brink of killing sometimes dismisses everything
the counselor has said except these personal statements. We have
later learned in some cases that such statements were the only thing
holding clients back from carrying out their threats.

Utilizing Community and Social Resources

Whatever the identified problem, a client in crisis has many
needs and can drain vast amounts of a program's time, energy, and
resources. Although there are some special issues to watch for with
abusers in crisis, these men are no more needful in crisis than clients
with other problems. Consequently, we do not think that family violence counselors are the only people with the skills to respond adequately to batterers in crisis. Therapists in abuser counseling
programs can mobilize a surprising number of situational supports
that can help a man through difficult times.

One major category of supports is found in the array of potentially helpful people in the abuser's family and social networks.
These are some of the most effective stabilizing elements available
for a person in crisis. They are supports that are already in place,
have a history with the batterer emphasizing stability and continu-
ity instead of change, and require little effort on the part of therapist
and client to mobilize. These are trusted friends and relatives who
may be capable of offering support in a familiar, relaxing setting.

A second major category of supports is found in the range of professional and paraprofessional community services (primarily social
services). Emergency service organizations in particular may be invaluable to a batterers' counseling program. For instance, we make
constant use of in-person and telephone crisis intervention services
as primary resources for our clients when our counselors are un-
available. Batterers' programs should establish links with these services and cultivate positive relationships, and, where necessary,
educate staff about the special issues inherent in providing service
to wife abusers. We believe the effectiveness of batterers' counseling
services can be increased when a network of reliable adjunct social
services is nurtured.

CASE EXAMPLES

Case Example 1

Harold, aged 35, was a corporate executive who was pressured by child protection authorities to attend batterers' counseling. As leverage in forcing him to get help, a social worker informed him that criminal proceedings for child abuse were possible.

Though he had been violent toward his partner in the past, the incident responsible for his referral involved his child. When intoxicated, he had a heated argument with his partner in the presence of their 2-month-old infant. When his partner picked up the child and threatened to leave the house, Harold attempted to take the child by grabbing the child by the leg. The child's leg was dislocated and required hospital attention.

Harold was attending individual sessions with the counselor while waiting to enter a group. Various stressors were taking their toll. He was deeply ashamed when relatives learned of the incident and became angry with him. His personal finances were in poor shape and he was having a difficult time coping with the requirement to live alone. His appetite decreased markedly and he began to suffer from insomnia. In sessions, he minimized the situation by claiming he knew how to "roll with the punches." He appeared exhausted and tense but smiled often (sometimes inappropriately). He spent his evenings and weekends watching television, an unusual activity for him. Furthermore, he resumed use of marijuana during leisure hours, after having quit ten years before.

Two days prior to his third session, Harold was passed over for an expected promotion. This event precipitated a crisis. He interpreted this as a sign that his employer knew about his personal situation. He was also convinced the entire organization knew, imagined everyone whispering about him, and concluded that his professional life was destroyed. During the session, he alternately cried about the situation and voiced anger at hospital workers and the protection worker.

The counselor intervened in several ways. He worked with Harold to help him identify feelings of helplessness and hopelessness and helped him see how aggression, directed at others or self, would be self-defeating. Though Harold initially resisted, he contracted to risk confiding in his one close friend at work and then ask him if his personal situation was known. He also agreed to take a brisk one-hour walk every evening to reduce tension. The counselor scheduled three appointments with Harold in the next ten days and secured an agreement from him not to use marijuana between the current session and the next appointment. Though Harold resisted initially, he agreed to attend a chemical dependency assessment at another agency. Additionally, the counselor referred Harold to the telephone crisis center and received permission to contact the center in advance so that staff would be aware of his needs.

When Harold returned, he had fulfilled all terms of the contract except the one specifying that he contact the friend at work. He still appeared exhausted and emotionally volatile. Under firm pressure from the counselor, he agreed to complete the contract. Added to the contract was the agreement that he seek the company of his brother and one other friend in the next two days.

Harold returned for the next session having completed all terms of the contract. The chemical dependency counselor, though concerned about use of cannabis as a coping mechanism, did not believe a treatment program was warranted as long as he could use healthier coping skills for the duration of the crisis. Through contacting his friend at work, Harold learned that nobody knew of his personal problems and that someone with more seniority was promoted. Though his friend was clearly shocked by the disclosure, he was supportive of Harold. Though Harold still appeared extremely fatigued, his tension level was markedly lowered and his thinking was clearer, and he was much less pessimistic and catastrophic.

Harold attended three more sessions, during which self-care was stressed. He also gained some insight into his tendency to assume the worst and use maladaptive coping skills. Equilibrium was restored and he entered group counseling.

Discussion

The counselor began intervention by concentrating on identifying a more appropriate emotional response than anger. This was important in assuring that Harold would not deal with his crisis through aggression. The careful but immediate focus on the emotional impact helped Harold feel understood, and consequently helped in bonding a therapeutic relationship. Also notable was the use of a contract in determining what Harold would do. The contract was highly specific in terms of particular actions and their timing. Because he followed through with this, the contract helped Harold restore feelings of competency and reduce his feelings of powerlessness.

Since Harold's crisis occurred prior to his entering a group, the counselor could not rely on the peer support of a group. However, Harold's eventual willingness to disclose to his friend served a dual purpose. It provided him with accurate information as well as reduced isolation, and it provided support. Calls to crisis telephone counselors, as well as time spent with his brother and another friend, filled in the gaps.

Case Example 2

Ian, aged 26, entered group counseling after his partner of eight years demanded that he leave the home. His abuse, while occasionally assaultive, consisted mostly of extreme isolation and monitoring, a pattern duplicating his father's behavior. Additionally, he was extremely sexually abusive. Being Roman Catholic, he believed birth control to be wrong. This couple already had six children.

He responded to the stress of separation by harassing his partner over the phone at all hours of the day and night to the point where she suffered physical and emotional exhaustion. Furthermore, he spent all his spare time watching her house and used their relatives to report on her activities. One evening, after his sixth group session, he saw her return from a party with a man who entered the house. Ian waited awhile and then entered the house, intent on catching them having sex. Instead, he discovered them drinking coffee. He raged at both of them, scared the man from the home, and lectured his partner for six hours. Complicating this issue was the fact that his partner, though wanting the harassment to stop, occasionally phoned him when she was lonely. He interpreted this as her giving him permission to contact (harass) her.

The discovery of a man in the house was a precipitating event for a crisis. Ian stepped up his monitoring and interpreted all of his partner's activities as a sign of final rejection. With continuing harassment, his partner was in danger of needing psychiatric hospitalization. Additionally, counselors feared that his rage would reach homicidal proportions.

In the group, he was confronted with his abuse on two occasions, and he promised to stop. When he did not, a counselor working with his partner helped her obtain a court order prohibiting contact and his presence in the home's vicinity. Simultaneously, he was informed in the group that any other reports of harassment would result in exclusion from the program. Ian obeyed the court order and accepted the counselor's ultimatum. Harassment ceased, he became more involved in the group, and the crisis abated.

Discussion

The key to resolving this crisis was so simple it almost eluded the therapists. Attempts to persuade, distract, and provide insight failed miserably. Ian's obsession with controlling his partner did not respond to normal counseling techniques. His need to monitor her greatly outweighed his willingness to mobilize self-control. As Ian continued to harass and watch her, he was totally occupied by rumination. Every observation was distorted to confirm his belief that she was rejecting him. As long as he continued to monitor her, he was trapped in a spiral of negative thinking and anger.

Because internal controls were lacking, external controls were imposed. In this case, the crisis was resolved by enforcing a change in behavior. Though cessation of monitoring did not completely stop his rumination, it helped in other ways. Because he no longer witnessed his partner's behavior, one powerful stressor was eliminated. Because he could not spend time parked in front of her house, he was diverted to more ordinary activities that distracted his concentration from the domestic situation. Furthermore, the monitoring taxed his time and energy; staying away from her allowed him to eat and sleep. A consequence of his getting some rest was that he was able to think more clearly about the situation and refocus his attention on himself.

It would seem inordinately simple and naive to expect an authoritarian approach to work with all clients experiencing this type of crisis. Many men who want to monitor their partners would not hesitate to disregard the court or the counselor. However, there are other men who seem to lack any ability to mobilize self-control but are surprisingly responsive to and respectful of imposed legitimate authority.

Case Example 3

John, a 20-year-old man with boyish good looks, was the youngest member in a group of batterers. He seemed to be slightly below average intelligence, was likable and shy, and exuded personal vulnerability. This elicited caretaking responses from most of the older men in the group. John had a history of abusing depressants but was struggling successfully in a chemical dependency program. He came to the group after his partner of three years left him due to his violence. He claimed that she promised to return if he could successfully complete the program.

John's participation in the group was at a minimal level. He was compliant but unimpressed with the skills being taught. Instead he was possessed by a tunnel vision concerning his partner. Whenever he spoke in the group, he analyzed her behavior in terms of it being a sign of either her returning to him or her dissolving the relationship. He reported many encounters with her and asked the group to predict the outcome on the basis of these reports. On several occasions he claimed he was unable to live without her. He also expressed anger and seemed genuinely convinced that she was punishing him.

Within the limitations inherent in a group, the counselors openly addressed his suicidality. Counselors arranged contracts between John and several group members to spend structured time together to reduce isolation. Additionally, a therapist arranged one individual session with John during which he convinced John to agree to a "no violence" contract. Though more sessions were needed, the combination of staff overload and the acceptance of his promise to maintain contact with group members precluded scheduling further sessions.

During group sessions, the counselors and the group members continually but gently chided him over his obsession and encouraged him to focus his energy on changing himself. His response was to claim that nobody understood his situation. He felt constantly criticized and barely suppressed his anger at the group. After each interaction with the group, he seemed to become more withdrawn and isolated.

Although John appeared to be moderately depressed, there was no obvious indicator of a severe psychological problem. His despair over the separation seemed only slightly more severe than that suffered by other separated men in the group. He continued to go to work and he came to group.

John missed the sixteenth group session. The program learned a day later that he had taken an overdose of drugs and hanged himself in his basement. The counselors and the group were plunged into grief. Some group members expressed this grief as rage and directed it at the counselors. Several group sessions were required before members could come to terms with this event.

Discussion

Unfortunately, the tragedy involving John is a reality that most programs working with abusers must face sooner or later. When it happens, therapists stop and perform a postmortem as a group or privately as individuals. They look for how they might have prevented the tragedy and experience a range of feelings that include inadequacy, guilt, anger, and sadness.

It is difficult to know whether a counselor could have prevented John's death. Hindsight, that wonderful teacher, compels therapists to agonize over numerous questions: Would more individual sessions have helped stop him? Were there signals the therapists failed to detect? Was hospitalization called for? Despite reasonable efforts to help him manage his despair, he made a choice to kill himself.

CONCLUDING REMARKS

Crisis intervention is sometimes regarded as a specialty service of therapists in hospital emergency rooms or community mental health centers rather than a basic intervention skill. We find variability among skilled therapists in the ability to intervene effectively in a crisis or in the appreciation for the importance of this counseling modality. We give special attention to crisis intervention in this book because domestic violence counselors are among those helpers most likely to encounter crises on a regular basis.

The imbalance or disequilibrium so characteristic of the crisis state ruptures the psychological, emotional, and social dimensions of the person's life. In view of the wife batterer's tendency to respond to stress with abuse and violence, counselors should be wary of an escalating risk when stressors become unmanageable. Behavior may be erratic and an increase in the frequency and severity of abuse may have tragic consequences.

As a result of these considerations, we make three basic recommendations. The first is that therapists who work with wife abusers be skilled in crisis assessment and intervention. The second is that therapists conduct crisis assessment formally with abusers at the intake/assessment stage and informally as needed throughout men's attendance in counseling. Finally, we urge that abuser counseling programs be designed with the recognition that they are dealing with a crisis-prone clientele. Because crisis response ought to be immediate, programs should have the flexibility to accommodate clients in crisis and should establish referral protocols with adjunct emergency services in their communities.

6

ASSESSMENT

Many treatment providers may feel that an initial intake interview should provide sufficient information on which to base a decision about whether or not a batterer is appropriate for their treatment program. This decision is often based on the batterer's presentation and the history and information available to the program or supplied by the batterer. We, however, would like to stress the importance of a thorough assessment of each client prior to admission into treatment.

There are a number of reasons for obtaining a thorough evaluation prior to deciding on the appropriateness of a particular form of treatment. Not all men will be able to participate in the type of treatment program we describe here. Some will not have the ability to comprehend the materials presented; some will not have sufficient motivation to benefit from the program; some will have significant emotional, psychological, and/or chemical problems that will interfere with treatment; and some will be too violent or too lethal to treat on an outpatient basis. Although some men may be able to benefit personally from a group treatment program, they may have significant behavioral or emotional problems that would be detrimental to the functioning of the group and may limit treatment benefits for other group members.

Dealing with men who are violent presents a number of legal and ethical dilemmas not found in other therapy practices. In a more general therapy practice, the therapist's first responsibility is to the client. In dealing with violent men the therapist also has a responsibility to the potential victims of the client's violence and to the community in general. Acceptance into an outpatient program may lead the victim and the community to believe falsely that the batterer is not a significant risk because he is in treatment. Assessment can provide not only criteria for appropriate decision making regarding program entry, but a data base for assessment of lethality.

On first contact, many batterers do not present as being significantly impaired, emotionally, psychologically, or chemically. As mentioned previously, Bernard and Bernard (1984) have described these men as being like Jekyll and Hyde in the differences between how they initially present themselves and their actual psychological characteristics. Additionally, research and clinical reports have suggested that batterers are not reliable reporters regarding either their level of violence or other emotional difficulties (e.g., Browning & Dutton, 1986; Ganley, 1981b; Hoshmand, 1987; Sonkin, 1987; Sonkin, Martin, & Walker, 1985). Discovering emotional and psychological problems during the assessment process can help therapists to predict treatment difficulties and, if possible, deal with them before they occur.

Finally, most programs are likely to include a number of batterers referred by the criminal justice system for treatment. Although many of these men may have had some form of court evaluation or have undergone presentencing investigation, these assessments may not be violence specific and may not adequately address the issues we are presenting here. A thorough assessment will begin a process of communication with the court, will inform the court of the counselor's predictions for future violence (note, however, that this may not completely satisfy the counselor's "duty to warn" as described at the end of this chapter), and, through the focus and content of the report, can educate the community and the courts to look at the perpetrator's responsibility for the violence.

COMPONENTS OF THE EVALUATION

A complete evaluation of the batterer prior to treatment should cover four main assessment areas. The first and most important topic to be covered is a thorough assessment of the batterer's violence; this will be covered in detail below. The therapist should always obtain information from as many sources as possible. The more information available, naturally, the better the assessment will be (Sonkin et al., 1985). Beginning the evaluation with an assessment of violence sets the focus for both evaluation and treatment.

The second area to be covered is an assessment of emotional and psychological functioning. This should include a thorough social, clinical, and medical history for the batterer and his family of origin. We recommend some psychological tests as routine with each batterer; we will discuss others that may be useful below. This is also an area where collateral information is essential.

Third, each batterer should be assessed regarding chemical usage. Although we do not believe that there is a causal relationship between chemical usage and wife abuse, most psychoactive chemicals tend to disinhibit behavior, possibly setting the stage for violence to occur. Sonkin et al. (1985) report increasing evidence that men who are predisposed to violence are more likely to be violent under the influence of alcohol or drugs. Additionally, Browne (1986) suggests that when batterers are under the influence, they are likely to cause more severe injuries than at other times.

Finally, an assessment of the batterer's motivation to change is also an integral part of the evaluation. Although part of the assessment will address this directly, it is also covered in each of the other three areas. Motivation to change is a complex issue, and a batterer's actual motivation may not correlate with his stated motivation. Most batterers come into treatment under external pressure, often from a partner or spouse or from the court, although they may state initially that they are personally interested in change. Additionally, motivation is not static and may change during treatment (Sonkin et al., 1985).

To assess the four major areas mentioned above, three main evaluation techniques are used: (1) clinical interview, (2) psychological and other forms of testing, and (3) gathering of collateral information. As with the first contact with the batterer, the clinical interview is a dynamic part of the treatment process. In addition to providing an opportunity to gather data, it sets the stage for the focus of treatment and can be used to enhance motivation. Psychological and other tests are used to obtain an objective measure of functioning separate from the batterer's report. In addition, they can provide a baseline with which to compare the effectiveness of treatment. Finally, collateral information from as many sources as possible—including partner or spouse, children, other family members, investigation and court reports, and treatment histories—is essential in forming a valid judgment as to the lethality of the situation.

Prior to the start of the assessment, the purpose of the assessment should be explained to the client. The limits of confidentiality should be reviewed with the client and signed releases of information should be obtained before beginning. Many programs, ours included, will not proceed with assessment or treatment without releases to any individual or agency that may have essential information regarding the violence or that we may have to contact to warn about or to prevent potential future violence. This generally includes spouse or partner, family members, previous treatment providers, the women's shelter program, the courts and other criminal justice agencies, and other community agencies.

Mental health evaluations are not considered by most courts in the United States to constitute a therapeutic relationship, and therefore information obtained in evaluations is not likely to come under therapist-client confidentiality laws. This means that if the evaluator is called into court, she or he can be directed to reveal any information to the court obtained during the evaluation. In addition, there are a number of instances in which client confidentiality must be violated by the therapist. If the therapist believes that a reasonably identifiable person or persons may be in danger from the client, she or he has a duty to warn and to take steps to protect, if possible, the potential victim(s). Also, if a therapist believes that a client may harm himself or someone else, the therapist must break confidentiality in order to act to protect the client or others. Finally, if, during assessment or treatment, the therapist learns from the client of any past or present abuse of an individual who is currently a child, the therapist is required by law to break confidentiality and report the abuse.

Although we believe that it is important to inform the client about these limits of confidentiality prior to beginning the evaluation, and although therapists do not need a release of information to violate confidentiality in the above instances, obtaining signed releases of information to contact significant others prior to and during treatment is still essential. As Sonkin (1987) points out, the therapist needs to have regular contact with the victim to determine reoffenses during treatment and treatment progress. Additionally, when the client knows that he is being closely monitored, he is less likely to be violent during treatment (Sonkin, 1987).

The assessment process usually involves from two to five hours of clinical interview with the batterer, from two to five hours of paper-and-pencil testing and/or evaluator-administered tests, and whatever time is necessary to obtain collateral information. In addition, the therapist should plan for time to consult regarding the information obtained with other therapists in the program and for time to prepare the written report. This can take place over a number of sessions rather than in one sitting. The following sections will discuss in detail each area of the evaluation.

VIOLENCE ASSESSMENT

Assessment of the frequency, extent, and lethality of violence involves interviewing the batterer directly regarding the violence, interviewing the victim separately, obtaining information from other sources, and gathering data regarding the batterer's attitudes about his violence and about violence in general. Ganley (1981a, 1981b) suggests that four distinct types of violence should be assessed: (1) physical violence, (2) sexual violence, (3) property violence, and (4) psychological violence. These types of violence should be examined in a batterer's current relationship, in his past relationships, and in his family of origin. Additionally, violence outside of the home—such as previous criminal history, acting out, violence with friends, relatives, or strangers, and occupational violence (e.g., military experience or police work)—should be evaluated (Sonkin, 1987).

Many counselors will approach the assessment of violence with some confusion as to what terminology to use with the man being interviewed. Violence toward spouses and partners, although strongly rooted in our society, is generally a shame-based topic for the violent male when dealing with counselors or authority figures. These men may respond with extreme defensiveness when asked about their "violence." Many batterers, as a result of their own internal defense mechanisms, will not define their behavior as "violent." On the other hand, the counselor should take care not to join with the batterer to minimize violent behavior by labeling it as something less serious. More detail on this process is presented in Chapter 4.

In discussing violence with men during the assessment, we have found a number of methods that address these issues. First, we begin the interview by discussing behaviors. The men are informed that we plan to ask them about a number of behaviors they might perform in their relationships, some of which may occur in the best of relationships. We begin with an inventory of behaviors starting with the least threatening (in terms of the man's embarrassment in reporting) and proceeding to the most violent. After obtaining a thorough inventory of what the man is willing to report at this time, we ask him how he would define his behavior. If he does not define his behavior as violent, then we will discuss with him the violent aspects of his actions and help him to then redefine his behavior as violence.

There are a number of questionnaires available that can be filled out either by the batterer or by the evaluator. Sonkin et al. (1985), Edelson, Miller, and Stone (1983), and Paymar and Pence (1985) all have developed excellent forms that may be useful in an evaluation. These forms attempt to identify all aspects of violent behavior.

The assessment of violence should begin with a history of violence in the current relationship. A detailed account of abuse should include a progressive history of the violence, noting when the violence started, how it progressed over time, the current frequency of violence, the highest frequency, the extent of injury inflicted, the general cycle of violence, legal consequences (if any), whether or not weapons have been used, what threats have been made, and whether or not chemical use was associated with the violence. To assess the cycle of violence, the counselor should examine events preceding a violent incident, thoughts and behaviors just prior to and during an incident, and thoughts and behaviors following an incident. One method of obtaining this information, suggested by Walker (1984), is to ask the client to describe four violent incidents: the last incident, the first incident, the most violent incident, and the incident most frightening to the victim.

Following the assessment of physical violence, an assessment of sexual violence is obtained. Our experience is that a large percentage of, if not most, batterers also are sexually abusive toward their partners. To assess this, the counselor needs to ask a series of questions regarding obtaining sex from a partner when she did not desire it. These questions should include manipulating, insisting, and/or threatening violence to obtain sex, as well as using physical force. The counselor should also inquire as to whether the batterer used these behaviors to compel his partner to perform particular sexual acts in which she did not wish to participate, such as anal or oral sex. In addition, sexual behavior before, during, or after physically violent incidents should be explored. This is an area in which it is important to obtain collateral information from the man's partner, rather than relying solely on his report.

In addition to sexual violence toward a partner, sexual abuse of children should also be examined. Although there is no clear research as to the incidence of child sexual abuse in homes where men are violent toward their partners, our clinical experience suggests that this is not uncommon. Given the legal consequences of an admission to child sexual abuse and the fact that the counselor has warned the batterer regarding responsibility to report child abuse, it is not likely that an admission will be forthcoming. However, it is important for the counselor to inquire, as it indicates that this is an area that she or he is willing to discuss if, during treatment, a batterer decides to disclose.

In addition to actual physical incidents of violence, it is important to assess the batterer's use of emotional and psychological violence. As with physical violence, there is a wide range of behaviors that may be categorized as psychological or emotional abuse. These may range from relatively subtle controlling behaviors, to the use of threats to kill the victim or her children, to killing or injuring pets to intimidate the victim. As with assessing physical violence, the counselor should ask about particular behaviors, rather than inquiring whether the batterer perceives that he is psychologically abusive.

One of the most common forms of psychological or emotional abuse we have found among batterers is the attempt to control partners in both social and financial ways. This often begins in relationships prior to the onset of physical violence. Batterers may stop their partners from seeing certain people or friends (both male and female), may control their partners' activities, may interrogate their partners regarding their activities, constantly accuse them of extramarital sexual relationships, and follow them or tap their phones. In the financial arena, batterers may force their partners to obtain permission to spend money, keep all the family's money (including the partner's money), and refuse to give out money for essentials, including food or children's needs.

Direct emotional abuse may be somewhat subtle in its presentation and is often not defined as abusive by the perpetrator. This may include berating his partner's family or friends, threatening to end the relationship to win an argument, criticizing and name-calling, and yelling. Divulging personal information about one's partner to others or telling others things about one's partner that are not true can be a form of humiliation and degradation. At the more lethal end of this continuum is the use of threats to injure or kill one's partner or her relatives or children, threats to commit suicide, and the physical torture or killing of family pets.

Batterers also may be emotionally abusive regarding sexuality. This may include making lewd or vulgar comments to their partners privately or in public and sexual name-calling. A more subtle form of sexual emotional abuse consists of creating a highly sexualized atmosphere within the family, where personal boundaries are violated both with one's partner and with her children. Often this is a form of child sexual abuse and should be assessed as part of the batterer's relationship to his children. However, it may be used as a method of threatening, degrading, or humiliating a spouse or partner.

Following an assessment of psychological and emotional violence, the counselor should obtain a history of violence in other relationships, outside of relationships, toward children, and in the batterer's family of origin. Obtaining a history of violence in previous relationships serves three main purposes: (1) It aids in assessing the potential for lethality in the present, (2) it may be used to help the batterer who blames his partner to see his responsibility for the violence, and (3) it may increase motivation for treatment if the batterer can see the pattern of violence in his relationships (Sonkin, 1987). The assessment of previous violent relationships should follow the same general guidelines as the violence assessment discussed above.

Violence outside the home may involve fights with neighbors, relatives, or strangers or previous criminal acts and/or legal charges, or it may be "occupational" violence, such as police work or military history. Nonoccupational violence outside of the home indicates a much higher lethality in general and suggests that a batterer may have progressed significantly in the cycle of violence. If the violence has occurred since childhood, it may suggest that violence has been "normalized," that is, that the batterer sees violence as a necessary means of existence in all areas of life. Additionally, a long history of generalized violence may indicate that the individual may be highly addicted to violence. Hanneke and Shields (1981) state that the evidence suggests that men who are violent inside and outside their homes (compared with men who are violent only in their homes) tend to be more violent, approve more of violence, and are less likely to seek help.

Violence in the client's family of origin should be explored as well. Batterers are more likely than men in the general population to have experienced violence as children (Rosenbaum & O'Leary, 1981a; Saunders, 1982; Straus, Gelles, & Steinmetz, 1980). A number of studies estimate that more than one-half of all men who batter were physically or sexually abused as children or witnessed violence in their homes (Fagan, Stewart, & Hansen, 1983; San Francisco Family Violence Project, 1982; Sonkin, 1987; Straus et al., 1980; Walker, 1984). Batterers who have been physically or sexually abused as children experience more anger than batterers who were not abused (Sonkin et al., 1985).

Most batterers who were abused as children either do not define their treatment as abuse or believe that the abuse was justified by their behavior. To examine this area, the counselor may explore with the batterer how the children in the family were "disciplined," asking how often this occurred, whether objects (e.g., belts or sticks) were used, and whether injuries were inflicted. The amount of arguing the parents did that the client was aware of and whether those arguments were physical should be assessed also. Whether or not the client admits to family violence, an important question to ask is whether or not the client was afraid of either parent. Finally, the counselor should ask each client whether he was approached sexually as a child by an adult or older peer. Although the client may deny this during the assessment, later in treatment he may admit to being sexually abused. Asking during the assessment raises the topic and may allow the client to feel less anxious later in talking about this issue.

The next section of the violence assessment is concerned with the batterer's attitudes toward violence. Much of the information for this section of the assessment will have been shared spontaneously by the batterer during the previous part of the violence assessment. In discussing violent incidents, the batterer will generally present the situations in a cognitive context that has allowed him to minimize his responsibility for his behavior. During this part of the assessment the counselor should clarify the areas above that have not yet been discussed or about which the counselor is not clear. In addition, the client's general attitudes toward women, men, interpersonal relationships, child rearing, and violence in general should be explored (Adams, 1988b; Sonkin, 1987). This can be done by interview and by paper-and-pencil testing.

Most people have a repertoire of personal defenses that they employ to maintain a sense of self-esteem and intrapsychic integrity. Most of these defenses are useful to us and assist us in daily functioning with ourselves and with other people. On the other hand, these defense mechanisms can prevent us from accurately examining our behavior, taking responsibility for our actions, and changing our behavior when it would be beneficial. Most batterers tend to employ a number of defense mechanisms that allow them to minimize or deny their responsibility for their violent behavior (Adams & Penn, 1981). These defenses will be major roadblocks to overcome in treatment and their extent and strength will give the counselor some idea of the difficulties a batterer may face in treatment.

A common defense seen in batterers is minimization. The batterer tends to minimize what happened during the violence, the amount of injury inflicted, or the level of fear created or emotional impact of the violence on the victim. Browning and Dutton (1986) state that "many assaultive husbands emphasize the frequency of violence while ignoring the fact that their actions caused severe injury or hospitalization to their wives." We often see this defense in statements made by the batterer such as "I didn't really 'beat' her, all I did was slap her once or twice," or, "It's only happened a couple of times."

Loss of control is also a common defense that allows the batterer to admit to the violence while claiming, in some sense, not to have really been there. The feeling of loss of control is more likely to have occurred prior to the violence and to have been one of the motivators for it than to have been a condition during the violence. Many men are violent in order to regain control, and the situational aspects of violent behavior suggest that batterers exert a great deal of control during these episodes. Most batterers choose a private, non-observable place to be violent (the home) and tend to have some conscious control over the extent and visibility of the injuries they inflict. Batterers will report, however, the feeling of "going crazy," saying, "I lost my head, I didn't know what I was doing."

Similar to loss of control are the defenses of confusion, lack of intentionality, and being intoxicated. A batterer may report that the situation was "crazy" and that he cannot remember how the violence started or what happened (confusion). He may state that he did not mean to be violent or that he did not mean to injure his partner (lack of intentionality). Finally, he may state that he was drunk or "stoned" and that was the reason he was violent (intoxication) (Adams & Penn, 1981).

Most batterers project some of the blame for their violent behavior on their spouses or partners, a process often called "externalization." They will spend a great deal of time talking about what their partners did or said while not talking about what they did. In addition to blaming partners, clients will blame outside situations or stressors as reasons for their behavior. While stress has an impact on violent behavior, it does not cause violence, nor is a change in stressors likely to stop the violence permanently. While it is important to assess current stressors, the counselor should also realize that this is a way for the batterer to avoid responsibility for his violence.

Finally, some batterers will absolutely deny their violent behavior. Most batterers will deny some part of their behavior or some particular incident. However, when a batterer denies being violent, it is unlikely that he will be amenable to treatment, and a criminal justice approach, rather than a therapeutic one, may be the most appropriate way to deal with the problem. The counselor should share these opinions and concerns with the batterer's spouse or partner.

In addition to utilizing defense mechanisms, many batterers cognitively distort their behavior. Cognitive distortion is a reinterpretation of events or thoughts that reframe a situation to the batterer's emotional or psychological benefit. Such distortions often sound like "I'm the victim here," or "Any man would do what I did." Often these distortions are directly related to attitudes regarding male-female relationships, what a "normal" man's role is, or an overall worldview ("This is the way things work"). Again, most of these attitudes will be apparent during other parts of the assessment and only need to be extracted from statements the batterer makes on other topics.

Evaluating the level and nature of the client's defensiveness and cognitive distortion will give the counselor a sense of how much the client is willing to accept responsibility for his violence. Acceptance of responsibility, like motivation for treatment, is not static. It may increase or decrease as treatment progresses. The level of acceptance during the assessment is one factor in the decision regarding a batterer's amenability to treatment in a community-based program.

In addition to the areas covered above, the therapist needs to obtain a picture of the client's current stressors in order to assess the current lethality of a situation. These stressors can be both within the family and external to the family. Common areas of stress to explore within the family are finances, living situation, relationships with extended family members, sexual relationship, children and disciplining of children, chemical use, and health problems of family members. Stressors outside the family often include unemployment or occupational stress, legal problems, relationships with friends, and extramarital relationships. Different individuals will respond to similar situations in different ways. Therefore, it is important that the therapist ask the client what he perceives as stressful in his life, rather than assume that a situation should or should not be stressful.

Psychological Testing

After the interview portion of the violence assessment has been conducted with the batterer, there are some psychological tests that may provide the counselor with information not yet obtained. A number of paper-and-pencil inventories have been devised in attempts to assess anger, hostility, attitudes toward women, hostility toward women, and attitudes toward violence. Some of the more general psychological tests that may also contain useful information regarding these areas are discussed in the section on psychological assessment below.

Although these tests may be useful, both as an independent measure of anger arousal or proclivity and in providing a baseline from which to measure progress in treatment, they should be used only as an adjunct to a thorough clinical interview. If the results of the tests are markedly different from impressions formed during the interview, neither clinical impressions nor test results should be abandoned without an attempt to identify the source or reason for the disparity. Additionally, studies indicate that psychological tests do not provide sufficient information to predict violent behavior in an individual (Maiuro, Vitaliano, & Cahn, 1987; Megargee, 1970; Monahan, 1981).

The most commonly used hostility inventory is the Buss Durkee Hostility Inventory (BDHI) (Buss & Durkee, 1957). Although designed to analyze an individual's preferred mode of hostility expression, most studies indicate that at best it provides a global impression of hostile feelings and tendencies to act out anger (Biaggio & Maiuro, 1985; Biaggio, Supplee, & Curtis, 1981; Maiuro, Cahn, Vitaliano, Wagner, & Zegree, 1988). The BDHI is a 75-item true/false test with subscales named assault, indirect hostility, irritability, negativism, resentment, suspicion, verbal hostility, and guilt. As with other hostility measures, its predictive validity has not been established, although the test has been shown to discriminate violent from nonviolent offenders in a criminal population (Selby, 1984). Additionally, the reliability of the BDHI subscales is problematic and the test is highly correlated with social desirability (Biaggio, 1980; Biaggio et al., 1981; Buss & Durkee, 1957; Selby, 1984).

Another commonly used scale, both clinically and in research, is the Conflict Tactics Scale (CTS) (Straus, 1979). The CTS was designed to measure intrafamilial conflict in the sense of the means used to resolve conflicts of interest, with the assumption that hostility is likely to be high when the existence of conflict is denied (Straus, 1979). The CTS has three main scales: the Reasoning Scale (the use of rational discussion, argument, or reasoning), the Verbal Aggression Scale (the use of verbal and nonverbal acts that symbolically hurt the other or the use of threats to hurt the other), and the Violence Scale (the use of physical force against another as a means of resolving conflict). Form N of the CTS is used in face-to-face interviews as a measure of child abuse and battering.

Hornung, McCullough, and Sugimoto (1981) modified the scale to be used by spouses to report on their own use of violence as well as their partners' on a 7-point scale ranging from "never" to "more than 20 times a year." Jouriles and O'Leary (1985) found that there was low to moderate agreement on reports of violence between spouses, with a slight tendency for the men to underreport their own violence and for women to "overreport" the violence performed by their husbands.[1] Szinovacz (1983) also found variability between men and women on the CTS, with men reporting a lower incidence of violence than their partners. The CTS produces information already gathered in the clinical interview. However, the counselor may want some quantitative format to use in assessing progress, comparing clients, or reporting to the courts.

Other tests that may be of interest are the Novaco (1975) Anger Inventory, the Brief Anger Aggression Questionnaire (Maiuro et al.,

1987), and the Hostility Toward Women Scale (Check & Malamuth, 1983).

The use of paper-and-pencil tests to measure attitudes toward women, attitudes toward battering, and attitudes toward interpersonal violence may produce material not obtained through clinical interview. While batterers may present themselves in a more socially desirable fashion on direct questioning, more subtle test questions might reflect underlying attitudes more accurately. The short form of the Attitudes Toward Women Scale (ATW) (Spence, Helmreich, & Stapp, 1973) has been found useful both in research and in clinical settings. Briere (1987) compared subjects' self-reported likelihood of battering to the ATW and found that likelihood of battering was associated with conservative attitudes toward women.

The Acceptance of Interpersonal Violence Scale (Burt, 1980) has been correlated with proclivity to rape (Briere, Corne, Runtz, & Malamuth, 1984; Malamuth, 1984; Stille, Malamuth, & Schallow, 1987) and with proclivity to batter (Briere, 1987). Briere (1987) has also devised the Attitudes toward Wife Abuse (AWA) Scale, which has been positively correlated with self-reported likelihood of battering.

EMOTIONAL, PSYCHOLOGICAL, AND SOCIAL HISTORY ASSESSMENT

Mental status examination is considered a mainstay of the psychiatric profession. In reality, mental status examination, as it is taught to psychiatric interns, generally involves finding out if the person knows who he or she is, where he or she is, and what the date is. Mental status then involves determining the level of general information available to the subject, whether long- and short-term memory is intact, and whether the person is psychotic, depressed, obsessive, or suicidal. Although this may be a useful examination in a general psychiatric population, most of us do not ask our clients if they know where they are unless something about the client has tipped us off that this may be an issue. Few batterers are actually psychotic, although under stress their jealousy and need for control may become delusional and they may have a psychotic "reaction" or breakdown (Elbow, 1977; Makman, 1978; Saunders, 1982).

In general, we want to be able to describe how a client presents himself, how he structures his inner world and what defenses he uses, and whether he has any significant problems with cognitive processing, thought disturbances, depression, or suicidal ideation. Defense mechanisms and cognitive processing can be deduced from the way the client presents during other parts of the evaluation. Thought disturbances may be asked about directly, with questions such as "Have you ever heard voices that other people did not hear?" Although not many clients in this population are likely to respond affirmatively, this is an area that should be examined.

The assessment of depression can be made both from direct questions and from observation of how the client behaves during the evaluation. Whether or not a client states that he is depressed, the assessment should be made from reports of symptoms common to depression. These symptoms might include sleep disturbances (e.g., difficulty sleeping, oversleeping, waking often in the night), appetite changes, loss of interest in activities (or, at times, overinvolvement in activities), crying spells, and loss of energy. All clients should be asked directly about suicidal thoughts or behaviors. (For a more thorough discussion of suicide assessment, see Chapter 5.)

There are a number of short tests for estimating level of intellectual functioning. These tests are not likely to be extremely accurate, are usually culturally biased, and should not be used when the question of intellectual functioning may have significant consequences (e.g., in the case of organic brain damage or specific learning disabilities). They can, however, be useful in assessing how a client will do in the educational aspects of the treatment program and in predicting problems in advance that, with some adjustment in treatment approach, can be overcome. A test that one of us generally uses in the assessment of batterers is the Shipley Institute of Living Scale (Shipley, 1940). This test not only gives a quick (20 minutes) assessment of intellectual functioning, it also provides a measure (the Conceptual Quotient) of how much stress or distress may be interfering with a client's ability to solve problems or process thoughts.

The social history section of the emotional assessment should cover a number of areas. A history of the client's life as he perceives it, it should include history of the family of origin, school history, legal history, military history, occupational history, and medical and psychological problems history. Previous mental health treatment of the individual, as well as a history of emotional problems in his family of origin, should be obtained. We also recommend getting a sexual history from childhood to the present.

In addition to discovering important milestones and traumas for the client during his life, the gathering of a social history presents an excellent opportunity for assessing defenses, cognitive distortions, how the client handles problem situations, and how the client makes choices. Focusing questions on the client's decision-making process sets the stage for dealing with the issue of choice and responsibility in treatment. A common question we use in this portion of the assessment, for example, is, "How did you make the decision to ask your wife to marry you?" (or "How did you decide to marry your wife?" if his partner asked him).

There are a number of psychological tests available for the assessment of personality and emotional problems. We have found two tests to be particularly useful with batterers: the Minnesota Multiphasic Personality Inventory (MMPI) (Hathaway & Meehl, 1951) and the Beck Depression Inventory (Beck, 1976). The MMPI is a paper-and-pencil true/false test with 566 questions. Scoring of the test produces three validity scales, ten primary clinical scales, and any number of new scales that have been derived from research since the test was first published. The resulting profile can be fairly complex to interpret and is limited to use mainly by licensed clinical psychologists. The MMPI has been used in research to attempt to identify personality traits of batterers (e.g., Bernard & Bernard, 1984; Sonkin et al., 1985; Sonkin, 1987); the results of this work are discussed in Chapter 2.

The purpose of using the MMPI is not to see if the client "fits" some modal profile for batterers, but rather to discover unique characteristics of the person being evaluated. Batterers present with some similarities, but also with remarkable individual differences. The use of the MMPI can identify general and pathological personality traits, defense patterns, level of distress, depression and anger, general ego strength, and level of identification with masculine sex roles. Because the test is not based on face validity, the counselor often will discover latent traits that are not revealed during the clinical interview.

Common themes found with batterers on MMPI profiles are anger and hostility, distress or depression, overidentification with masculine sex roles, low ego strength, proclivity to chemical abuse, and problems with impulse control and "acting-out" behavior. Although these themes are common, we have seen almost every possible MMPI profile with batterers. These data can be extremely important for appropriate treatment planning and should be obtained whenever possible for clients who have the necessary reading skills. When clients lack the ability to take the test, some clinicians may administer projective testing. We tend not to do this, as the data obtained are not always as useful, the tests take a great deal of time to administer, and most projective tests have been criticized regarding reliability and validity.

The Beck Depression Inventory is a short, easy to administer paper-and-pencil test that can give the counselor a comparative rating of the level of depression a batterer is experiencing. Although much of the information it provides should already have been covered in the clinical interview, an independent measurement is often useful in communicating evaluation results to others, such as the criminal justice system.

ALCOHOL AND DRUG EVALUATION

Many domestic violence treatment programs have found it useful to have either an addiction counselor on staff or some form of consulting relationship with an addiction treatment program. Given the significant incidence of chemical abuse in a battering population (Bernard & Bernard, 1984; Sonkin, 1987; Sonkin et al., 1985), we recommend that every evaluation include an assessment of drug use. We recommend that this evaluation be done by an addiction counselor when possible. If that service is not available, the following guidelines should help to identify potential or actual chemical abuse problems.

The first part of the chemical use assessment is a thorough history of drug and/or alcohol use. This should include the client's first experience with each chemical, the first intoxication, the chronological pattern of use (times of heavier or lighter use), and the client's current use. The counselor should inquire as to whether the client has ever experienced blackouts while using (periods of time when the person carried on activities without being aware of what he was doing), binge drinking, morning drinking or drinking to relieve the effects of a hangover, and drinking more than he had planned to drink (for example, deciding to have a drink and having ten). Men with chemical use problems tend to minimize or deny their usage. As with assessing violence, counselors should expect minimization and should obtain collateral information to assess the validity of the client's report.

The dynamics of drinking should also be explored. These would include "relief drinking" or drinking to escape from distress or to relax, need to drink when with others, and ritualized drinking (e.g., always having one or two martinis immediately after work). A client's attitude toward the use of chemicals may be used as a defense to minimize or deny a drinking problem. Some clients will associate chemical use with maturity, independence, sophistication, or revolt against conformity. Many batterers will use alcohol or drugs to try to "cool down" their anger and may believe that they would be much more violent without this chemical "safety valve."

Chemical use often leads to legal, medical, family, and occupational problems, and these should be explored. Some clinicians will request that clients undergo a physical examination when there is a question regarding chemical use. Indications of possible chemical problems include elevated liver enzymes, blood pressure, or, more directly, blood alcohol levels. Previous treatment for chemical problems should also be examined, along with the client's attitude toward treatment, if necessary.

Although the client may or may not have a chemical use problem, he may be affected by others' usage. Growing up in a family where a parent has a significant alcohol problem is in some ways comparable to growing up in a violent family. For example, the parent's behavior may be unpredictable, may be violent, and may be embarrassing to the child. The counselor should ask about usage in the client's family of origin and in his extended family. Having one or two siblings with significant alcohol problems may suggest a proclivity for addiction. Finally, the client should be asked about his partner's usage (or previous partners' usage). As with exploring with him his views about his partner's violence, this is a subject that he is likely to raise anyway.

There are a number of addiction questionnaires available to assist in assessing chemical usage. The vast majority of these have high face validity and ask what the counselor has already covered in the face-to-face interview. The McAndrews Scale from the MMPI is extremely useful in assessing proclivity to addiction and has the added advantage of not relying on face validity. The scale does not tell whether or not someone has an addiction problem: Clients could score high on the scale and never have used alcohol, or they could score low and have a significant problem. It does, however, give the counselor some indication, in addition to the general profile, that a person may have personality characteristics that would put him at risk for chemical addiction.

Clients may have no addiction difficulties, may have periods when they abuse chemicals, may be more violent when they use chemicals, or may have a moderate to severe addiction problem. With each client, program staff will have to make some decision as to amenability for treatment given the client's chemical usage. If the decision has been made that chemicals are a problem for the client, some programs will admit the client to treatment only if he is concurrently participating in addiction treatment. Or the problem may not be seen as severe and the client may be admitted with a contract not to use chemicals during the time he is in treatment. Some clients will need to complete inpatient addiction treatment and be chemical free prior to admission to a domestic violence program.

When in doubt, we recommend consulting with an addiction counselor or addiction treatment program. Drug or alcohol usage can complicate diagnoses of emotional problems such as depression, anxiety, or organic components of major mental illnesses. In addition, a person with a drug or alcohol problem will have a difficult time comprehending the material in the program and may use chemicals between group sessions to avoid processing uncomfortable emotions raised by participation in the group.

COLLATERAL INFORMATION

It may come as no surprise to seasoned counselors that batterers generally lie to therapists. Clearly, the research on batterers (e.g., Bernard & Bernard, 1984) suggests that they not only minimize or deny the violence in their relationships, they tend to present themselves on interview as functioning better than they are. Attempting to determine lethality or amenability to treatment solely from an assessment of the batterer would not be good practice in this field. As time-consuming as it is to gather, collateral information is essential to a good evaluation. All collateral information should be gathered in separate, individual sessions rather than in conjoint sessions, unless a child is too young to be seen without the mother present. We recommend sharing the same limitations on confidentiality with collateral contacts as were shared with the batterer, especially regarding the reporting of child abuse.

The primary source of collateral information will be the batterer's spouse or partner. Most programs, ours included, tend to assume that both the batterer's and the victim's report of violence are minimized. Victims tend to minimize the violence in their relationships in order to feel as though the situation is not as dangerous as it is, to justify their decision to stay in the relationship, and to maintain their own feelings of self-esteem and control. Victims may also feel as though the violence is their fault and may be embarrassed about reporting what they feel they are responsible for. Nonetheless, the victim is likely to be closer to reality in the report of violence than the batterer.

The general format of gathering information from the spouse or partner regarding violence is similar to the format presented above with batterers. A history of violence and a picture of the cycle of violence should be obtained. As with batterers, level of violence, sexual violence, extent of injury, and violence toward children should all be explored. In addition, the counselor should try to assess the level of fear and distress experienced by the victim.

Additional information regarding the batterer's social history, chemical use history, legal history, and emotional and medical health history should also be obtained. This will generally be markedly different from the information gathered from the batterer.

Many spouses or partners will be involved in women's treatment programs. However, some will not. The counselor may have information available regarding the victim's own family of origin history, chemical use, and mental health history. If not, these may be important areas to explore. Some programs also administer psychological tests to spouses or partners. If this is an issue in the woman's treatment, then testing may be appropriate. If not, we recommend against this practice. Exploring emotional or personality characteristics through the use of testing instruments tends to carry the message that the victim's personality or behavior may be part of the cause of the violence, rather than the violence being the batterer's responsibility.

The information given to the counselor by a spouse or partner should be shared with the batterer or used to confront the batterer only if (1) the woman is informed beforehand and has given her permission, and (2) the counselor is able to determine that sharing this information will not endanger the woman or her children in any way. If the counselor feels that sharing information might threaten the woman's safety, the information should not be divulged, even if the woman gives the counselor permission to do so. It is important to remember, without becoming "paternal," that victims minimize and deny the extent of abuse and may perceive that they are safer than they are in reality. If information obtained collaterally is part of a determination that the batterer is suicidal and at high risk, then the counselor will have to divulge this information in order to take appropriate action.

The gathering of collateral information from the victim may be used as an opportunity to educate her about the dangerousness of her situation. At this point in the evaluation the counselor may not have all of the information from the evaluation analyzed and may not be able to make a determination as to whether the situation constitutes one that involves the legal duty to warn. We recommend that the final evaluation report be shared with the victim in a separate session following the completion of the evaluation.

Having the spouse or partner fill out some of the violence inventories mentioned above may be useful. The CTS, if used, should be completed by both the batterer and the victim. Additionally, Hudson and McIntosh (1981) have developed a 30-item Index of Spouse Abuse that can be completed in a few minutes and that measures both physical and nonphysical abuse.

In addition to the spouse or partner, the children in the family should also be interviewed. Children often present information that neither the batterer nor the victim has revealed. Additionally, children should be assessed as to the emotional or psychological impact of the violence they have witnessed or experienced. Most, if not all, children will have suffered traumatic effects from living in a violent home, and when it is appropriate they should be referred to a children's treatment program or to a counselor familiar with the dynamics of domestic violence.

Additional sources of collateral information may include police or court reports (the counselor can get copies and/or speak with the investigating officers), neighbors, previous spouses or partners, extended family members, employers, school personnel, and previous mental health and medical treatment providers. Naturally, signed releases of information need to be obtained to gather this information.

PREPARATION OF THE REPORT

At this point a sizable amount of information has been amassed, much of which is contradictory and confusing. Sorting and integrating these data, making treatment decisions, preparing a written report, and informing the batterer, the victim, and, when applicable, the court is a complex task. Even though some of the information may be labeled as "objective" (such as test results), much of the decision making will depend upon "clinical intuition" used in integrating the data. In many instances, when compared against a template of treatability or dangerousness, the objective data may look promising, but the clinician may have a "gut level" feeling that some factor is not right.

A book is generally insufficient to teach a counselor either how to use and evaluate intuition or how to integrate multiple levels of information internally. In order to evaluate the data collected, they first must be placed against the framework of what is known about the dynamics of domestic violence, lethality or dangerousness, and amenability to treatment. In addition, some determinations must be made based on conditions that may vary unpredictably, such as motivation for treatment.

Issues to be examined in the determination of amenability to treatment would include (but may not be limited to) the following:

(1) level of motivation of the batterer

(2) safety of the family and the community if the batterer is treated as an outpatient

(3) use of weapons or the extent of injuries inflicted by the batterer

(4) frequency of the violence

(5) amount of responsibility the batterer is willing to accept for the violence

(6) whether the violence has generalized to victims outside of the family or whether the batterer has a history of being violent in previous relationships

(7) whether child physical or sexual abuse is occurring in the relationship

(8) level of fear and distress experienced by the victim or the children in the family

(9) whether alcohol or other drug use has been associated with the violence or whether the batterer has a chemical abuse or dependence problem

(10) whether there is some external control over the batterer's violence in effect (e.g., court order, probation, protection order)

(11) level of current stress experienced by the batterer or the family

(12) significant problems in psychological, emotional, or organic functioning

Motivation for treatment is not a static condition. It can be either internal (desire to change) or external (wife has left, court ordered). Men often come to treatment after a partner has left them, convince their partners to return, and drop out of treatment. Our experience is that the vast majority of batterers come to treatment because of external pressure. If this pressure continues through treatment, the batterer may develop more internal motivation. If the pressure ceases before treatment has had a chance to cultivate internal motivation, batterers often leave. More information on assessing and nurturing motivation is available in Chapter 4.

Having gathered and incorporated this information, and assuming that the client is amenable to a community-based program, the counselor needs to determine whether the client can benefit from the type of program presented here. Some batterers may be amenable to treatment but may not be good candidates for a group-based program. Some clients may not be able to function in a group, because they are too psychologically disturbed, need too much attention, or have too few skills in social interaction. Other clients may be able to benefit from a group, but their participation in the group might be detrimental to other group members. This is often the case with highly defensive or rigidly sex-role stereotyped batterers. A batterer who maintains an adamant stance in blaming his partner or external influences for his violent behavior can mobilize other group members in resisting information presented by the group leaders.

Whatever determination is made regarding admission to the program, a thorough report should be produced. Even when a person is found not to be amenable to treatment, the report is an important document to inform the court regarding the clinician's assessment either for current legal problems or if there are future criminal charges.[2] The evaluation then becomes part of a permanent (or semipermanent) record of the batterer's violence. This has some importance, because courts usually treat first offenses as though they represent the first time the behavior occurred. Mental health professionals, on the other hand, simply assume that this was just the first time the person was arrested for the behavior.

We recommend formatting the report by addressing the assessment of violence immediately following the identifying data. Prior to presenting the body of the report, along with the usual identifying data and referral source, the warnings regarding limits of confidentiality and the batterer's understanding of these warnings should be documented. The assessment of violence should be thorough, containing the statements made by the batterer and the clinician's assessment of the validity of those statements.

Collateral information should not be identified in the report unless the information has been shared previously with the batterer. General statements are more appropriate, such as, "From other information obtained, it appears that Mr. X minimized the frequency and extent of his violence." The clinician should remember that evaluations are not considered confidential by the court, and the situation may occur where the report is introduced as part of a legal action, at which time the batterer will have access to the entire report.

Following the assessment of violence, each section of the evaluation described above should be included: intellectual functioning, social history, chemical assessment, and emotional and psychological functioning. These sections should contain any relevant data from which the conclusions and recommendations are drawn.

Diagnosis, using the *Diagnostic and Statistical Manual of the American Psychiatric Association* (third edition, revised), will help to consolidate and organize information and serves as a form of shorthand to translate information to other treatment providers. Additionally, diagnosis is essential to third-party insurance payment. The most common diagnoses used with batterers tend to be intermittent explosive disorder, antisocial or narcissistic personality disorder, and depression and anxiety disorders.

Finally, the report should include the counselor's conclusions and recommendations. These should be specific, with as little ambiguity or hedging as possible. The counselor should note the main points on which recommendations or conclusions are made. If the report is going to the court, the counselor should try not to usurp the judge's responsibility to sentence. The report can state that the client is not amenable to outpatient treatment, will not be accepted into this program, and is likely to be violent again if not incarcerated. The report should not state, however, that the client *must* be incarcerated.

After the report is completed, the material in the report should be shared with the batterer and the victim. We recommend first informing the victim of the results of the evaluation, so that if the report is going to increase the batterer's stress and/or dangerousness she can take steps to protect herself and her children. When the information from the evaluation is shared with the victim, she should also be warned regarding the counselor's assessment of dangerousness in the situation. Additionally, even if the counselor may not perceive the situation as highly lethal, she should be warned that any violent situation is unpredictable and that she is at some risk.

Alternatives to living in a violent relationship should be explored with the victim, such as separation, use of a shelter, criminal justice interventions, and civil options. If she does not have a protection plan developed, she should be assisted in developing one. Although counselors have a duty not only to warn but also to take reasonable care to protect intended and unintended victims, overreaction on the counselor's part can ultimately be harmful to a victim. Novice counselors (generally men) who experience the frustration of seeing victims choosing to stay in dangerous situations have at times tried to commit women to hospitals in order to protect them. This tends to undermine the empowerment of the victim and increases her feeling of helplessness and powerlessness.

The counselor may then decide either to share the results of the report privately with the batterer or to do this with the victim present. This is a clinical decision that should take into account the victim's wishes and the assessed level of risk in the situation. Having the victim present may help to reduce the amount of distortion by the batterer and may reinforce the notion that his behavior is being monitored.

Finally, if the batterer is ordered into treatment by the court, copies of the report should be distributed to the probation officer, the judge, and/or the prosecuting attorney. If the batterer has been found to be amenable, the treatment program now begins. Therapists should continually assess lethality from first contacts to termination from treatment and should take steps to warn or protect potential victims. Before we present the group treatment program, however, the issue of "duty to warn" is discussed in detail below.

A SPECIAL ISSUE: DUTY TO WARN

Previously, the right of a client to almost absolute confidentiality was considered necessary for successful psychotherapy. Clients were supposed to be able to come into the therapist's office and tell the therapist about anything they had done, legal or illegal, and expect that the therapist would not divulge this information to anyone. Recent court rulings and new legislation have changed this dramatically.

A therapist must now violate confidentiality in cases where the therapist, using professional judgment based on the standard of practice of the profession, concludes that the client is a danger to her- or himself or a danger to others. Additionally, where a therapist has reason to suspect that child abuse is occurring or has occurred toward a person who is still a minor, the therapist must file a report of suspected child abuse with the proper authorities.

There are some instances in which client-therapist confidentiality is never considered to exist. Psychological evaluations are not considered confidential by the courts, because the courts reason that no therapeutic relationship is created. Essentially, a therapeutic contract of some form between the client and the therapist must exist before the client can expect the therapist to be bound by the laws governing confidentiality. In addition, in some states or provinces, only some professions are covered under patient-therapist privilege rules.

One of the major issues in working with violent men is the therapist's duty to warn and to take reasonable steps to protect *others* if the therapist should perceive that the client may be a danger to another person or persons. This duty to warn has been mandated and delineated by a number of recent court cases in which therapists have been found liable for not taking steps to warn or protect others.

A landmark case, *Tarasoff v. the Regents of the University of California* (1976, 17 Cal.3d 425), first defined a "duty to warn" when the court decided that the special relationship between a therapist and client imposed a responsibility to use care to protect others. Although the arguments were made that therapists may not be able to distinguish between hostile ideation and real danger, and that free and open communication is essential to therapy, the court felt that professionals *should* have expertise in deciding when a threat is serious and considered the public interest to be more important than the policy of confidentiality. The court mandated that when a therapist determined that the client may be a danger to another person, one or more steps should be taken: The therapist should get a second opinion or consult, warn the likely victim, warn others in the victim's environment, notify the police, or take whatever other steps appear to be reasonable.

Other court rulings have either limited or broadened the scope of the *Tarasoff* ruling. In *Thompson v. the County of Alameda* (1980, 27 Cal.3d 741), the court stated that the county did not have a duty to warn the public at large. Similarly, in *Brady v. Hopper* (1983, 570 F.Supp. 1333 Denver, Colo.), the psychiatrist of John Hinckley, who shot President Reagan and William Brady, was not found to be liable as there was no readily identifiable victim the psychiatrist could warn.

Therapists, however, may have a duty to take steps to uncover the identity of potential victims, if the identity could be determined "on a moment's reflection" (*Mavrudis v. Superior Court of San Mateo*, 1980, 102 Cal.3d 594). In addition, therapists may have a duty to warn or protect others who might logically be in danger as a result of their proximity to the identified potential victim (*Hedlund v. Superior Court*, 1983, 34 Cal.3d 695).

A number of states have recently introduced or passed legislation aimed at limiting a therapist's responsibility to warn potential victims (Bales, 1988). California passed a law in 1986 that "provides immunity from liability for a therapist who, in the event of violence by a client or former client, might be charged in other states with failing to predict, warn, or protect others from the client's behavior" (Bales, 1988). If a client makes a serious threat against a reasonably identifiable victim, however, the therapist must make reasonable efforts to communicate the threat to the potential victim and to the police. Other states have introduced legislation that protects therapists from being sued for breach of confidentiality when fulfilling in good faith their duty to warn (Bales, 1988).

To fulfill his or her duty to warn others, a therapist must make some decision regarding the client's potential for violence. Research in predicting dangerousness generally suggests that therapists have either less ability or no more ability than the general public to predict whether a person may or may not be dangerous in the future (Allgood, Butler,

Byers, et al., 1978; Hamilton & Freeman, 1982; Hinton, 1983; Kozol, 1975; Megargee, 1970; Monahan, 1981; Quinsey & Ambtman, 1978; Sonkin, 1986; Steadman, 1977; Steadman & Cocozza, 1974; Werner, Rose, & Yesavage, 1983). Sonkin (1986) points out that false positives (predicting violence that then does not occur) are more probable than accurate predictions. The best predictor of future violence appears to be past violent behavior (Monahan, 1981), although even this criterion is not very accurate.

Whether therapists are accurate predictors of violence or not, generally the courts have decided that they should be able to draw inferences regarding the dangerousness of their clients. Hoshmand (1987) suggests that therapists' judgments, in spite of the poor research results, are presumed to be more trustworthy than those of laypeople. Our perspective, supported by research and clinical reports (e.g., Finkelhor, 1984; Groth, 1979; Sonkin, 1986; Sonkin et al., 1985; Walker, 1984), is that men who are violent in their families will continue to be violent until some significant intervention is made that either controls their behavior or removes potential victims from their control (e.g., incarceration, treatment, court order, departure of the victim). A number of studies examining family homicides report that most cases involved a history of physical abuse prior to the homicide (Boudouris, 1971; Browne, 1983, 1986; Chimbos, 1978; Thyfault, 1984). Even when a man enters treatment, the likelihood that he will continue to be violent either during or after treatment is high (Ganley, 1981b; Halpern, 1983; McNeill, 1987; Sonkin, 1986, 1987; Sonkin et al., 1985). Sonkin (1986) reports that the long-term effectiveness of treating male batterers has not been demonstrated.

In predicting violence with batterers, any history of violence may be significant enough to justify warning potential victims. Nevertheless, a thorough assessment of lethality is essential. This assessment of lethality should occur not only at the beginning of treatment, but should be a continuous process during treatment. Assessment of lethality prior to entering treatment is discussed above and in Chapter 4. Sonkin (1986, 1987) advises that therapists should assess the following eight factors during the treatment process in deciding to warn or protect potential victims:

(1) if violence is escalating in frequency or severity during the course of treatment

(2) if explicit or implicit threats are made

(3) if the client is in crisis and is unable to assure the therapist of his ability to control himself (even with assurance, the therapist may need to issue a warning)

(4) if the victim expresses fear for her own or another's safety

(5) if there is an escalation in the client's use of drugs or alcohol

(6) if the client refuses to cooperate with the treatment plan

(7) if the therapist discovers that the client has not talked about acts of violence committed while in treatment

(8) if the client has committed life-threatening acts of violence or made specific threats to kill prior to entering treatment (not discovered until in treatment) or during treatment

When working with violent men, we recommend a number of steps be taken with each client. First, we suggest obtaining signed releases of information to communicate with the man's partner and significant others, the criminal justice system, and any other individual or agency that may be important in his treatment. In this way, the legal problems of violation of confidentiality without permission are avoided, and the client has the expectation that his partner will be interviewed, so that he is not surprised and angered by this.

As mentioned earlier, we recommend that each man be thoroughly evaluated prior to being admitted to the treatment program. Following this evaluation, the results should be reviewed with his partner in an individual session. If his partner is involved in a women's domestic violence program, a staff person or counselor from that program should sit in on this session, when possible. Additionally, if the potential victim is not in treatment or has not been evaluated, it is important to assess her ability to comprehend this warning. As mentioned above, victims also minimize and deny the extent and lethality of the violence in their relationships. Sonkin (1986) suggests that the counselor should take into consideration the potential victim's perception of the seriousness of the threat, the batterer's perception of the seriousness of the threat, the batterer's psychological condition, and the availability of the victim to the batterer.

In addition to warning the potential victim regarding the client's dangerousness, exploring possible alternatives with her, such as separation, use of a shelter, and/or criminal justice and civil legal options, is very useful. A periodic assessment of dangerousness with a client should be made and noted and, whenever a warning is issued to a potential victim, the warning should be documented. Warning the victim, in reference to the legal precedents noted above, is not likely to be sufficient in many cases. Clinicians must use reasonable care to protect both intended and unintended victims. This may involve warning the victim, calling the police, hospitalizing the victim or client, informing a probation or parole officer, requesting revocation of parole, informing the shelter, or informing the family or friends of the victim (Sonkin, 1987). In addition, it is important for the counselor to consult with colleagues on a regular basis to review the ongoing assessment of a client and to get support if a decision is made to warn a potential victim.

Although many therapists were rather shocked and upset by the *Tarasoff* ruling, the practice of therapy does not appear to have been destroyed, as many predicted at the time, but it has changed dramatically as a result of the duty to warn and child abuse reporting laws. This may not, however, be due solely to legal changes, but may also be influenced by a change in the practice of therapy in general, and the changing value systems of therapists. More therapists are now involved in the work to end violence and in many ways see their clients as being the community and its interrelationships, rather than the individual. In addition, some therapists feel that the new laws are beneficial not only to potential victims, but to the potentially violent client as well (Bales, 1988). Our position is that if the setting characteristics (releases of information and the like) are handled well and the warning itself is framed in a therapeutic intervention, warning potential victims becomes an integral part of helping the batterer to focus on his responsibility for the violence and the effects of his violence on others.

NOTES

1. The word *overreport* is placed in quotes here because there is not likely to be any accurate base to which to compare these reports. Clinical impressions indicate that both husband and wife tend to underreport the actual level of violence in the relationship.
2. When a person is ordered into treatment by a court, in most instances, the order applies to the individual and not to the treatment program. If a person is not amenable to outpatient treatment, the court should be so informed and the person should not be accepted. Once the court is informed, the disposition is then up to the court and/or the individual.

PART III

TREATMENT

7

THE USE OF GROUPS

Counselors have intervened in wife assault with a variety of approaches: separate individual counseling for men and women, couple counseling, couple groups, family counseling, and gender-specific groups have all been utilized in the attempt to terminate the cycle of violence. For reasons discussed in this chapter, we strongly prefer to counsel abusers in groups. Although other modes may be helpful at later stages, we believe the immediate and primary goal of stopping the violence seems best attained when a man is in a group of his peers.

Groups for assaultive men differ in several important ways from most other problem-oriented groups, general therapy groups, and personal growth groups. Counselors who have been unaware of the differences in structure, objectives, goals, counselors' roles, and facilitator styles have had difficulty when beginning these groups. Failure to tailor an approach in the planning stage to suit the characteristics and the needs of abusers and the aims of an assaultive men's counseling program can produce regrettable results; dropouts, group rebellion, therapist frustration, and marked deviation from the goal of the group can occur. In addressing many of these issues, we aim in this chapter to help counselors prepare for productive, efficiently operated groups.

GROUPS FOR ASSUALTIVE MEN

Individual Counseling Versus Group

We have counseled batterers both individually and in groups. These contrasting experiences have led us to choose a group setting for this work whenever possible. In part, the reasons emerge from the inadequacies of individual counseling. This mode of helping an abuser is slow and arduous. The requirement to address minimization, externalization, and other problem behaviors overtly is not only difficult, it has the potential to create an adversarial atmosphere in which two roles can be highlighted—persecutor and victim. If a man regards us as persecutors we become his enemies, and it is then only natural that he strengthen his defenses. Where social and emotional isolation are problems for the man, individual meetings with a therapist are a poor remedy. Because an individual counseling relationship occurs behind closed doors, violence remains a secret and the shame associated with it remains. Furthermore, the one-to-one relationship risks reinforcing notions of psychopathology rather than the sociocultural, learned aspects of violence against women.

While the individual approach presents obstacles to change, the use of groups is based on what we believe to be the overwhelming advantages of this mode. Distinct and separate from content or counselor skill level, the group environment itself facilitates change. We can think of at least nine reasons to counsel abusers in groups:

(1) A group helps decrease a batterer's isolation. The group counseling environment requires taking risks, self-disclosure, and being vulnerable in the presence of others. It promotes trust while eroding the harmful facade of pseudoindependence demanded by the traditional male sex role. Social and emotional isolation from others is a mental health deficit, particularly when a man must deal with mounting stress levels. A group provides opportunities both to learn to rely on others and to help others.

(2) A group promotes improved interpersonal skills. A man in a group engages in discussion and role play, learns to give and receive feedback, and must do these respectfully.

(3) A group offers mutual aid among peers. The mutual aid process created by ten men multiplies the potential number of creative responses to any one man's struggle. This maximizes the self-help el-

ement while reducing the counselor's responsibility always to have an answer to a problem.

(4) As men learn to be helpful to each other, each individual's status as a batterer makes him a special kind of expert. His credibility stems from "having been there." Additionally, because help comes from a number of individuals, men's authority issues with the counselor are deemphasized.

(5) The effect of confrontation is maximized in a group. When a therapist confronts one man on an issue, other men who struggle with the same issue are indirectly confronted. When the group observes one man struggle with an issue, each member identifies with that struggle as if he were looking in a mirror. However, because only one man is being confronted directly, defensiveness on the part of others in the group may be diluted.

(6) As a group works for change, a norm is established for attaining group objectives within a certain time. This sense of group time functions as a reference point for members who lag behind, encouraging them to keep up with the group.

(7) A group maximizes rewards for change. As each man reports a success, he is reinforced by the entire group instead of by the therapist alone.

(8) The secrecy surrounding male violence against women and children often leads both perpetrators and victims to believe they are exceptional or sick. A group helps to dispel this notion. When a batterer enters a group, he meets ordinary men who have the same problem. This event begins the consciousness-raising process whereby men learn about the prevalence of abuse and the sociocultural factors influencing ordinary people to be violent. Beyond the educational value of this revelation, we believe shame is reduced.

(9) In view of incessant funding difficulties in social services, the group approach is cost-effective.

A Psychoeducational Approach

The term *psychoeducational* has been used to describe groups for assaultive men (Ganley, 1981b). Although the implications of the term might vary according to who is using it, it seems to be one of the best available for describing a recommended overall approach in batterers' groups. When violence is viewed as learned behavior, it follows that it can be replaced by new learning. Therefore these groups are partially oriented to educating batterers. Counselors teach skills, lead discussion on various issues, facilitate role plays, and assign homework. Interestingly, the learning aspect of abuser groups is reflected by many men's tendencies to refer to the group as a "class."

Education in these groups differs from that found in most classroom situations. Classroom education is most often concerned with subject material that is external to the learner, such as facts, figures, and concepts. Although this does occur in a batterers' group, we select most material for its personal relevance to assaultive men. Members are really learning about themselves. For instance, when we teach a man that certain ways of thinking about a situation profoundly affect the way a person feels about it, he must apply this information to his struggle to be nonviolent through his participation in group exercises and self-disclosure. Therefore, there is a marked personal slant to all material.

The psychoeducational approach that we present also allows for each man to present personal issues and receive help from the counselors and other members. Although this occurs at special, predetermined points in each session, portions of these groups bear strong resemblance to ordinary therapy groups.

Counseling Duration

The duration of a man's counseling varies from one program to another. One New York program provides only 6 sessions in an "educational workshop" format (Frank & Houghton, 1982). A Minneapolis program offers 32 group sessions of assaultive men's group counseling as well as a variety of other services (Stordeur, 1983). Programs differ not only in length, but in philosophical assumptions, subjects covered, and techniques used. Hence comparing programs is complex if not unrealistic.

Our emphasis on violence as learned behavior leads us to believe that eradicating violence and replacing it with alternatives is a long process. Twenty or more years of learning cannot be altered overnight. Herein lies a problem; few agencies or communities have the resources to provide one or more years of counseling to each man.

Seen in this light, most programs fall short of an ideal and simply provide what they can. Knowing that there is an ever-present discrepancy between men's needs and service availability, we chose to offer group counseling, specifically aimed at stopping the violence, that has ranged from 24 to 32 sessions. When possible, we now choose the higher figure.

Group Structure

Although we feel most comfortable with eight to ten clients in a group, we typically attempt to begin a group with ten to twelve clients. This is to account for men who drop out at some point along the way. Assuming that the majority of men are not mandated to attend, it is usually necessary to perform assessments on twenty or more men to produce the desired ten to twelve clients. Of the number of men assessed, some will not be appropriate for the group and are refused, some will openly decline an offer to enter, and some who are accepted will not show up. From our experience, we think it is advisable to have approximately fifteen men assessed and appearing to be committed to enter a group. Normally, ten to twelve will follow through and attend the first session.

Although it is possible to operate a group with more than twelve men, it makes it difficult to develop a trusting atmosphere, to give each man the attention he needs, and to finish on time. When beginning with fewer than ten men, the group may stabilize (after dropouts) at a number that decreases the program's efficiency. Sometimes it is advantageous to postpone the beginning of a group until a sufficient number of men are available.

We operate closed groups, meaning that we will not accept new members into the group after the second session. Excepting dropouts, men who begin this group finish with the same group of men 32 sessions later. Although many programs choose to operate open groups and admit new members at any point, we favor the closed group option for two reasons. The first is that it is difficult to integrate new members when considerable amounts of material have been taught prior to their entry. It would involve prohibitive amounts of group time to help new members catch up to the group. Alternatively, it could consume hours of a counselor's time in individual sessions to do the same thing. Attempting to do this would be analogous to admitting students to a course that was half finished. A second reason for running closed groups is that admitting new members after a certain point of group development destabilizes the group. The men will be familiar with each other and a bond of trust will be growing. The addition of new faces can interfere with this process by temporarily reducing spontaneity, comfort, and self-disclosure.

While closed groups have definite advantages over open ones, not all agencies are able to accomplish this. In locales where only one closed group is offered, men who miss an entry deadline could wait several months for the next group. This is no small consideration. In light of the dangerousness of battering, a shorter waiting period may better protect the battered woman. Closed groups may also be unrealistic for programs in small, rural communities, for there may never be enough men at one time to start a closed group of sufficient size. Such communities frequently use open groups and gradually build up their membership.

Our groups meet for approximately two and one-half hours each session.[1] The first two-thirds of the session consists of structured activity, such as teaching a skill, facilitating discussion, or involving the men in an exercise. After a coffee break, the last one-third of the session is Sharing Time—a period in which any man can present an issue or seek help for a problem.

While it is possible to reverse the order by beginning with Sharing Time and then proceeding to structured activity, there are two reasons not to. It can be difficult to terminate Sharing Time in favor of other tasks if many men have problems to present or if there is a man in crisis. Additionally, a man may want to discuss material from the structured portion as it relates to himself during the Sharing Time that follows.

We have also experimented with the frequency of meetings. In one of the best arrangements, the group meets twice a week for the first 16 sessions and once a week for the remainder. One reason for this is that a 32-session group that meets only once a week takes a long time to complete. A more important reason is that the portion most concerned with imparting the skills to avoid abuse needs to be completed without delay. At minimum, we believe counselors should quickly complete what we refer to in the next chapter as the Beginning Phase by meeting twice a week.

Confidentiality and the Group

Most counseling relationships are private affairs; the flow of information from that relationship to outsiders is strictly regulated according to "right to know" rules. Almost always it is the client who determines who has a right to know this information. The flow of information in the reverse direction is not so stringently governed. Although it is normally necessary to secure a client's permission to seek information about him (e.g., contacting previous therapists), a therapist sometimes receives information volunteered by others. In everyday therapeutic relationships, therapists often feel uncomfortable receiving unsolicited information about their clients. The ethics and the consequences of using these data in counseling can be perturbing.

Counseling offenders requires the ability to enforce accountability. To aid in this, we have made some changes in the normal flow of information. Programs in which we have worked often have men's partners attending battered women's groups, either in the same agency or in another community service. In this situation we are sometimes informed by the woman's counselor, or the woman herself, of abusive behavior between group sessions. If the woman feels safe enough to allow us to use this information in the men's group, we will confront the man if he chooses not to report it. There are other information channels we keep open. We provide probation workers of court-mandated men with general progress reports and specific reports on abuse or threats of abuse. Child protection agencies are sometimes involved in a case and may delay final disposition pending the outcome of treatment. We sometimes provide them with progress reports. The end result of this regular flow of information is that our groups are much less confidential than other counseling endeavors.

Counselors should consider the effect of these practices on the group's members prior to beginning a group. In every group we have conducted, the first time we confront a man with accounts of his abuse that he has chosen to conceal, the entire group seems shocked. The man under scrutiny may feel angry and betrayed. Similarly, a member may have strong reactions when he discovers that his probation worker knows something that he discussed only in group. For this reason, we strongly recommend that therapists discuss the confidentiality policy with each man carefully during the intake process and that each man sign a form indicating he understands the policy. Therapists should address this issue again in the first group session. If these policies are explicitly outlined and explained as non-negotiable conditions for participation in the program, clients are more likely to accept them and less likely to feel betrayed later.

Readers may wonder if these alterations of normal confidentiality practices interfere with trust and openness in counseling. Some men become guarded and suspicious, but, in our experience, they soon regard these practices as normal. We do not see a harmful effect. Men still disclose very sensitive information under these conditions. Some men even seem motivated to disclose abuse precisely because they do not know if the therapists have knowledge of these events in advance of a group session. They prefer to take the initiative in disclosing rather than be caught trying to conceal abusive behavior. The effect is negative only when policy is explained after the fact.

THE GROUP COUNSELOR

Leadership Style

Assaultive men are generally not self-reflective, self-disclosing, or self-motivated. They are often highly anxious about relating to others on the level called for in a counseling group (Ganley, 1981b). They also employ defenses that are incompatible with addressing the issue of battering. If the therapist waits for anxiety to disappear and for desirable behaviors to emerge, the group will likely flounder and men will drop out. For these reasons, a nondirective counseling style is inappropriate in these groups.

We agree with Ganley's (1981b) recommendation that counselors adopt a directive leadership style that implies certain counselor behaviors. The directive counselor is actively involved in the group process. The counselor teaches not only through words but also by modeling or demonstrating skills. Interaction among members is facilitated through structured activities. Member participation is elicited by asking questions. The counselor assigns homework, follows up on assignments, and confronts individual men and the group on their resistance to changing thoughts and behavior. When appropriate, the counselor tells members what to do and what not to do. Furthermore, the counselor sets clear limits on behavior and enforces consequences for violation of those limits.

These examples describe someone who is a very central figure in the group. The term *authoritarian* may come to mind for some readers. This pejorative term suggests a leadership style emerging from a need to wield power over others, a rigid respect for hierarchical structures, and an inability to tolerate dissent. In recommending a directive style, we are not promoting authoritarianism. While the therapist definitely assumes the position of authority in the group, the directive style is not that of a martinet. Power for its own sake is not an issue here. The therapist is always respectful of group members' feelings and rights. While also being a caregiver, the therapist maintains control over the group so that it may do its work.

We believe the directive style is most needed in the earliest stage of the group. As time passes, the therapist can relax this stance as the group gradually develops some measure of constructive autonomy. Group norms emerge, a mutual aid process is born, and members slowly learn to do with each other what the therapist modeled in the earlier sessions.

Guarding the Time

These groups use a highly structured format because the psychoeducational approach necessitates covering much material in a relatively short time. If the group is planned as having a maximum number of sessions, we guarantee that a counselor will feel pressured to keep to the schedule. Many situations will seem to conspire against accomplishing what was planned.

The reader should not underestimate the difficulty of keeping to a schedule. In any single session, a number of factors can wreak havoc. Members may arrive late. Men who have difficulty understanding material may necessitate longer periods of discussion than planned. One or more men may be in crisis while several men may be required to report abuse; a sense of urgency often develops around competing demands. It is common for novice therapists to have difficulty covering the agenda. Consequently, we advise meticulous planning of time in each session. As the therapist becomes more familiar with the material, he or she will develop the sense of timing needed to cover it all.

Two and a half hours of group time can easily be consumed by attending to men's individual problems. Therapists trying to keep to a schedule are often deeply affected by the men's needfulness. There can be a temptation to postpone the educational portion of the group for that session so that men can be cared for. This is a common dilemma. Because we recognize that counselors often have to make judgment calls, we are not inflexible on this issue. However, we must caution the reader that the postponing of educational material in a batterers' group might be tempting fate. In particular, the first half of the program contains anger control skills that must be learned rapidly. A particular skill scheduled for a certain night may help prevent an assault.

Group Cofacilitation

A result of adopting a directive style in these groups is that the therapist assumes much responsibility. Attending to the resistance to change, maintaining awareness of group process, and the demands of teaching are a huge load for one person. Those who facilitate these groups alone often perceive the competing demands as an impediment to doing their best work. For this reason, having a cofacilitator, though not absolutely essential, is of tremendous value.

Cofacilitation allows one person to be engaged with the group while the other observes specific interactions and the group's process. It fends off therapist exhaustion by allowing for periodic switching of roles. Additionally, dealing with difficult clients may be easier because the differing characteristics of each therapist offer a greater variety of constructive responses. Often the best qualities in each therapist are complementary and result in effective teamwork. Furthermore, for between-session problem solving, two therapists are better than one.

Counselor's Gender

The subject of the gender of group counselors for batterers raises some interesting issues. Although there seems to be little in the professional literature concerning the gender of therapists in this specific field, most programs face this question sooner or later. The basic question is, Does it matter whether it is men or women who conduct groups for batterers? In some quarters, this is a controversial question.

In conversations with some counselors who believe men alone should do this work, we have heard a number of reasons used to support their position. There is the politically based argument according to which men have an obligation to assume the responsibility of working with other men in stopping violence against women. This frees women to work with victims. Other reasons stem from beliefs about the positive impact of male facilitators in a batterers' group. Some believe it is advantageous when two male therapists model cooperation rather than traditional male competitive behavior. Some believe that the presence of men alone will facilitate disclosures of violence in general and sexual violence in particular, while the presence of a woman would inhibit these. Also stated is the belief that an all-male group forces batterers to learn to accept nurturing from other men and thereby decreases their dependency on women.

While these are intriguing notions, we know women who have successfully conducted these groups with other women. In conversations with those who use mixed-gender teams and seem less concerned with the gender of therapists, we have been told that many North American programs seem no less successful with this approach to abuser counseling. They believe that abusers who practice traditional sex-role stereotyping may benefit from observing women demonstrating strength and equality in relationships with male coworkers. Finally, from a pragmatic perspective, many communities with scarce resources are lucky to find knowledgeable staff to run such programs. Whether these are men or women may seem a luxurious worry in many locales.

While the issue of counselor gender is certainly important in services to female victims of male abuse, we do not believe gender is a key issue in counseling male abusers. Consequently, we do not support exclusionary policies or practices based on gender as some service providers do. A therapist's personal suitability, skillfulness, and general awareness of issues surrounding violence against women seem much more relevant to working well in this area.

Women Counselors in a Batterers' Group

While it is difficult to justify claims that either gender has an advantage in counseling batterers, the presence of women counselors will affect the group in some manner. The effect is neither good nor bad; it will simply be different from groups operated solely by men. A woman entering a group should consider in advance how she will respond to a variety of special issues.

A first issue arises from batterers' curiosities and fears. The group may want to know if the woman has been battered. Beneath this question may be the hidden concern that she will be angry, harsh, and rejecting of abusers if she has been battered. We believe honesty is probably the best policy in this situation. Although she can reassure men that she is there to help, not to punish, the group will ultimately be reassured by how she behaves rather than by a statement of intent.

If she has been battered and this is revealed to the men, the group may attempt to treat her as an expert victim. They may routinely turn to her for the "battered woman's point of view." While this is not necessarily negative, it can become so if the members become preoccupied with victims and lose the focus on themselves. If she feels constrained because her role is too narrowly defined by the group, the cotherapist team should find a way to broaden her role.

A second issue stems from male sex-role conditioning. We believe this conditioning predisposes men to seek nurturing from women. Consequently, the group may attempt to relate to a woman cotherapist exclusively as the nurturer (mother). If she feels pulled in this direction, some planning with the cofacilitator may be necessary to ensure that her role is not narrowly defined for her by the group. For example, in establishing a balance that is not based on sex-role stereotypes, cofacilitators may determine that the man should consciously adopt more than his share of nurturing tasks while the woman assumes more of the directive or confrontive tasks.

Finally, and most important, a man and a woman should be conscious of how they share power between themselves in the group. Assaultive men should witness a working relationship characterized by mutual respect and equality instead of male domination. In a situation where a female trainee works with an experienced male counselor, the difference in experience and the educational aspect of the relationship should be announced to the men. This will provide an accurate interpretation for whatever degree of uncertainty and dependency she may exhibit.

Keeping Records

While there are more interesting aspects to our work, our roles also involve keeping reasonably accurate client files. Although most agencies have specific policies in this regard, we find that many counselors are irregular in making entries to client files. In extreme cases, a therapist may work with a client for months and not make entries until closing the case. We have good reasons for emphasizing this mundane activity. The first stems from our experiences in court. In our work with court-mandated abusers, we sometimes have to terminate their involvement with the program. When termination carries the threat of other penalties, some men will ask for a hearing. Whenever this has happened, we have felt relieved to have reliable, detailed records when called to testify. Second, all of our clients are more susceptible to court involvement because of assaultive behavior. Counselors may be called to court in the event of an assault, a homicide, or a suicide. Finally, detailed records are absolutely precious if the program is ever accused of negligence or malpractice.

Detailed record keeping should extend beyond assessment and individual sessions. We make file entries after every group session for every man. We record his presence or absence, his contributions to the group, and the substance of any personal issues he raises. We are particularly diligent in recording exact details of his abuse accounts or threats of violence. We also note the specifics of any intervention we make.

COMMUNICATION WITH MEN'S PARTNERS

Disclosing Information

In Chapter 6, we underlined the necessity of seeking collateral information during assessment. Part of this task involves interviewing the man's partner whenever possible for general information and, in particular, violence data. We believe that, once communication channels between abuser counselors and victims have been established, they should be kept open. One reason for this is that men's partners should have access to reliable information about abuser counseling. Abusers too often lie or distort information about their participation in counseling during disputes with their partners. In misrepresenting the program as supporting them in their behavior, they perpetrate a form of psychological abuse. To help reduce the impact of this tactic, the program should develop a method of imparting the following information to victims:

(1) The program views the man as entirely responsible for his behavior. His partner and children are never responsible for his actions.

(2) The man's partner is in no way responsible for his success or lack thereof in abuser counseling. He is entirely responsible for utilizing information from counseling. Additionally, the program will never attempt to intervene in her life through him. For instance, he cannot correctly claim that she must cooperate with him in some manner when he uses a particular anger control method.

(3) The abuser counseling program content is outlined for her.

(4) Counselors will never take the man's side if he describes a domestic dispute in the group (although other men often do).

(5) Abuser counseling is not a "cure" for a man's abuse. Indeed, he is not diseased. It is no more than an opportunity for him to learn how to handle himself nonabusively in relationships. Whether he learns the material and uses it in his relationships is entirely up to him. This also means the fact of finishing a group program is no guarantee that he will be nonabusive.

(6) The program unequivocally supports her and her children's rights to be free from all kinds of abuse. We will provide as much information as we can on alternatives to enduring abuse or will facilitate a referral for this purpose to an appropriate service.

(7) If the agency offers battered women's counseling, the woman is informed of this and given the opportunity to attend counseling.

This information can be given to women in two ways, each of which will depend on how the agency's abuse services are organized. The first option is that each female partner can be invited to attend an individual session with a counselor. A second, more efficient option is possible when the agency operates battered women's group counseling and a significant number of women have partners attending abuser counseling. A counselor from one of the abuser groups can be invited to a women's group session to give this information and answer questions.

Receiving Information

A second reason to maintain communication with men's partners is that counselors can periodically receive valuable information from partners. Because some men will continue to conceal their abusive behavior while enrolled in a group, we believe it advantageous to invite women to inform men's counselors of abuse. If a man decides not to report an incident of abuse to the group, counselors can confront the man with the incident and with his decision to conceal it. Counselors should never disclose a woman's report without her permission and without being confident that she has made reasonable efforts to protect herself from retaliatory abuse. To facilitate safety when women report abuse, those agencies offering group counseling for battered women should ensure that there are reliable communication channels between men's and women's counselors.

We cannot overstate the counselor's and the agency's obligation to be cautious and vigilant in attempting to ensure the safety of anyone who is a potential victim of violence. We believe this goal should always have the highest priority. As the counseling of abusers becomes more routine within an agency, and as the program proceeds, therapists may slip into complacency. We urge therapists to avoid complacency by beginning service to each abuser with the assumption that he constitutes a lethal danger to others and to himself.

ISSUES RELATED TO THE USE OF GROUPS

Group Heterogeneity

Most of our groups include a broad spectrum of men. They come from a variety of socioeconomic groups, racial and cultural backgrounds, and educational levels. We have had white, upper-middle-class businessmen, teachers, and bank officials blending with the poor, the working class, new immigrants, the physically disabled, and the learning disabled. We have had educational levels ranging from fourth grade to the master's degree in a single group. In groups with a high number of court-mandated men, we have had a higher than usual number of disadvantaged clients; these groups seem to attract more frequent attention from the criminal justice system than groups made up of the more privileged elements of society. In groups containing larger numbers of voluntary clients, the privileged sectors of society have greater representation. Although each group is unique, all groups are heterogeneous.

The heterogeneity of these groups is a challenge for therapists. The program's educational facet, with its emphasis on skill development and attitude change, must be planned and conducted with foresight and care. Members differ in their abilities to read, to abstract, and to follow through with homework assignments. Written material must be selected not only for its content but also for its coherence to a range of members. Unlike a university course, in which written materials are primary learning tools, most written materials in batterers' groups should be supplementary rather than essential to the program's core requirements. Because we never assume that an abuser will gain essential knowledge from handouts, we always cover core material through lecture or discussion during group. Counselors following this strategy will minimize a class bias in their approach and be more certain that all members are learning the core material.

When we discover a man having difficulty with the material, we take remedial action. For example, one of us conducted a group in which a blind man attended. His lack of sight sometimes interfered with his remembering lecture material. We remedied this in two ways. Whenever possible, we avoided overreliance on visual aids. When a chart was presented, we took pains to explain the content and assure he understood. Second, we recorded lecture and discussion portions of each group so he could review them between sessions. Programs serving the blind might consider translating written material into braille. In other instances, when we have had semiliterate men in group, we have scheduled occasional individual sessions to be certain they are learning the material. When we present material, we watch the group and look for signs of losing some men's attention. Glazed looks or staring at the walls or out the windows might suggest that therapists should change their language or strive to be more concrete.

Group Members Perpetrating Violence

Clients in batterers' counseling will experience failure from time to time. Particularly in the early portions of a group, it is common for a member to come to a session and report that he was violent. While this behavior contravenes a group rule, we expect this to happen. While a prohibition against violence is obviously necessary, it is unrealistic to expect total compliance. The learning of nonviolent alternatives is a gradual process. Initially there will be awkwardness with new skills and mistakes will abound.

Two of our colleagues began their first group by making any violent behavior automatic grounds for expulsion from the group. Very early in the group, a man was expelled. Thereafter, not a single man spoke about current violence. Instead, the group pretended everything was fine while undercurrents of hostility and suspicion made for a truly miserable experience. Although the counselors abandoned this policy, the group in question remained suspicious of the program.

Although some degree of failure is normal, readers should not infer that we indulge violence. Backsliding in a batterers' group is cause for grave concern. The counselor should feel compelled to reserve time in the group session for any man who has been violent between sessions. At the beginning of each session, we determine if this is an issue by asking the group if any man has been violent or abusive since the last meeting. If anyone has, he is directed to share this with the group and be the first to speak during Sharing Time.

We have several objectives in mind when dealing with a violence report in the group:

(1) The man should relate his version of the events.
(2) When details are lacking (as they often are), the counselor should seek more information.
(3) The therapist should respond to apparent inconsistencies, distortions, blaming of the victim, and other defenses that are obstacles to the man's accepting responsibility for his behavior and understanding his mistakes.
(4) The counselor should help the man understand as precisely as possible the points where he made mistakes.
(5) The man should be helped to see specific alternatives to abuse in that situation.

(6) Input from group members should be encouraged.

(7) If possible, those alternatives should be role-played.

Failures provide opportunities. Each man will learn some of his best lessons from a detailed analysis in group of how he and other group members went wrong. Additionally, each man will be in a better position to avoid abuse in similar future situations if mistakes and nonabusive alternatives are highlighted.

There will be situations where a member has difficulty choosing nonviolence, but counselors are reluctant to expel him from the group because he seems motivated and cooperative. Before expelling the man, counselors can try a less drastic course. For instance, they can offer the man the option of separating from his partner for the duration of the program as a condition of remaining in the group.

Toleration of mistakes, however, does have a limit. When a man is repeatedly violent and this is not remedied by counselor or group input, his continuation in the group becomes an issue. Whether it is an unwillingness to stop his abuse, inability to learn, or habitual defiance of authority, a batterer should not remain in counseling if he is not changing. Counseling may not be the appropriate response to his violence.

Contact Among Clients Outside of Counseling

To address batterers' isolation and to structure support for nonviolence between sessions, group members should be encouraged to rely on each other outside the group. Usually, counselors feel reassured about the developing mutual-aid function of the group when relationships between men grow. While this is generally a positive development, it is occasionally destructive. Subgroups of men may form and coalesce around viewpoints that erode the purpose of the group. These subgroups may meet informally over coffee either before or after a group. Favorite activities include criticism of the counselors and program content, and group support for sexist and violent behavior. This may be signaled by a subgroup spokesperson seeming to speak for a number of men by using the pronoun *we*. For instance, "Last week after group we were talking about what you said and we disagreed with ... " might be a sign that bonding is a problem instead of an asset.

We have encountered very rare, but horrific instances of

subgrouping in which the subgroup's behavior was intolerable. In one case, two men formed a subgroup in which they sexually abused the partner of one of the men. While therapists might be tempted to censure the behavior and continue working with the perpetrators, this crosses all reasonable boundaries for toleration of backsliding. When a member uses the group as a recruiting ground from which he can form abusive teams, it is insufferable. As a remedy, we favor ejection of this subgroup. To keep these members in the group is more than a mockery of the program—it communicates an ambiguous message to other members about behavioral limits. We terminate members for other, less harmful transgressions than this.

Requests for Advocacy

Occasionally a member will ask a counselor to intercede on his behalf in difficulties he has with other people and systems. Most often it is a request that the therapist be his advocate. Some common requests are listed below:

(1) With an imminent court appearance on assault charges, he asks the counselor to write a positive personal reference that will help his defense.

(2) He asks the counselor to provide a positive personal reference to help in his child custody dispute.

(3) Fearing the loss of his children, he asks the counselor to intervene in a child protection investigation.

(4) Anxious about losing his partner, he asks the therapist to convince her to remain in the relationship.

Counselors would be justified in feeling discomfort about any of these requests. All of them represent a man's attempts to escape the consequences of his abuse. Counselors complying with these requests may be in an untenable position. While working in a program that ought to support protection of victims and the ability for appropriate social systems to censure abuse, they adopt a stance that undermines these goals. They compromise their own integrity and that of the program. Each of these requests also puts counselors in the position of seeming to support the promise that the batterer will not be abusive in the future. This prediction is impossible to make with any accuracy.

One way to curtail these requests is to formulate a policy outlining what kind of support can be offered to abusers. This policy can be announced to men at intake or at the first group meeting. One kind of representation we believe is appropriate is a written or verbal statement indicating that the man has enrolled in the program, and what portion of the program he has completed thus far. Additionally, an explicit, carefully worded statement concerning outcome separates the fact of completion from an assumption that the man has achieved nonviolence. For example, we commonly qualify letters confirming program participation with this statement: "Completion of this program does not guarantee that the man will not be abusive. Completion indicates that he is equipped with the skills to stop his abuse. The decision to use these skills is entirely his."

We do not mean to dismiss all forms of advocacy. There is another kind of advocacy that is both appropriate and helpful. Since many abusers come to counseling facing criminal charges, separation and divorce, the need to find new living quarters, and other serious stressors, they can benefit from help in negotiating strange systems and from receiving accurate information. This kind of assistance can reduce stress levels and indirectly help prevent abuse triggered by these stressors. Ideally, this as an adjunct service that is not part of the therapist's role. Specialized advocates operating out of a separate program within the agency or from a different social service may be helpful with these matters.

Use of Anger in the Group

The subject material in a batterers' group, the use of confrontation, and the stress associated with struggle periodically elicit powerful reactions from the men. If the arousal were labeled appropriately, it might more often be recognized and expressed as feelings of vulnerability, sadness, helplessness, or confusion. More often these are transformed into anger and there is the danger, however slight, that an angry member will be violent in the group. Interestingly, this occurrence in the group replicates his problem in his home. The same escalation mechanism is played out except that, in the group, it is less likely to result in him choosing violence.

Although violence in these groups is exceedingly rare, extreme anger can be frightening to therapists and clients. While an angry outburst can be a means of personal tension reduction, it can also have an external function; anger can be used as a conscious or unconscious attempt to control the behavior of others. People the man perceives as threatening will likely alter their behavior if they feel intimidated by his anger. A group in which one or more men frighten others will lack the safe atmosphere necessary for effective counseling. It is the counselor's job to halt such a development.

When a man becomes excessively angry in group, he should be reminded that he is capable of temporarily leaving the room to "cool down." Leaving is not an offense and it is not a sign that he is a coward fleeing confrontation. Instead, it is a sign of self-control. It demonstrates that he is able to make a choice between staying in the situation and being abusive and leaving to avoid abuse.

CONCLUDING REMARKS

In this chapter we have made a case for considering batterers' groups as a special phenomenon. While all counseling groups are similar in some ways, groups differ in other ways as a result of the focal problem, any special characteristics of clients having this problem, and the choice of interventions. We have described issues or concerns that may be peculiar to abuser groups, and in so doing, have sought to prepare readers to plan their own group programs.

For therapists beginning this work, we want to stress the need for careful, thorough preparation. Of course, clinical readiness, in terms of counseling skills and group content, is necessary, but clinical preparation is not enough. Though detailed coverage is beyond our scope, we remind the reader of another realm in which it is important to prepare for assaultive men's group counseling. That is the level of program readiness in its relationships with other community services. The professional education and networking aspect of beginning this service should not be neglected. It is important that links among services be established, that respective responsibilities be negotiated, and that other services have a general understanding of the program's approach to men who batter.

NOTE

1. The group structure and many of the group rules were adapted from those employed by the Domestic Abuse Project, Minneapolis.

8

THE BEGINNING PHASE

A group is much more than a simple collection of individuals who happen to gather in one place. Such a description suggests stagnancy and lifelessness. An astute observer would acknowledge that a group has a life of its own. That life is dynamic, rich, and complex, for it is composed of individuals whose lives are similarly vibrant, multidimensional, and varied. Those who work frequently with groups recognize that the coming together of several individuals creates a new life. In the beginning, this life has a tentative, awkward quality in which the separateness of each individual person stands out. However, this predominant sense of everyone's separateness does not prevail. As with individual people, a group grows, changes, and develops an identity of its own. It continues to develop as an entity until it dies. For this reason, not only can group therapists talk about individuals in a group, but they can talk meaningfully about the group as a unit of attention.

We are continually fascinated by the life processes of groups. Our fascination stems from observing the unique identity of each group. It is as if each group has a special signature; no two groups are ever the same, just as no person is ever a replica of another. If each group is so special, how can we talk about groups in general? Despite their special qualities, we are able to talk about groups in a generic sense because of aspects that are common to all. For instance, groups for batterers surely demonstrate predictable characteristics that are peculiar to those kinds of groups. These peculiarities, however, are usually related to the content. For instance, in batterers' groups there is much talk about violence, abuse, and the skills necessary to avoid violence. Such content will not likely be found in groups formed to deal with chemical dependency, life skills, or cancer.

Beyond differences in content, there is a dimension in which groups are more similar than different. Regardless of the kind of group or the special concerns it addresses, there will be a predictable group process—a perceptible growth and development over time. For example, all groups have a Beginning, a Middle, and an Ending Phase, and with each of the rudimentary phases predictable themes will emerge. The inevitability of certain themes and the manner in which they are expressed in each phase lend a familiarity to group process. Experienced group counselors come to depend on the expression of those themes and look for problems when they are delayed or suppressed. So inevitable are some of these that Yalom (1975) claims that a knowledgeable therapist could accurately estimate the age of any group by observing the emerging themes and the manner in which they are acted out.

BEGINNING PHASE THEMES

We chose a framework within which the reader can view the content and the process in batterers' groups. That framework consists of phases of group development. Balgopal and Vassil (1983) write about three phases: Beginning, Middle, and Ending. While sacrificing some of the precision of other group theorists, we like this division for its clarity and simplicity. It allows the reader to compare and contrast groups for assaultive men easily with other types of groups.

Within each of the phases there are a number of themes common to most groups and described by various group theorists. We will highlight those that illuminate events in a batterers' group. According to Balgopal and Vassil (1983), the Beginning Phase consists of three subsets of activities or themes. The first, labeled *pregroup*, involves a set of interconnected activities occurring before the group meets. Essentially, the pregroup activities comprise the preliminary groundwork and planning for the group, the enlistment of clients (often called intake), and the setting of client expectations (for instance, positive or negative expectations about gains and outcome).

The second theme is *exploration*. It describes the members' uncertainty, vigilance, and testing characterizing their anxious participation in the first meetings. The third theme is *involvement*. It describes the ambivalence of group members as they struggle with the two competing needs for achievement and affection.

Particularly important in batterers' groups are three additional themes. Yalom (1975) mentions dependency and counterdependency as inevitable initial concerns. In this context, *dependency* describes the force behind the tendency of the group, or of particular individuals in the group, to look anxiously toward the therapist for structure and for answers as well as personal approval and acceptance. *Counterdependency* describes the force behind the tendency to attack, resist, or express hostility and suspicion toward the counselor.

The themes of dependency and counterdependency naturally lead to the issue of authority, a major concern in batterers' groups. Though most salient in the Beginning Phase, it is a thread running through all phases of batterers' counseling. We can think of two reasons for its importance. Because minimization, denial, externalization of responsibility, and other behaviors are obstacles to change, the therapist often must be directive and confrontive. When therapists adopt this style, members' sensitivity to authority is heightened. We would expect this reaction from members of any kind of counseling group. Second, assaultive men in particular have usually experienced authority as abusive, either in their families of origin or in the manner in which they wield authority as adults. Hence it is reasonable to expect abusers to be aroused when others exercise authority over them.

We believe the developmental themes and the phases of a group are important considerations both in understanding and in designing group counseling programs. As we describe activities in this chapter and the two that follow, we ask the reader to consider the material against the background of these developmental themes and phases. At particularly important points, we will highlight these themes as they relate to program content.

THE MODULE FORMAT

Considerable deliberation preceded our choice of a method for relating how we conduct a batterers' group. Most books we have seen provide an overview of content. Although this approach is valuable, it leaves the therapist guessing at the details. Other publications, which we class as manuals, assume a detailed, session-by-session approach. These can appear to be as inflexible as recipes. As a middle ground, we chose a thematic approach, in which we specify our activities and interventions but do so within topical headings. Hence activities have been organized as modules. Some therapists may want to follow our approach verbatim. Others, however, may decide to modify their own programs by simply adding one or more of our modules. In either case, the module format provides both specificity and flexibility.

The description of each module begins with a section titled Rationale, in which we state our reasons for pursuing that module's topic or activity with batterers. We then describe the material and how we use it in the group. Following this, a statement of completion criteria briefly describes what should have been accomplished before leaving that module, and a rough estimated completion time is given for the module. Since there is an attempt to preserve 45 minutes to an hour for Sharing Time at the end of each session, note that the psychoeducational portion of the session consumes approximately 1½ hours. Estimated completion times are normally expressed in terms of 1½-hour sessions. Most module descriptions conclude with a discussion that provides additional comments or case examples.

While we have stated our preference for a 32-session group, the reader will note that the modules can be completed in much less time. This allows sessions at the end of the program to be used as traditional process sessions, in which there is no set agenda. In those sessions, the focus is on the concerns men bring to the group that day. Alternatively, supplementary modules can be included to address any special needs of a particular group.

MODULE 1: INTRODUCTION, RULES, AND CONTRACTS

Rationale

Each man inevitably arrives at the first session feeling anxious. Group counseling is a new experience for most men. While counselors cannot take away this discomfort, they can soothe group members by providing information about the journey they are beginning.

A structured introductory exercise requiring men to speak with each other will set a precedent for member participation.

We are convinced by our experiences that it is essential to be explicit and unequivocal with participation rules. There are several reasons for the special attention given to rules in this kind of group:

(1) Batterers have a history of violating others' personal boundaries with abusive behavior. Group rules help protect therapists' and members' boundaries from this violation.

(2) Batterers frequently test the limits of acceptable behavior in a group. Behavioral limits must be defined explicitly before problem behavior occurs.

(3) Explicit rules coupled with the will to enforce consequences for violation help build an "accountability structure," a new but necessary experience for many abusers.

A written, signed agreement known as a participation contract can help bolster each man's commitment to ending his violence and completing the program.

Introduction to Group

We begin introducing men to the group by making a statement about the group's purpose. We tell the men in plain terms that we know that every one of them has a problem with violence and that the purpose of the group is to help them learn to handle conflict and powerful feelings without violence or abuse. They also probably feel bad about themselves because of the way they handle situations in their relationships. The key to raising self-esteem is to find other ways of handling those situations. Learning these will help them to deal with stress, lead to better self-understanding, and develop the potential for better relationships.

Many men who enter the group have one primary goal: reconciliation with their partners. They expect that their participation in this experience will be the key to strengthening a relationship that is currently either tenuous or so damaged by abuse that it would take a miracle to survive. Because of this it is important to be realistic with them. We tell men that the group's purpose is not to save their relationships. Its sole purpose is to stop their violence. A man's relationship may get better or it may get worse while he is in group. By entering counseling, he is entering a time of accelerated personal change. If we could assess whether his relationship will survive, ceasing abuse and reestablishing trust constitute only one important factor. His partner also has to adjust to changes in him. Although the changes may be positive, all changes create stress in the relationship.

Changes in his partner further complicate the situation. As he demonstrates an ability to tolerate stressful situations without lashing out, she may feel free to experience and express her anger over past abuse. This development is more pronounced if she is involved in a battered women's group in which victims' anger is seen as healthy and independence is encouraged. This can be confusing for him, for, ironically, her anger emerges when he is trying his best to change. To decrease men's reliance on their partners for support and nurturing, we warn the group of this possibility and constantly encourage them to turn to the group for these needs.

Although we attempt to decrease men's dependencies on their partners, we encourage members to keep their partners informed about what they are learning in the group. One reason for this is that it can be helpful for the partner to know about particular anger control techniques, so that when they are used those techniques are not misunderstood. For example, her awareness of him leaving an argument as an attempt to avoid abuse rather than as an attempt to punish or control her can help deescalate anger in the relationship. An exception to this recommendation are situations in which a man's partner does not want any contact with him. In other words, a woman's attempt to protect herself takes precedence over our recommendations.

We ask the group to protect each man's right to confidentiality. Although information is always more difficult to control in a group than in individual counseling, men are asked to be discreet about events in the group. Most indiscretions involve giving sensitive information to a partner. This can be a serious problem when a man's partner is in a concurrent women's group consisting of partners of the men in his group. As a guideline, men can tell their partners about their own participation and about group issues, but must not talk about another man's struggles or reveal his identity without that man's permission.

We make a statement to the group about inevitable complacency in an attempt to reduce the dropout rate. Because incidents of violence may have ceased since a man first contacted the program, he may convince himself that his problem is not as serious as first imagined. We predict to the group that every man will think this and will be tempted to leave the group. Essentially this is a warning against self-deception.

Introducing Group Members

Group facilitator manuals detail many creative methods of having men introduce themselves to each other. We typically use one method that is relatively nonthreatening, simple, and gets men to talk to each other and the group. Men are asked to form dyads. Each man is to spend a short time introducing himself to the other man by addressing the following: (1) Who are you? (2) Why are you here? (3) Tell us something about yourself. When the group reconvenes, each member of the dyad must introduce the other member.

Group Rules

We discuss the group rules with the men and give them in a written statement. Some of these are typical group rules, such as those calling for participation in the group and completion of assignments. Listed and discussed below are others that are less common in other kinds of groups but are important here. Though men can ask for explanation or clarification, these rules are nonnegotiable. The first three rules are considered so important that violation of any one of them can be grounds for expelling a man from the program.

(1) *There must be no violence or threat of violence directed at a therapist or any other group member.* While we are generally successful at the intake stage in screening out men who are judged to be dangerous to staff or clients, on rare occasions we have been threatened by clients. The group must be an environment as safe as possible from violence if both therapists and clients are to be able to perform their tasks.

(2) *The man must not use alcohol or drugs on group meeting days.* It is necessary for a man to be free of chemicals so he can concentrate fully on group proceedings. Although counselors cannot always be aware of a man's chemical use, particularly when he has con-

sumed chemicals several hours prior to group, the expectation must be stated.

(3) *The second time a man does not report in group that he has perpetrated violence, he must leave the group.* Although a man may not report violence he has committed between group sessions, his partner may inform the therapist. A man cannot effectively work to change his behavior if he refuses to use the group to learn from his errors. The choice of the second time as the point to enforce severe consequences is simply an allowance to make one mistake.

(4) *A man must not hit his partner or his children while involved in counseling.* Despite the complexities noted in the previous chapter concerning violence perpetrated while enrolled in a group, it must be clear that this behavior is unacceptable. We recommend that the reader review discussion of this problem in Chapter 7.

(5) *A maximum of two missed sessions are allowed during the first sixteen sessions.* A man who misses more than this number is required to drop out and begin again with a new group. This is not punishment. Because the program is concentrated with information and skill development, a man can fall behind very quickly.

(6) *A group member should not hit, push, or point at other group members.* While hitting and pushing are obvious concerns, some readers might raise eyebrows at prohibiting pointing. Pointing at another can be an aggressive act when it is done during a discussion, argument, or angry moment. Some men point their fingers at their partners during conflicts that precede violence. Used in this way, it is an emphatic gesture that may be intended or interpreted as a warning.

(7) *A man may not touch another group member without first getting permission from him.* Violence is an extreme violation of another's personal boundaries. The requirement to get permission prior to crossing personal boundaries of any kind is useful training.

(8) *Each man must refer to his wife or partner by her name.* When recounting an argument, a man often automatically refers to his wife as "that bitch" or some other pejorative term. In a milder vein, without thinking about it, a man often will refer to his partner as "the wife," "my wife," or sometimes "my old lady." While this is so common in this culture that it usually passes unnoticed, it has the subtle effect of objectifying the woman and depersonalizing the relationship. Additionally, the word *my* denotes possession. The choice of language in this situation is important. When a woman's humanity

is diminished by inhuman labels or she is referred to as a possession, she is made less worthy of respect. In the heat of anger, it is easier to hit or otherwise abuse someone who is reduced to this level. In groups, we consistently correct men in this regard.

(9) *A man may not bring a weapon into the group.* We decided on this rule after observing that it was common practice for some men to wear hunting knives on their belts. One of us worked in a setting where concurrent battered women's groups were held. The knives were frightening to the women and the practice of carrying them was quickly prohibited. Additionally, the men's group facilitators noticed that men who did not carry knives eyed those who did nervously. In any event, allowing weapons to be within reach of men who have a problem with violence is probably ill advised.

Contracts

Contracts for participation can be arranged individually prior to the beginning of group sessions, or at the first group session. If the contract at the end of assessment is verbal, a written contract signed by the man and the therapist is advisable before ending the first group session. The substance of these contracts may vary from one program to another. In general, they specify the men's commitment to end violence, to attend group, and to participate fully.

Completion Criteria

In gauging the completion of this module, therapists should perceive that men understand the purpose of the group, agree to abide by the rules, have participated in member introductions, and have signed participation contracts.

Estimated Completion Time

This module would normally consume half of the psycho-educational portion of a session.

Discussion

If intake and assessment tasks have been handled well prior to the first group meeting, pregroup issues (Balgopal & Vassil, 1983) will not devour valuable group time. We cannot overstate the importance of attending to these issues prior to the first group meeting. The client's admission that a problem with violence exists and the mobilization of his motivation to change consume time and energy. We have noticed three negative outcomes of failure to deal with these issues prior to group. First, instead of this module being an introduction to group, it becomes an introduction to the basic issues of responsibility for violence and responsibility for change. This can turn the group into a battlefield in which therapists become mired in confronting an entire group over these concerns. Second, men who would have been screened out prior to group because of responsibility, motivational, or other issues are successful in entering group. Finally, an unnecessarily confrontational atmosphere may prompt some men to flee the group.

The effect of reading rules and announcing expectations is that the men learn immediately who will control the group. As counselors provide structure and are in charge of intake sessions, so are they in charge of the group. Members respond with ambivalence. On the one hand, this fits with the men's dependency needs—an inevitable theme in the Beginning Phase. Each man is anxious about the unknown and feels secure in knowing that he can rely on authoritative leaders to guide him in this new experience. This feeling of security emerges toward the end of the first session. On the other hand, counterdependency needs, also an inevitable theme, usually result in some feelings of hostility toward the leaders. These may initially be expressed by one man or a subgroup of men, and they are often expressed through challenges to the rules or questioning of the counselors' expertise.

Though they describe it in a more behavioral sense, Balgopal and Vassil (1983) refer to the same phenomenon as "exploration." While reassured by structure and authority, the men also explore the new environment by testing and challenging the limits.

MODULE 2: DEFINING THE PROBLEM

Rationale

Though an abuser has taken a giant leap by admitting at intake that his behavior is violent, he is only beginning to learn what behaviors constitute violence. Additionally, his definition of abuse is usually limited to physical violence.

At this early point, the group needs a working definition of abuse that encompasses a broad range of conduct. This module makes explicit the range of behavior that men must change. Furthermore, the structured activity in this module reinforces the norm of group participation.

Defining the Problem

While family violence researchers and therapists are often concerned with the intricacies of defining abuse, such precision is not necessary in a counseling group. Two things are necessary in defining abuse for batterers. The first is a set of categories for abuse. The second is a lengthy list of examples under each category.

A typical set of categories would include the following:

(1) physical abuse
(2) psychological abuse
(3) sexual abuse

Ganley (1981b) adds a fourth category—destruction of property and pets. This category could be considered a form of psychological abuse, or it could be considered separately.

A useful method of determining a group definition of abuse is to begin with a short lecture roughly defining the terms *abuse* and *violence.* In group, we use *abuse* as a general term that refers to all cruel, hurtful, controlling, and violent behavior. The term *violence* refers to one form of abuse and is characterized by physical expressions. Although we rarely initiate the use of the term *battering* in groups because of ambiguous connotations, we treat it in group as synonymous with *violence.*

After defining these terms, we tell the group about the categories of abuse. In stating each category, a therapist will probably offer a few simple examples of each form. Listing these categories on a blackboard as separate headings is preparation for a group activity. Counselors direct the group to brainstorm a list of examples under each heading. Alternatively, the group can be broken into smaller working groups to accomplish the same tasks, with, perhaps, each group working on one category. After completion, each small group reports to the larger group on its findings.

At this stage we explain brainstorming to the group. Members should realize that it is not a debate; the goal is to list as many examples as possible in a short time. At this early point, members may prolong the activity by minimizing the importance of others' examples. When there is argument as to whether or not a certain valid example is abusive, therapists can defuse this by reminding the group that the list is a group list rather than one that signifies agreement from each individual.

Completion Criteria

Though not all members will agree with every item, there should be some degree of consensus on the validity of the list.

Estimated Completion Time

This module would normally consume half of a session.

MODULE 3: CONTROL PLANS

Rationale

It is common for an abuser to say, "I was doing just fine but then I suddenly flew into a blind rage." Though this claim seems suspect, the experience is genuine. A man who batters is often unclear about preceding events, his responses to them, and the connection between these and the anger and aggression that follow. A first step in intervention is to train clients in the skills of self-monitoring. When these men are able to identify both their personal responses to arousal and behavioral chains and their antecedents, they can begin to alter them.

Because there is always danger of serious injury or death, we begin to address the violence as soon as possible. Although the Control Plan is placed within the first three group sessions, at a time when men are new to the group and lack sophistication in abuse issues, this tool is conceptually simple. The inclusion of a basic, relatively concrete skill at this early point coupled with assignments also reinforces the expectation that members participate fully. Furthermore, the program and the counselors gain credibility if we can immediately demonstrate that we have practical solutions. This can help encourage further attendance.

Cues for Violence

A Control Plan[1] consists of three basic parts. The first part lists categories of cues that are signals of arousal or escalation. The categories are physical, fantasy/images, emotional, and red-flag words and situations. Though there are many cues that are common to most men, each man's final list of cues reflects his personal response to arousal. It is, if you will, a customized list.

Physical cues include all sensations in a man's body or physical behaviors occurring when he is angry. These cues can be identified by the man prior to his behaving abusively. For instance, muscular tension, rapid movements, pacing, unusual stillness, changes in breathing, feelings of great physical power, and clenching of fists are all common physical signs of growing anger.

Fantasies or images are internal phenomena that often precede violence. Typically, these occur very rapidly. A man may report "seeing" himself hit his partner prior to actually doing it. Occasionally, a man will report having vivid images of a hated person doing him an injustice. The person is often a cruel parent or other authority figure who is physically punished by the man at the end of the fantasy. Another common fantasy theme is that of escape. The man responds to the painfulness of the situation by imagining himself escaping both his partner and the dispute.

Emotional cues are emotions preceding abusive behavior. While men may initially have difficulty identifying anything other than anger or rage, they eventually learn to identify such things as feeling put-down, inadequate, hurt, misunderstood, needful, and ashamed.

Red-flag words are words or phrases a man either verbalizes or recites internally when he is angry with his partner. For instance, "I'm warning you," "I don't want to hear anymore," and "bitch" can be words he uses prior to being violent. Red-flag words also can be words or phrases a man's partner uses to which he is highly sensitive. Red-flag situations may be sensitive topics or relationship issues that prompt arguments. Examples of these are child rearing, money, sex, domestic chores, and in-laws. Situations can also include places. If assaults have occurred most often in the kitchen, any argument occurring in the kitchen might be considered a red-flag situation. One of us knew a man who almost always assaulted his partner in the car. As it turned out, his dissatisfaction with the way she maintained and drove the family vehicle was a trigger for his anger.

We introduce the notion of cues with a short lecture. Cues are explained as warning signs that a man may choose to be violent very shortly. Although learning to recognize them can at first be difficult, vigilance and practice make it easier. We ask the group to brainstorm examples of each cue category and we give them homework. Each man must come up with a list of his cues for the next session. During the next session, each man takes a turn reciting his cues. While the first few men usually need some assistance, the rest of the men who witness this process are helped to enhance their lists.

Control Plans

Although the first Control Plan session is concerned with cues, the second session is concerned with the Control Plan itself. Recognizing cues is only one part of this tool. The other part consists of a plan of action that must be instituted once a man recognizes the presence of his cues.

At this stage in the program, every man's plan must include taking a time-out, which essentially means leaving the situation to calm down. However, the successful use of time-outs involves several conditions. In taking a time-out, men must observe the following:

(1) If a man still lives with or has contact with his partner, he must explain this tool to her before the next meeting. It is important that she know in advance that a time-out is not a manipulative technique but, instead, a tool for the man to use in avoiding abuse.

(2) Time-out means not only leaving the immediate vicinity, it means leaving the entire vicinity. That is, instead of simply leaving the room, a man must leave the premises to avoid the temptation of returning to finish an argument before a time-out has been completed.

(3) Time-out must be taken for a period of one hour. Because anger escalation results in physiological change, a suitable period must be allowed for physiological processes to return to normal.

(4) During a time-out, the man should not think about the issue that triggered his anger. He should use any method available to distract himself from ruminating about the troublesome issue (e.g., counting passing cars, concentrating on the feeling of the wind on his face, counting his steps). The purpose is to calm himself, not to maintain anger by ruminating.

(5) During a time-out, brisk physical activity is encouraged (a walk, jogging, or the like).

(6) For the sake of safety, a man should not operate machinery or drive a vehicle during a time-out. An angry man in a vehicle is dangerous to himself and others.

(7) To maintain personal control, the man must not use alcohol or psychoactive drugs during a time-out.

(8) When a man decides to take a time-out, he must say aloud to his partner, "I'm taking a time-out."

(9) A time-out is for self-control only. The man's partner does not have to stop talking or do anything else when he calls a time-out. It is not a way to control her behavior.

(10) After he successfully completes a time-out, the man should return to the situation and, if his partner is willing, again attempt to resolve the conflict. It is important that he respect her right not to resume the discussion. It is also important that the group understand that the recommendation to return to the situation is not permission to violate restraining orders or otherwise harass the partner.

Counselors model a time-out by doing two short role plays in front of the group. In the first scenario, counselors assume the roles of a man and his partner. An argument occurs and after a short time one therapist simply says, "I'm taking a time-out." He then leaves the room. In a second scenario, a similar scene is enacted but the man's partner does not stop arguing. Instead, she follows him about the room, demanding that he stay after he has stated his intention. The therapist demonstrates how the man is tempted to stay in the situation, but leaves nevertheless.

In the discussion following this modeling, there are inevitably objections to what has occurred. Men object on the grounds of pride. They argue against it because it leaves the issue unresolved. They ask an abundance of questions beginning with "What if." The therapist's basic response to all of these is to remind them that a time-out has one goal: avoidance of abuse. The goals of resolution, maintaining pride, or winning ought to be much less important than avoiding abuse. From the program's perspective, the man is a winner if he successfully uses a Control Plan.

The Control Plan becomes customized as each man determines exactly what he will do during a time-out. He might call or visit a friend, a relative, or another group member. He might go jogging, swimming, or shopping, or call a crisis hotline. Any activity that distracts him from his anger, provides support for nonviolence, or expends physical energy in a nonviolent manner may be appropriate.

We demand that a man be specific and exact in designing his plan now, since clear and logical thinking cannot be expected when he is escalating. Some practical preparations are often necessary. For instance, some men will pack a small bag so they are always ready to leave the house at a moment's notice. Some have called friends in advance to ask their permission to contact them day or night. Counselors will ask, "What if your friend John isn't home? What else will you do? What if you take a time-out at 3:00 a.m. and the swimming pool is closed? What is your backup plan?"

As homework, each member must design the specifics of his Control Plan. In the next session, we ask each man to recite his plan. The therapists and the group offer suggestions, praise, or criticism about the elements of each man's plan. When this is completed, each man signs the agreement to be nonviolent, and both the man and the program retain a copy.

Completion Criteria

Each man must understand the concepts of cues and time-out. He must also have discerned his cues and developed an acceptable Control Plan in writing. It must be fairly specific and include contingency plans, and the agreement to be nonviolent must be signed.

Estimated Completion Time

This module consumes approximately two sessions.

Discussion

The Control Plan, the most basic tool in these groups, functions as the cornerstone skill of the program. Though we teach other, more sophisticated skills, a man who reoffends at any point during the group must examine his failure to use his Control Plan. We lead the man through a detailed analysis. The core of this analysis can be summarized by the following questions: Did he recognize his cues prior to being violent? If so, how did he stop himself from taking a time-out? Are there certain cues to violence that occurred but were not included in his list? Did his plan of action prove to be inadequate or unrealistic? Why? How can his plan be improved so this will not happen again?

We insist that men adjust and improve their plans continually while attending the program. Indeed, they should always bring them to group and should carry them whenever possible. We refer to their cues and their plans at every reasonable opportunity—even when violence is not an immediate issue. For instance, when a man talks about a relationship problem and says he feels put-down, we ask him if this is an emotional cue for violence. If it is, we tell him to get out his written plan and add it to his list of cues immediately. Therapists who work with Control Plans in this way will notice that these tools evolve into sophisticated aids bearing little resemblance to the rudimentary plans formulated at intake.

In terms of group process, some interesting dynamics are apparent. By this time, the group will have met for several sessions. One or more men will be exhibiting what Yalom (1975) terms counterdependent behavior. This can be expressed overtly or covertly. Challenging what the counselors say, refusing to follow directions, and questioning the usefulness of suggestions are overt expressions. The more covert expressions may occur as hostile or suspicious glances or feigning boredom and disinterest. There are at least two ways to understand this behavior. Yalom (1975) believes:

Those members who are earliest and most vociferous in their attack, are heavily conflicted in the area of dependency and have dealt with intolerable dependency yearnings by reaction formation. These individuals . . . are inclined to reject prima facie all statements by the therapist and to entertain the fantasy of unseating and replacing the leader. (p. 308)

Another, less pathologically oriented, way of viewing this is to frame this behavior in terms of the group's struggle with the issues of exploration and involvement (Balgopal & Vassil, 1983). If members could voice their concerns directly, they might state them as questions: Am I in or out of this group? How can I tell if this is a place for me? Can I trust the counselors? Do they know what they're talking about? What can and can't I do here? These and other questions stimulate the variety of testing found in the Beginning Phase.

Also of concern is the issue of authority. It would be a mistake to view members as simply fleeing from or fighting against the authority of therapists. Whatever discomfort men have about authority, accountability, and structure, most men choose to stay in the group. While remaining suspicious of the counselors and the idea of group counseling, members communicate a need to know that the counselors are experienced, knowledgeable, and benevolent. Responses to the issue of authority are complex, exhibiting elements of approach and avoidance. Witness the following exchange between group members and a therapist:

JIM: You just said that there are no guarantees that we'll change. If that's true, then I don't know what I'm doing here. I've got to change or my marriage is finished.

COUNSELOR: I meant what I said. I can't guarantee you'll change in this group. That's going to be up to you. If you attend, participate, and do the assignments, the chances are good that you'll learn to give up your violence. I'll do my best to help you and probably others in the group will too, but the key ingredient is going to be your effort.

JIM: Well, how successful have you been? Have you led one of these groups before?

C: Yes, I've done this before. From what I've seen, not every man, but most men make big changes. Again, it's up to each individual man. It's what he puts into it that really counts.

JOHN: I've been to my family doctor, two shrinks, alcohol treatment, and marriage counseling. They didn't help. In fact, it always sounded like they didn't want to hear about my temper.

C: I can't speak for other counselors, but not every counselor has been trained in this area. Sometimes they don't know what to do and sometimes they don't see it as a problem. However, this is a place where you're going to talk about your anger and your abuse a lot.

JOHN: Have you ever had the same problem that we have?

C: No, I haven't.

JIM: Well, then how can you understand us and help us? I've got to know that you know what you're doing.

C: I can understand that this experience is new and a little scary for all of you. Talking about your abuse isn't fun. But if you're saying that I can only understand and help you if I've had a problem with violence, I think you're wrong. It may help to think of me as a teacher. A teacher isn't an expert on who you are and hasn't always had the same experiences as you have. However, as a teacher, I can know a lot about violence and how to help you get rid of your violence.

LEN: I don't have problems with you leading us. You've done these sessions before with other men and you've been trained. I think we should just get on with it.

One notices immediately how important the therapist is to the men. Two men challenge him and seem to border on hostility. Another man expresses his faith in his competence and becomes an ally. Though each man differs in how he regards the leader, the group tends to elevate him. He may be benevolent or malevolent, trustworthy or treacherous, but he is of paramount concern. At this early stage there is little awareness of the possibility of learning from other members. Though that awareness typically emerges in the Middle Phase, therapists nurture it now by structuring activities requiring member interaction. For the moment, however, the therapists are responsible for the group.

MODULE 4: SHARING TIME AND VIOLENCE REPORTS

Rationale

Lecture, discussion, and role plays must be balanced by attention to men's individual concerns. Sharing Time at the end of every session allows therapists to monitor each man's progress and provide individualized help. Sharing Time is also used for abuse reports. In helping a man to analyze his mistakes, he and other group members learn more specifically how the skills learned in group can be applied to everyday situations. This period is also a powerful tool in building a sense of "groupness"—a change in identity whereby the assortment of separate individuals merges into the growing entity known as group.

Men learn valuable skills from this activity. They learn to use others for support, to take care of themselves, and to take risks. Furthermore, they learn to be accountable for their abuse.

Sharing Time

Though modules usually describe activities corresponding to certain sessions, Sharing Time is different; it is an ongoing activity occupying the last portion of almost every session in the Beginning and Middle Phases. We begin every group with two questions: Who has been violent and abusive? Who wants time tonight? Those who have been abusive always receive first priority during Sharing Time.

Since time is a scarce commodity in these groups, two problems commonly plague Sharing Time. The first is that the psychoeducational or topical portion of the session runs overtime and limits Sharing Time. While this is sometimes unavoidable, careful planning and time management will limit its occurrence. The second problem occurs when many men want time, or when one problem seems so serious or complex that one man's problems threaten to consume Sharing Time. While the second problem cannot always be remedied, it is less often a problem when counselors approach Sharing Time with the following guidelines:

(1) *Retain a focus on the issue at hand.* Intervene respectfully but firmly when a man tells long, roundabout stories. Help him get to the point and stay with it.

(2) *Avoid long, introspective journeys.* Though they may be appropriate in individual counseling, they cannot be accommodated in group counseling. Groups for assaultive men operate best with an efficient problem-solving approach.

(3) *Recognize when a man needs more than Sharing Time.* Men in crisis or men with chronic difficulties may need individual attention outside the group.

(4) *Be willing to be directive when necessary.* It is not always possible to allow a man to labor through an issue and come to his own conclusions. For instance, if a man's Control Plan needs revising, he should be told this rather than being aided in arriving at this conclusion.

(5) *When possible, partition Sharing Time according to demand.* When three men want time and there is one hour available, the therapist should be aware when one man is taking too much time. As an alternative to this silent awareness, a more mature group can openly negotiate a system for partitioning Sharing Time.

Some men will naturally utilize Sharing Time more frequently than others. Some men never ask for time but are active in helping others with their problems. Still others remain totally silent. Although some imbalance is normal, we insist that every man take some time to talk about himself. We advise counselors to ensure that each man has done this at least once by the eighth session.

Although more common in the first few sessions, there are meetings at which nobody wants time. We think this is unacceptable. It is inconceivable that men enrolled in batterers' counseling would have no need to talk about their struggles. When a group resists Sharing Time during any session, we immediately institute a "check-in." The check-in simply consists of having each man in turn tell the group how he is doing now and how his week has progressed. A check-in inevitably turns into Sharing Time, since somebody will mention an issue and then gloss over it. We respond by asking questions, making observations, and seeking more details until the man is quickly and thoroughly involved in exploring the issue. In other words, we begin a check-in and rapidly transform it into Sharing Time.

Readers who are familiar with other programs may be confused about our use of the term *check-in*. Many programs use this term to describe the same activity that we call Sharing Time. Still others operate both a brief check-in at the beginning or end of a session and an equivalent to Sharing Time. In our approach, Sharing Time is indispensable. Although adding a check-in has its merits, we have found that using both in one session (particularly during the modules) consumes a lot of time.

Completion Criteria

During the first eight sessions, each man should have utilized Sharing Time at least once.

Estimated Completion Time

Available time will depend on the activities of the particular module. We prefer to have 45 minutes to an hour at every session.

Discussion

Control Plans are not only useful tools for avoiding abuse. Their existence also limits the usefulness of various excuses to deny responsibility for violence. Once a man has identified his cues, the claim that "suddenly something came over me" loses credibility. Once a man has identified a plan of action as a response to his cues, the claim that he had no other choices is no longer credible. Thus the exercise of developing a Control Plan weakens his usual defenses and helps move the man another step closer to accepting responsibility for his behavior.

When men report being abusive between sessions, the counselors invariably ask what cues were present. *Whether* they were present should no longer be relevant; they were identified in the exercise. Successful completion of that exercise implied a responsibility to identify them in the future. At this stage, many men will admit that they had at least a minimal awareness of their cues but mistakenly thought they had everything under control.

If a man claims he had no awareness of his cues during a dispute with his partner, we help him examine that situation in minute detail. A detailed analysis almost always produces some recollection of cues. Again, this places responsibility for cue identification with the man. When a man did identify his cues but nevertheless chose to be abusive, he may try to justify his actions by reporting his partner's objectionable behavior, implying that anyone would have reacted as he did. It is essential that counselors reject descriptions of a partner's behavior as justification for violence. Confronting a batterer in this situation might sound like this:

MAN: I didn't say anything back to her and she screamed at me. She called me a wimp!
COUNSELOR: What did you do then?
M: I got up and I hit her ... I think.
C: What do you mean, "I think"?
M: Well, I hit her in the face and I left the house.
C: How many times did you do it and exactly how did you do it?
M: I slapped her once with my open hand. She pushed me too far that time! Anybody in this room would have done it!
C: Which of your cues were present before you hit her?
M: I had a lot of tension in my face, and my shoulders, and my breathing

was shallow. I was clenching my fists. Look, how come you're taking her side?

C: You seem angry right now and that's understandable if it looks like I'm taking sides. I'm not taking anybody's side. I'm just trying to get an idea of where you went wrong in this situation so I can help you. So, you recognized your cues but you didn't take a time-out or do anything else in your Control Plan.

M: [loudly] Look, you're making it sound like she was totally innocent in this situation! She wouldn't shut up! What am I supposed to do when she's like that? She should be here answering for what happened, not me!

C: This is a violence group and your partner doesn't have a problem with violence. I can only help you look at how you handled yourself in that situation. It sounds like you want me to believe that you had no choice but to hit her. Do you want me to believe that you're like a robot and she pushes your buttons? Is that it?

M: No. I'm not a robot. But she should learn when to quit too!

C: What you're not seeing is that you're the one who raised his hand and hit her. You made the decision, not her. You had a Control Plan but you decided not to use it.

M: I thought I could stick it out and stay cool.

C: Did your pride get in the way?

M: Yah, I guess so.

C: How did you feel after you hit her?

M: I felt lousy. I failed.

C: Do you see that by trying to control her actions, you set yourself up to choose violence? You won the argument, but you really lost because you used violence.

M: Yah.

C: Under the section "Red-Flag Words and Situations," maybe you should add "when she doesn't stop talking" and the word "wimp." Now, how are you going to handle yourself in this kind of situation in the future?

At several points, the man invited the therapist to debate the issue of his partner's behavior. Instead, the therapist either side-stepped the issue or stated who was responsible for hitting. The major task was to return the focus to the man, his behavior, and his responsibility.

Occasionally a man who has been violent will claim that his partner used violence against him. Although this is sometimes true, it is usually a distortion or a lie. When working with a man in group on his failure to avoid abuse, we choose not to concentrate on this issue for two reasons. First, even if his claim is true, it is largely irrelevant.

Violence against him in any situation does not justify returning the violence. The only exception we would consider is a justifiable claim of self-defense in the face of threat to his life. These "do or die" situations are exceptionally rare. When a man persists in citing self-defense as the only option because of inability to leave, closer examination usually reveals that he was unwilling to leave. If he had any opportunity to take a time-out, that is what he should have done. If he chooses to stay in the situation and retaliate, he must be accountable for that choice. Again, the focus of our intervention is on his behavior.

A second reason we avoid pursuing this issue in the group is that it is impossible to verify the truthfulness of such a claim at that moment. Attempts at verification in the group would be a waste of energy and group time. By inviting fruitless discussion on whether or not partners provoke violence, this tack removes the members' ability to concentrate on their own need to change. Alternatively, we can (for the moment) either accept or ignore a man's claim that his partner assaulted him. We are then free to concentrate on his behavior in that situation. The therapist's response in this situation might sound like this:

M: I'm telling you, she slapped me in the face. What would you do?

C: What did you do?

M: I threw her across the room. What else could I do? Stand there and let her beat me?

C: You could have taken a time-out. You could have left the house immediately. You had choices, but you chose to throw her across the room.

M: No, I couldn't leave. She screamed and swore at me when I said I was leaving. She demanded that I stay! She told me that if I left, she'd lock the doors. Then I wouldn't be able to get back into the house.

C: Are you always this obedient when your partner gives you orders? I remember you saying several times during this group how you never let her push you around. And yet this time you seem to be saying she forced you to stay.

M: How could I leave? I wouldn't be able to get back into the house!

C: It sounds like you made a choice to stay and hit her rather than choose to risk being locked out of the house. I'm using the word *choice* on purpose. You could have left but you decided not to.

This kind of interaction between counselor and client could be quite lengthy. We have included enough of it to provide a sample of how the counselor responds to a claim of mutual violence and the perpetrator's claim that he was forced to be violent by his victim. The counselor is paying special attention to cognitive distortions and externalization. Equally important is the attention given to the misuse of the term *couldn't*; if this man were accurate, he would have accepted responsibility by saying *wouldn't*.

Confrontation of this sort is difficult for both the group and the therapist. It creates a tense atmosphere in which men silently stiffen and watch. Occasionally, a member who empathizes with the man will attempt to interrupt and defend him. When we encounter this, we acknowledge the other member's input but quickly return the focus to the offender.

The limitations of printed dialogue could make our examples sound like a harsh interrogation. Although we strive to be clear, incisive, and unrelenting when we confront men's defenses, we always deliver confrontation respectfully. The message is modulated by a voice tone and facial expression that communicate care and respect for the offender.

MODULE 5: USING PEERS FOR SUPPORT

Rationale

Because assaultive men are isolated and lack emotional and psychological support, we attempt to reduce this isolation by setting a precedent for contact between members outside the group. The importance of support is apparent in view of the grueling struggle to attain nonviolence and the consequent potential for personal crisis. Men learn to take risks with each other and open the possibility of mutual aid.

Calling a Group Member

Counselors tell the group that each of them is to find another man in the group and make arrangements so that each of them will telephone the other once in the coming week. These arrangements usually consist of planning for days and times when each man is available. The content of these calls is not important; they can be long conversations or they can simply consist of "hello" and "goodbye."

Though this seems to be a simple task, we have found that this requirement elicits great anxiety from the men. They often display this anxiety by asking an endless number of questions or by criticizing the requirement. Therapists may avoid this by leaving the room for several minutes after giving simple instructions.

Therapists should stress that they are serious about this requirement and that they will follow up on it the next session. We have found it helpful to recite the various excuses used by men in the past in not completing this assignment. We sometimes relate preposterous, humorous excuses to help reduce tension.

Completion Criteria

Each man must call, and be called by, another man.

Estimated Completion Time

This task, along with a group follow-up, consumes one-fourth of a session.

MODULE 6: STRESS REDUCTION THROUGH EXERCISE

Rationale

Since an inadequate response to high stress levels is one factor contributing to wife assault, regular, nonviolent discharge of tension may help a man to cope better with stress.

The Exercise Program

Therapists explain the rationale for an exercise program. The men are instructed to choose an exercise that they will perform for a minimum of 20 minutes, three times per week. This exercise must not involve obvious suggestions of violence; any exercise requiring hitting (e.g., boxing, squash, chopping wood) will not satisfy the requirement. Men who have a problem with violence should learn to reduce tension without a hitting motion. We recommend exercises such as walking, cycling, and swimming. Counselors should follow up this requirement at the next meeting.

Completion Criteria

Each man must report back to the group on the exercise program he has chosen.

Estimated Completion Time

Giving instructions and group follow-up consume one-fourth of a session.

MODULE 7: CYCLE OF VIOLENCE

Rationale

Walker's (1979) "cycle of violence" describes the cyclical nature of wife assault as experienced by battered women. This simple model is helpful in explaining the notion of "escalation" to batterers and aids in teaching self-monitoring. Additionally, predicting recurrence of violence can underscore the need to continue with counseling and the futility of mere promises to change.

Explaining the Cycle

Although we briefly explain the cycle of violence to men at intake, we cover it in much greater detail in the group. After drawing a bell curve on a blackboard, we ask the men to imagine a particularly horrendous day in the life of a man who hits his wife. We explain the concept of escalation by describing a series of stressful events that happen to the man. It begins in the morning when he gets up and ends with violence when he returns from work. The description of a condensed escalation phase might sound like this:

> You wake up late in the morning because you forgot to set the alarm. You rush to take a shower and there's no hot water. You rush to work but you get a speeding ticket. At this point you're really steaming. But you can't be abusive to the cop, let alone hit him, because of the consequences. Your boss snaps at you for being late and you have to take

it. . . . [Description of more stressful events.] . . . You arrive home after a long wait in a traffic jam. You walk in the door and find a letter from a collection agency. At that moment, your partner comes home from work. You fling the bill at her and demand to know why she didn't pay it. She replies that she thought you were going to pay it. You hit her.

Of course, we explain that this description encapsulates escalation into a one-day period. More realistically, men experience many small stressors over a longer period of time and suppress the effects. Hence the escalation period is variable, although the outcome is the same.

Pictorial representations of the cycle commonly utilize a bell curve with gentle slopes to signify gradual escalation and de-escalation. This conforms to the observations of victims, who quickly become attuned to danger signals in the batterer. Although we utilize this model, we present an additional diagram in which the gradual slopes are absent; instead of a bell curve, we plot a spike graph to represent how a man perceives his violence. According to this, a man relates that he was doing fine before being violent, that there was no warning, and that it "just happened." This perception is a consequence of not knowing one's cues and a general tendency to ignore or suppress the effects of stress.

When explaining the third phase of the cycle (contrite and loving behavior), we stress how sorry the man is and give examples of how he expresses this. He lavishes her with presents, apologizes, and begs her not to leave. Of particular importance is how often men make promises to themselves and family members never to do it again. The fact that they usually break these promises demonstrates that they are involved in a cycle of behavior that is difficult to break without help.

We also devote some time to describing the woman's perception of his escalation (the bell curve) and her consequent escalating tension. To counter claims that she invites the abuse by doing something she knows will aggravate him, we explain that a woman sometimes intentionally triggers his anger to "get it over with" (Walker, 1979).

We return to the escalation phase and utilize another visual tool; we draw an analogy between escalation and rising mercury in a thermometer. We present a vertical scale, similar to a thermometer, as a relative index by which each man can note the effects of stress at any moment. We ask the group to remember this "thermometer," and to ask themselves daily where they are on the scale. When they note a high level, they must do something to lower it. As practice, each man is asked in turn to assign himself a number corresponding to how escalated he feels at that moment. Often a man may appear angry or tense but give himself a low number. In this case, we describe his behavior and urge him to raise the number. Any man scoring a high number is urged to participate in Sharing Time.

Following the explanation of the cycle and the group discussion, we ask the men to identify their own personal behaviors from one situation as they apply to the cycle. We assign this as a homework task and ask that they complete it before the next session. We collect these, review them, and give written or short personal feedback to the men during the group.

Completion Criteria

The group should understand the notion of escalation and the cycle theory of violence. Each member should have personalized the cycle in writing, with revisions made from the therapists' comments.

Estimated Completion Time

This module consumes approximately one-half of a session.

Discussion

When teaching the cycle, counselors should try to make it personally relevant to all members. We do this by offering many concrete examples. A highly theoretical presentation, though suitable for therapists in workshops, will sound irrelevant to many men. The reader must remember that this is a heterogeneous group; each man will have a different capacity for abstract thinking. When the cycle is introduced in a meaningful way, men are usually riveted to the presentation; they nod and seem thoughtful. Their feedback reveals that this module illuminates behavior that previously puzzled them.

We provide examples of all forms of abuse when talking about Phase II of the cycle of violence. Sexual abuse is particularly important. This form of abuse is rarely acknowledged by men because of intense, shameful feelings. We formally address this form of abuse in the next chapter, describing the Middle Phase of treatment, where up to two sessions concentrate on sexual abuse. Its placement at that late point is intentional; few men are ready to face the issue until trust has been developed in the group. Nevertheless, it is wise to mention this behavior at this early point. It lets the group know that therapists are aware of its reality in men's lives. Additionally, it communicates the counselors' willingness to talk about it in Beginning Phase Sharing Times.

MODULE 8: ANGER EDUCATION

Rationale

Assaultive men have difficulties with anger because they experience it too often. However, the frequency of angry feelings is not the only problem these men have with anger. They come to counseling with erroneous ideas about anger and other emotions that contribute to their problems with anger and abuse. Many batterers regard anger as the only acceptable emotional outlet for men; anger, aggression, and masculinity seem almost indistinguishable. At the same time, abusers are often frightened of anger because they have seen it expressed abusively so frequently by themselves and others.

In this module, we begin a process in which batterers are enabled to make conscious choices about whether to utilize anger as a response to arousal. We begin two types of anger education. The first is to correct misconceptions about anger and other emotions. The second is to promote personal integration of these ideas by teaching the men to monitor their specific occurrences of anger closely.

Introduction to Anger

Counselors approach the topic of anger through either a short lecture or a discussion on anger. Examples of questions that can serve as a guide include the following:

(1) What is anger?
(2) Is anger "good" or "bad"?
(3) Under what conditions is anger a problem?

(4) What are the differences between anger and aggression?

(5) Why do we get angry?

(6) Why is anger often called a "secondary emotion"?

Several ideas should be conveyed in this discussion. Anger is a feeling or an emotion. In and of itself, it is neither good nor bad; it is often an appropriate response to an event. However, anger becomes a problem when someone habitually responds to many situations by becoming angry. Anger is also a problem when it lasts too long (e.g., fuming, carrying a grudge). Often people who try to hide or deny their anger carry it with them for a long time. Later, they explode with an intensity that is totally out of proportion to the precipitating event.

One can be angry without being abusive. Anger is a feeling and abuse is one way of channeling that feeling. They are two very different phenomena. By far, the worst problem with anger arises when it is expressed abusively. The aim of the group is to change how men express their anger, not to take this feeling away from them.

One way of answering the question, Why do we get angry? is to present a model of anger that focuses on the key role of thoughts in the production of anger. We tell group members that anger is often a result of the violation of one's "root expectations." Root expectations are very basic beliefs people have about themselves, about their relationships to others, and about how the world should operate. They usually govern either how people believe they should perform or how they believe others should treat them. When root expectations are perceived as being violated in a situation, an emotional response of some kind can be expected. One kind of response is called a primary emotion. The label *primary* is derived from an assumption that these feelings are the more genuine, emotionally honest responses to a situation. For instance, when one comes to grips with the death of a friend, sadness is an appropriate (and therefore primary) response.

At other times it is possible, and even appropriate, to defend against the experience and expression of a primary emotion by replacing it with anger. Used in this way, anger is a secondary emotion. In illustrating this for the group, the therapist may cite an example unrelated to abuse, such as the following:

If someone breaks into my home, ransacks and steals, my root expectation that I and my belongings be safe from molestation has been violated. In responding to this event, a number of primary emotions are possible. Fear is one that comes to mind. Yet fear, while appropriate, also involves an uncomfortable degree of vulnerability. It might become so overwhelming that I decide to do nothing about what has happened. While feeling vulnerable is understandable, in this situation it is a stressor that threatens my mental health. Anger, on the other hand, gives me more of a sense of personal power and safety. It may energize me to call the police, change the locks, and so on. Anger as a secondary emotion is useful and adaptive in this situation.

Although anger is often appropriate, the model we suggest uncovers two problems for assaultive men. The first concerns root expectations themselves. Since it is impossible always to control other people and situations, expectations that are unrealistic or rigid will be violated. As a result, the one who holds these expectations is doomed to feel perpetually angry and victimized. One key to identifying unrealistic and rigid root expectations is to determine if they use qualifiers such as "must always" or "should always." We urge men to explore this aspect of their thinking when they become angry.

The second problem stems from men's discomfort with vulnerability. This discomfort can be so pronounced that men rapidly and indiscriminately replace primary emotions with anger. This can be demonstrated graphically for group members with a diagram illustrating the male emotional funnel system (RAVEN, 1980), which was discussed briefly in Chapter 2. This simple but effective analogy utilizes a simple funnel, into the top of which are placed a variety of primary emotions. As these primary emotions travel downward in the funnel, they enter the neck in the form of anger and emerge from the funnel as rage. The model suggests that the assaultive man must develop the ability to label arousal more accurately, and must learn to be more comfortable with a broad range of feelings.

A group of men discussing their anger presents a prime opportunity to introduce ideas about male sex-role conditioning. At various points in the discussion, counselors should introduce questions about the differences between the way women and men deal with emotions. The male emotional funnel system analogy is useful in demonstrating how men suppress the experience of many feelings.

Counselors should suggest that the normal prescriptions for adequate masculinity are incompatible with good mental health.

In group, we call this suppression of feelings *stuffing*. A common metaphor used to describe this process and the outcome is that of a man stuffing his feelings in a huge sack. Soon the sack will become so full that it explodes in rage. The group can brainstorm lists of emotions that are permissible for men and those that are permissible for women. This activity often produces controversy in the group, with some men arguing that recent changes in sex roles make this dichotomy obsolete. We have found it useful to redirect an over-intellectualizing group to their own experiences as men. In other words, we ask them, "What emotions do you definitely feel free to experience and express as a man?"

The Anger Log

An anger log or journal is a self-monitoring tool that helps a man identify and record anger cues, differing intensities of escalation, triggers for his anger, the cognitive process feeding his anger, and any deescalating self-statements he may use to reduce his anger. Many North American programs use this tool, forms of which are described by Ganley (1981b) and Sonkin, Martin, and Walker (1985). We assign two anger log entries per week and require that men submit these on a weekly basis. We peruse them and then return them with comments and suggestions. To aid men in labeling emotions, we give them a long list of "feeling" words.

Completion Criteria

Therapists should feel confident that the group understands the theoretical material on anger and the anger log assignment.

Estimated Completion Time

This module normally consumes 1½ sessions.

Discussion

We always attempt to maximize men's involvement in discussion during this module. This helps avoid the dry, theoretical realm and makes the material relevant to men's experiences. In doing this, we ask men for examples from their lives. We seek discussion and debate. We also are vigilant in scanning for glazed looks or other telltale signs of boredom.

We believe that anger logs ought to be a central component of anger education in every batterers' counseling program. Although many programs assign this tool as regular homework, logs tend to fall by the wayside. Men will often perform this assignment several times and then forget it. Counselors are so pressed for time that regular follow-up during group is difficult.

This module marks the beginning of gender-role consciousness raising. Although one module is formally devoted to this topic, we like to take advantage of many opportunities to comment on sex-role issues through the course of the group.

MODULE 9: MOST VIOLENT INCIDENT

Rationale

This is one of the longest modules, and one of the most difficult, grueling activities for the entire group. Each man must undergo an extremely detailed examination of the time he was most violent toward a partner.[2] There are several reasons for conducting this activity.

At this point in the group, the members are aware of the group's purpose and their reasons for being there. Nevertheless, almost all of them are still minimizing their violence. The fact that they cooperate with the requirement to use a Control Plan guarantees only that they are using a tool—not that they see themselves as truly responsible for their behavior. Their responsibility is underlined in this module.

In the Beginning Phase, group cohesion is hampered by each man's desire to hide the true extent of his abuse from other men. Beneath this need to hide is fear. Fear that he may be the most violent, fear of vulnerability, fear that others will judge him harshly, and fear of exposing his shame and low self-esteem are some of the major factors inhibiting openness in the group. The group pays a price for this; mutual support for change is limited. Instead, there is pretense and an illusion of good work.

Exposing the full extent of a man's abuse can reduce his shame. Shame is an important reality in abuser groups. Guilt (born of the recognition of bad behavior) is an appropriate experience for a batterer. Shame (born of the belief that one is essentially a bad person) is counterproductive to change. When a man continues to cling to the notion that he is essentially a bad person, he is more likely to turn shame, or anger at himself, into anger and abuse against others. If shame over past behavior plays a part in his choice to batter in the future, a destructive cycle is operating.

Finally, though the group has heard that stress is a major factor in wife assault, this knowledge is abstract and remains disconnected from daily life experience. Detailed exploration in the group of each man's violent behavior can demonstrate specifically how stress is connected to his abuse.

Most Violent Incident

We prepare the group for this activity by delivering a short lecture on shame. We discuss shame as a negative phenomenon—as a burden wearing men down and maintaining low self-esteem. To begin extricating themselves from the spiral of violence and shame, men need to be completely open about their violence in the group. We tell them that the activity is difficult and that it is natural to want to avoid it, to claim they do not remember, or to minimize the accounts. Nevertheless, we encourage them to risk being truthful.

Each man receives a sheet of paper with the following questions:

(1) Describe the situation in which you were most violent. What was the nature of the conflict leading up to your violence?
(2) Were there any events that led up to this situation?
(3) At what point did you decide to use physical force?
(4) What kind of physical force did you use?
(5) List the advantages and disadvantages of using physical force in this situation.

We give them 10 minutes to recall the essentials.

We ask for a volunteer to be first in relating his incident. The volunteer relates this by responding to each of the questions except the last one; the entire group will examine these after each man has had his turn.

Because this activity is unpleasant, we expect each man will try to race through his response to each question. If this happens, the purpose of the exercise is defeated. Instead, each man should take approximately 20 minutes to complete his story. In attempting brevity, a man offers very few details unless specifically asked for them. We strive to elicit minutely detailed accounts of what transpired.

A batterer often presents his incident in a way that suggests his partner was mostly (if not entirely) to blame for the conflict and the abuse. We seek information about the conflict not to help him justify his behavior, but to elicit a well-rounded picture of the event and to uncover the particular stressors the man responded to with abuse.

Examples of the questions we use to elicit details include the following: Who broached the subject? What did she say? What did you say in response? How did the argument proceed from there? Where were you in the house? Was she sitting or standing? Where? What were you doing with yourself physically throughout this part of the argument? Do you remember any of your cues? Were the children present? Was anybody else there? Did either of you raise your voices? Did either of you move to another part of the house? Did the other follow? Were you verbally abusive? In what way exactly? Did you threaten her directly or indirectly? How?

We also seek information about events leading up to the argument and the violence. Typically the acute battering phase is a culmination of long periods of mismanaged stress. The man may have had trouble at work, marital tension, problems with extended family, or other difficulties. He was likely ignoring the effects or "stuffing" the feelings. Though less time is used exploring these stressors than is used in establishing details about the conflict and the abuse, it is important to explore the man's quality of life prior to his abuse. It will help him see the costs of responding to stress in his usual manner.

A crucial point in the process is marked by the question, At what point did you decide to use physical force? The question has been carefully phrased; we always assume that the man made a decision. An abuser typically responds by claiming that he did not make a decision. Instead, he claims his partner pushed him to his breaking point and left him no choice. Another common claim is that he lost control of himself. A therapist and group member discussing this issue might sound like this:

MAN: I didn't make the decision. She did! She pushed me too far that time! She knows I don't like her bringing that up.

COUNSELOR: She made you lift up your hand and hit her?

M: Well, . . . no. She didn't make me lift up my hand but she pushed me too far. What was I supposed to do?

C: You're still saying in effect that she made you hit her because she wouldn't keep quiet. I don't buy that for a second.

M: Look, maybe I'm not saying it right, but I never decided to hit her. I just lost control. It was like I was crazy.

C: You also said earlier that you only hit her below the shoulders and you said a few sessions ago that you never hit her when the kids were around. In the past, you stopped hitting her when the police arrived. You also have never hit her in public. That sounds to me like you're making definite decisions how, where, and under what circumstances to hit her. You're very much in control.

M: Well, I can see what you're saying, but I was like a crazy man.

C: If you were crazy and out of control as you claim, why didn't you kill her? Why did you stop?

M: She was moaning a lot. I was afraid I'd hurt her badly.

C: So you made decisions—when to start, how to hit, and when to stop. You were definitely very much in control of your behavior, weren't you?

We also seek details about the kind of violence used. How did he hit her? Did he use an open hand or closed fist? How many times did he hit her? Did he use his feet? Did he use other weapons? What injuries did she suffer? Did she get medical care or did he stop her?

After every man has had his turn, therapists ask the group to tell of the advantages and disadvantages of using violence in the situations they described.

At the end of both sessions, we always warn the men to monitor their cues during the coming week. Since the activity is highly stressful, men should be careful not to respond to the stress by becoming angry and abusive.

Completion Criteria

Each man, in turn, must participate in this activity.

Estimated Completion Time

Two sessions are consumed by this module. Since these are often lengthy, Sharing Times may be short.

Discussion

During these sessions, a man may act on his fear, anxiety, and shame by escalating his anger. Though violence in group is rare, counselors should be aware of the potential for it. If any man becomes angry with anyone in the group, counselors should remind him that he can take a time-out during the group.

At other times, a man might express his feelings more appropriately by crying. When a man cries in group, he breaks a sacred masculine rule, and will be worried about what others think of him. He often appears ashamed and believes he has failed. Men witnessing this appear uncomfortable, avoid eye contact, and remain silent. Therapists should not underestimate the impact of this event. If it does not receive attention and care, the one who cries can feel so humiliated that he drops out of group.

When the group is asked to tell of the disadvantages of using violence, men usually have no difficulties listing these. The disadvantages stand out, for it was these that brought them to the group. When asked to list advantages, they often claim there are none. Instead of abandoning this portion, therapists should offer a couple of examples to stimulate thinking (e.g., She stopped what she was doing; I won the argument). When members are aware of how abuse functions for them, they will have a better appreciation of the difficulty in giving up violence.

This module always has a personal impact on therapists. Although we discuss in a broad sense the impact of working with violence in Chapter 11, at this point we must mention some ways in which counselors are affected by this module. When seeking information and confronting men about their abuse, the counselor's style is highly rational and methodical. Counselors beginning this work can have difficulty maintaining this style. Men's denial and the horrifying accounts of violence can create anger and a desire to punish the men. We find we must retain awareness of our anger and avoid directing this at the group. This particular session is easier to conduct if one has a cocounselor to share the load.

A second issue is that of therapist self-care. Listening to graphic accounts of violence leaves one feeling raw, vulnerable, and offended. These effects can be limited if a therapist debriefing session is available after the group. At that time, we talk to our cotherapists about the personal impact of the session.

A third issue is concerned with a response more common to therapists who are beginning their work with abusers. As a man recites the details of his violence, his attempts to blame his partner may actually sway the therapist's judgment of the situation. A batterer can sound so rational and logical as he describes her "irrational," objectionable behavior that the unwary counselor's perception of reality can be blurred. The counselor may begin to feel sympathy for the man, begin to wonder if his circumstances are special, and be blunted in ability to confront the man's externalization of responsibility. We believe the therapist feeling influenced in this way should initially strive to remain skeptical. Additionally, we urge the therapist having this difficulty to consult all alternate sources of information available in an attempt to regain a balanced perspective.

Transition to the Middle Phase

The module dealing with the most violent incident produces truly remarkable group counseling sessions. They stand out because portions of them are so emotionally charged. Also salient are the "battles" between counselors and men over the issues of personal responsibility for abuse. Confrontation and resistance clash, and men cling desperately to the illusion of justified violence. There are dramatic moments resembling television portrayals of psychotherapy sessions. However fascinating, it is not entertainment.

The energetic clash is much more than drama. It represents a culmination of everyone's work in the Beginning Phase. Counselors have provided a preliminary education on violence, abuse, and anger and have given men a tool to help achieve nonviolence. However, the group's awareness of some issues has not been sufficiently personalized. Each man needs to examine his own violence thoroughly to help integrate his knowledge with his personal experiences. On the surface, the clash seems to be between therapist and client. Below the surface, a more crucial battle is waged; it is a fight between each man and himself. The part of each man that deceives himself into believing that others are responsible for his abuse must be at war with another part that sees the truth as reflected by the therapist. If he cannot assume responsibility for this one part of his life, the chances of nurturing peace and gentleness in him are slim.

In terms of group process, this module usually marks the turning point from the Beginning Phase to the Middle Phase. Men have done what they have dreaded: They have exposed their dark sides in the presence of others. Their counselors and peers have not judged them, and they realize they are not that different from others in the group. In enduring this experience they have gone through a rite of passage.

There are unmistakable changes born of this experience. These may be quite marked or they may be subtle. One change is a consolidation of group identity. From this point onward, men more often use the word *we*, when in the past it was always *I*. They talk about the men out there who are not changing in contrast to group members. We hear of men gathering informally for coffee and other leisure activities. They phone each other more frequently for support. We often notice a second kind of change in which men seem to possess a new readiness to work for nonviolence. At approximately this time, some of them ask, with an air of impatience, when we will teach them more skills for avoiding abuse. This need to learn and achieve also signals their transition into a more serious work phase, which we will call the Middle Phase of group development. Though the journey to peace has only begun, we sometimes see a glint of pride.

So far, our description of the changes in this transition is positive and optimistic. We feel compelled to balance this with another picture. Batterers entering the Middle Phase of group have a long, grueling struggle ahead. They are comparatively unskilled and have not reached the point of giving up their violence. Despite any positive, work-oriented atmosphere in the group, there will be violence reports in the Middle and Ending Phases. As a result, the physical and emotional well-being of each man's partner is still at risk. Furthermore, the group has yet to consider thoroughly and work on their abuse in the psychological, emotional, and sexual realms. Further difficult work on these types of abuse, as well as physical abuse, and a concerted effort to confront and change the belief systems supporting violence against women and children will occur in the Middle and Ending Phases.

NOTES

1. Self-monitoring or attention control techniques are now common elements of behavior therapy (e.g., Novaco, 1975). This particular tool utilizing these principles was borrowed from the Domestic Abuse Project, Minneapolis.
2. This module was adopted from the Domestic Abuse Project, Minneapolis.

9

THE MIDDLE PHASE

The remaining modules described in this book fall within what we term the Middle Phase of the group, divided into two parts. Group process in the Beginning Phase began a transformation: A collection of diverse individuals gradually formed a group—a new and vital organism. They formed a group identity based on the realization of shared problems and common goals. That process was a prerequisite of what is to occur in the Middle Phase.

Balgopal and Vassil (1983) state that the Middle Phase is recognizable by members' emerging realization that they are in charge of their lives. An authority vacuum created by gradual therapist withdrawal from the role of expert leaves members having to seek help from other members. Northen (1969) notes that the group learns to be less dependent on the counselor and begins to rely on the group for help. While we regard this dynamic as a sign of health in all groups, it is carefully regulated in our approach. The defenses employed by batterers that require counselors to assume a directive role still exert a counterproductive influence in the early portions of the Middle Phase. In addition, there is still a great deal of education and behavioral intervention to be accomplished. For this reason, counselors relinquish their directive, policing role much more gradually than is common in other kinds of groups. The rate at which this can be accomplished depends on the quality of member interactions. Interactions based on support of program tenets (e.g., personal responsibility, nonabusive behavior) suggest the counselor may experiment by tentatively withdrawing as the authority figure.

Northen (1969) emphasizes the problem-solving function of the group in this phase. Members discover that they can be helpful to each other, signaling the birth of what Shulman (1979) calls a mutual aid process. This is evidenced by a sharing among members of feelings, ideas, skills, and possible solutions to problems. In our groups, this mutual aid process is most visible in (but not restricted to) Sharing Time. Behavioral role playing of new skills, such as assertiveness, also encourages mutual helping. As mutual aid becomes a group norm, demands on the counselors decrease as men learn to respond to other members.

Equally characteristic is a sense of cohesiveness (Northen, 1969) usually signaled by members being attracted to the group and to the work being accomplished in the group. Evidence of cohesiveness or solidarity is often found in the choice of language: Members more often use *we* and *us* in contrast to the *I* of the prior phase. This is not to say that conflict and disagreement are absent. Overt conflict, however, seems more tolerable with the common assumption of everyone's right to membership despite individual differences.

Balgopal and Vassil (1983) summarize several theorists' observations on this phase by noting the group's emphasis

on work and exchanges of skills; feelings of security and freedom; mutual give and take; a sense of intimacy with one's self and the group; marked degrees of personal and interpersonal empathy; experimentations; valuing novelty and newness; acceptance of individual idiosyncrasies; affirmation of one's place, and of being right in what one is and does. (p. 205)

We look for all these qualities in our groups in gauging their health. However, the Middle Phase is also a time of work and struggle different from the struggles of the prior phase. Members sometimes find it grueling and even painful. It is concentrated with skill building and consciousness raising, and the therapists exert constant demands for work, accountability, and change.

The first part of the Middle Phase covers four cognitive-behavioral intervention techniques: covert sensitization, conflict management and assertiveness, cognitive restructuring, and relaxation. The second part of the Middle Phase expands identification of abuse to include psychological, emotional, and sexual abuse, completes the educational component on male socialization, and examines experience and learning from one's family of origin.

PART 1
MODULE 10: COVERT SENSITIZATION

Rationale

Covert sensitization addresses the batterer's violent behavior directly and reemphasizes the message, first imparted in the Control Plan, that the batterer is solely responsible for his violent behavior and that he has the ability to control it. This intervention increases awareness of escalation, awareness of cognitive distortions, and options to being violent. The constant rehearsal utilized in covert sensitization employs a behavior interruption technique that can generalize to high-risk situations, increasing the likelihood that the man will use a time-out when his anger escalates.

Covert sensitization builds on previous modules, and the homework first assigned in this module generally continues throughout the program. Training and education that take place in the group allow many opportunities for counselors to identify and confront defenses, distortions, and power and control issues. It is also useful as an ongoing monitoring process of how much the men learn about these issues, as they present new taped scenarios throughout the program. As the men learn about psychological, emotional, and sexual abuse, they can incorporate this new information into their tapes. Counselors can have some impression of whether this information is understood by the men by how they use it in their taped scenarios.

This module was incorporated into our program from a similar component developed by Redirecting Sexual Aggression, a sexual offenders' offense-specific treatment program in Denver, Colorado (Ryan, Lane, Davis, & Isaac, 1987). The cyclical nature of sexual deviancy and battering, as well as the use of cognitive distortions and defenses by offenders in both categories, suggested that similar treatment modalities in some areas might be useful. Indeed, we have found this module to be a valuable component in the behavioral part of our program.

Behavioral Chain

In order to develop scenarios for covert sensitization, we have each man build a behavioral chain of his violent behavior. This is similar to his work on his Control Plan, the personalization of the cycle of violence, and his presentation of his most violent incident. However, in this case the counselors and the batterer agree on a point in the sequence of behaviors where the behavior could be safely interrupted.

We often use the most violent incident presented in the previous module to develop the first behavioral chain with a group member. The information is fresh in his mind, and he is likely to be willing to continue to examine this incident. After having him briefly review the incident again, we start by having him describe what happened, especially his cues and distorted thinking, backward in time from the violent incident. The man should be encouraged to keep exploring backward to identify the point where the tension-building phase of the violence cycle moved into an escalation stage preceding his violence. The counselor and the client can then look at the chain and find a point where they both feel that, if the client had interrupted the chain, the violence could have been prevented.

Once the man has defined a chain, which we put on a blackboard and have him write down, we ask him to go through the chain in the first person and in the present tense. We ask him to try to imagine, as best he can, that he is in the situation now, to present it as though he is seeing it happen in the present, and to interrupt it at the stopping point previously agreed on. This description often sounds like this:

> I see myself getting in my car after work. I am very angry. I see myself rehearsing things to say to my boss. Now, I am driving very fast and I feel like making other cars get out of my way. I see myself wondering if Dorothy has picked up the kids' toys in the living room today. Now, I am calling her names in my head and saying, "Why did I ever marry a sloppy, lazy person like you?" This makes me even more angry and I am driving even faster. I am pulling into the driveway and I can see one of the kids' bikes in the driveway. I am getting out of my car and I am shaking, my muscles are tight, my face is hot. I am yelling for Dorothy.

At this point the client would say, "Stop," and stop the behavioral chain. The entire monologue should last approximately 1½-2 minutes. Once the client can do this fairly well in the first person, the behavioral chain is developed and covert sensitization can begin.

Covert Sensitization

Covert sensitization in this program involves verbally presenting a sequence of three scenarios, separated by the command, "Stop." Each of these scenarios is presented in the first person, as though the events are happening now. The men, when working on these scenarios, should be encouraged to attempt to put themselves in the situation in their imaginations, rather than reciting scripts. Counselors should monitor group members' tapes of their scenarios for tone of voice, as well as content, to identify when the men are truly involved in the exercise.

The first scenario is the behavioral chain developed above. Once a man has completed this and said, "Stop," the next scenario involves imagining the worst possible outcomes if the man is violent. In other words, the man presents a behavioral chain of escalation, stops it at a point where he can interrupt prior to violence, then presents a first-person account of real-life consequences to his violence. We often have to encourage the men to look at possible consequences, including incarceration, serious or fatal injury to their partners or children, the loss of their families, or loss of their jobs. This scenario often sounds like this:

> I see myself being arrested and taken out of my house. I am embarrassed. My children are looking at me with disgust and hate. I see my wife leaving, telling me she has filed for divorce and has a restraining order against me. I see my son and daughter saying they don't want to see me anymore.

This scenario should also last 1½-2 minutes. At the end of that period, the client should again say, "Stop," and move on to the next scenario.

The final scenario, again done in the first person, describes the possible positive outcomes of being nonviolent. Counselors should never allow clients to use fantasies that would involve violation of court orders or that would be very unrealistic. On the other hand, men should be encouraged to see positive relational consequences for nonviolence, even though those outcomes may seem somewhat distant at the time. Counselors should also encourage the men to look at positive outcomes for giving up their power and control behaviors, in addition to their violence. A final scenario might sound like this:

> I see myself more in control of myself. I am not trying to control my wife or children anymore. I see my wife starting to trust me again. I see my children looking less afraid of me than they have been. I see us doing things as a family without my ruining everything.

Once these three scenarios are explained and the men can do a fair job of each of them, we ask them to put them together in an uninterrupted sequence. We generally have them rehearse their scenarios in front of the group at least once, giving them feedback and encouraging the group to give feedback. We then ask them each to record at least one sequence on cassette tape before the next session. We review the tapes the men have made between sessions, especially for distorted thinking, blaming their partners, and ability to stay in the present. When each man has made an acceptable tape we ask the group to record two complete sequences between groups. Each sequence should take 5-6 minutes.

Completion Criteria

Each man should have developed an acceptable sequence and recorded it. Once the tape is acceptable, recording should continue until each man has completed 150 minutes (2½ hours) of taped sequences.

Estimated Completion Time

This module takes two group sessions to complete the training and start the men on the recording. Additional counselor time outside of group is required to review the tapes and give the men written feedback on their efforts. Most men will finish the 150 minutes of recording time just prior to the end of the program.

Discussion

As a behavioral intervention, covert sensitization can be a very powerful technique. It reinforces awareness of emotional arousal, reminds the client of the consequences of violent behavior, and reiterates the client's ability to control that behavior. It also provides an opportunity for the counselor to give individual feedback and attention to each man's cognitive distortions, defenses, and rationalizations. Finally, through constant rehearsal and sensitization, it provides each man with a new skill to interrupt his escalation to violence.

MODULE 11: CONFLICT MANAGEMENT AND ASSERTIVENESS TRAINING

Rationale

Lack of assertiveness and inadequate conflict management skills have been noted in Chapter 2 as characterizing men who are violent with their partners. In addition, a number of studies have demonstrated that assertiveness skills can reduce aggressiveness (Huey & Rank, 1984; Lange & Jakubowski, 1976; Saunders, 1982, 1984; Watts & Courtois, 1981). Most psychoeducational group programs for batterers use some form of assertiveness training (Deschner, McNeil, & Moore, 1986; Edelson, 1984; Ganley, 1981b; Saunders, 1982, 1984).

Assertiveness training is often misinterpreted by clients as a method of "getting what you want" or "winning." Indeed, Ray (1986) found that assertiveness may be correlated with an authoritarian personality. Assertiveness training should, when presented and taught correctly, be a skill that gives individuals more control over themselves and less control over others. If clients are able to control their own behavior and not feel manipulated or trapped by others' demands, they may have less need to control others.

Appropriate assertive reactions and conflict management can also prevent anger buildup. Saunders (1982) describes assertive behaviors that are incompatible with aggression as follows:

(1) handling criticisms and put-downs
(2) making requests constructively

(3) saying no when desired in a calm manner

(4) tuning in to the feelings of others

(5) recognizing, labeling, and appropriately expressing feelings

Conflict management includes assertive behavior as one of a number of skills that must be learned to resolve conflicts non-violently. Edelson (1984) lists six behaviors that must be accomplished in order to achieve peaceful conflict resolution:

(1) the ability to identify and state the parameters of a problem situation

(2) the ability to identify and express feelings

(3) the ability to identify and state one's partner's point of view

(4) the ability to offer solutions

(5) the ability to negotiate a final compromise

(6) the ability to extricate oneself from increasing stress, that is, take a time-out

Conflict management involves using a number of different behaviors that have been learned previously (time-out), are learned in this module (assertiveness, compromise), or will be learned throughout the program (cognitive restructuring, empathy).

Assertiveness Training

We often use a short lecture to introduce the subject of assertive behavior. Contrasting Smith's (1975) basic assertive rights with power and control behaviors offers a strong introduction to the usefulness of these skills. Smith (1988) has also recently released a condensation of his assertiveness training book on tape. For men who would have a difficult time reading the book, we have recommended the tape as a basic primer. We review some basic assertive behaviors and set up role-play situations for each of the men to participate in. We also teach the men the utility of employing these skills early in a situation as a means of maintaining their feeling of integrity and self-respect. It is important to emphasize to the men that they will not always "win" or get their way by being assertive and that winning is not the point of using the skills.

When a men's program is coordinated with women's services and the men's spouses or partners are in a concurrent women's group, it is very important to use the same materials and language for both programs. It is also helpful to coordinate the training so that the material is presented to both groups at the same time. If the women are presented with the material before the men, the men may be confused and angered by new behavior they do not understand.

One of the last assertiveness skills introduced is the ability to compromise, and we use the training in this skill to introduce conflict management skills, including the six skills mentioned above. We also discuss setting boundaries for oneself and respecting the boundaries of others. As we work through compromise, empathy, and conflict management, we point out to the men that this is the beginning of learning intimacy without coercion and control.

Completion Criteria

The group should demonstrate an understanding of conflict management and assertive behavior. Each man should have completed a successful role play and reported on one practice situation outside of group. Each man should have read the assigned readings and/or listened to the assertiveness tape.

Estimated Completion Time

This module should require approximately two sessions.

Discussion

There are a number of books and training manuals on assertive behavior, most of which would be very good in this program. We tend to use Smith's (1975) *When I Say No, I Feel Guilty*, Lange and Jakubowski's (1976) *Responsible Assertive Behavior*, or Alberti and Emmons's (1978) *Your Perfect Right*. In addition, there are a number of audiotapes available on assertiveness training, including Smith's (1988) audiotaped book. Given the time allocated to this section, this can be only an introduction to assertiveness training. Some men may follow up on their own for more training while others may not, especially if they feel confused. We recommend using very simple models and examples. It is important to evaluate each man's understanding and individualize assignments for the men if they appear to be lost.

Throughout this section, power and control issues of violent men need to be addressed. Men may attempt to use assertiveness as a means of dominating and controlling others, rather than as a method to gain control over their own behavior. The rights of others need to be emphasized as strongly as individual assertive rights.

MODULE 12: COGNITIVE RESTRUCTURING

Rationale

When violent men discuss their anger, their violence, and their cues to escalation, it is clear that their self-statements and cognitions influence their violent acts. An otherwise neutral event can become a violent situation as a result of distorted perceptions and cognitions and unexamined expectations. In Module 8, we educated the men regarding the role of root expectations in the escalation of anger. In this module, we work with the men to examine and reframe or restructure their cognitive responses to neutral events. We also teach them some basic thought-blocking techniques to interrupt cognitive processes that increase anger.

Most of the men will define their anger as purely emotional and will discount the process of thinking as having a part in their rage. Once men have examined their cognitive cues to violence, they begin to see that their thinking in a previous situation was irrational. The difficult part of this module is teaching them to pay attention to their cognitions during anger arousal and to use the techniques at that time.

The term *cognitive restructuring* has been used to describe a variety of interventions similar to one another. Meichenbaum (1977) has defined the term as

> a therapeutic approach whose major mode of action is modifying the patient's thinking and the premises, assumptions, and attitudes underlying his cognitions. The focus of therapy is on the ideational content involved in the symptom, namely, the irrational inferences and premises. (p. 183)

Some examples of beliefs wife abusers hold can be found in three of Ellis's (1977) irrational beliefs: (1) One must have certain and perfect control over things, (2) one has virtually no control over one's emotions and cannot help feeling certain things, and (3) human misery is externally caused and is forced on one by outside people and events. In addition, Beck (1976) talks about faulty styles of thinking, which include the following:

(1) *arbitrary inference:* drawing conclusions from insufficient evidence (if late = having affair)
(2) *magnification:* magnifying situations beyond reality (talking to a man = having affair)
(3) *cognitive deficiency:* inability to see other alternatives
(4) *dichotomous reasoning:* oversimplified perception of events as good/bad or right/wrong
(5) *overgeneralization:* making assumptions about partner from beliefs about others

These beliefs are similar to the root expectations discussed in Module 8 (see Chapter 8). When working with these styles of thinking, the counselor can build the men's awareness of their social, cultural, and childhood conditioning and give them tools to examine and reject abusive behaviors acquired from this conditioning (Saunders, 1982).

Identifying Red-Flag Thoughts

When the men first worked on their Control Plans in Module 3, they identified cues to violence, including thoughts they had prior to being violent. In this module, we expand this to look at how these thoughts increase arousal. One of the simplest examples and the easiest to understand for most batterers is jealousy. We use a four-stage example of a neutral situation that is converted into a jealous situation by the batterer's thoughts, thoughts that have no factual base.

The first part of the example is the neutral incident. In this case, a man's partner is half an hour late getting home. There may be numerous reasons for this, the vast majority having nothing to do with jealousy. The second stage of the example is the self-statements that the man makes. These can start out somewhat distorted and increase in irrationality. These statements sound like this:

If she cared, she would be home on time. She is showing me that she doesn't care for me. This is a slap in the face to me. She is probably with someone else. She doesn't care for me and is going to sleep with someone else just to hurt me. I can see her having sex with someone else. I hate her for what she's doing to me. She should be punished and she should hurt as much as I do.

The third stage in the example is the emotional consequences of this distorted thinking. These consequences generally progress from rejection, hurt, fear, and anger to rage. This emotional state then propels the man into the fourth stage, behavior. This may include, in our example, calling bars or her friends, driving around looking for her, and the like. These behaviors tend to reinforce the irrational self-statements as being valid.

By going through this example and challenging the men as to whether they know such self-statements to be true, men can then start to identify how they personally use such distorted thinking in their own anger escalation. We then ask the men to come up with examples from their own lives and to increase their writing in this area in their anger logs.

Cognitive Restructuring

Cognitive restructuring involves teaching men to interrupt and reframe distorted thinking patterns, such as the one in the example above. Once the men are able to identify irrational thoughts, they can learn to stop them, challenge them, or reframe them. The simplest technique is thought stopping or thought blocking. Similar to the external verbal command, "Stop," used in the cognitive sensitization section, once the men identify anger-escalating thought patterns, they simply say to themselves, "Stop," and attempt to refocus their attention elsewhere. They may need to do this numerous times in any situation. Each man should have some plan before a situation as to where he could best refocus his attention.

Before distorted thinking can be challenged successfully, the men may need to use the relaxation techniques taught in the next module. Once a client becomes aware that he is intensifying his anger with distorted thinking, he is directed first to use relaxation techniques. Then, he can examine and challenge the validity of his statements and the unrealistic expectations he may be responding to.

Using the assertiveness training technique of "negative inquiry" (Smith, 1975) in an internalized conversation can help to test the roots of his thinking. Once calm and relaxed, a client may ask himself, "What is it that causes you to think that, because Mary is a few minutes late, that she is looking for another man? First, is there any real evidence for this? Second, what am I responding to? Is this thought coming because I can't believe that Mary would want to be with a guy like me? Am I responding to my own bad feelings about myself? Or do I expect Mary to take care of every anxiety I have? Is this why I control her?"

We work through a number of role plays with the men in the group and then ask them to use this during the week at least twice. As with other behavioral techniques, the role plays, examples, and rehearsals present excellent opportunities to reiterate power and control dynamics. When the men can work with these dynamics in behavioral role playing, they can digest and incorporate these principles much more than through education alone. This form of self-awareness also increases the men's ability to recognize their own feelings.

Completion Criteria

Each man should have presented an individualized scenario from his own experience of how he distorts events through his cognitions. Each of the men should have participated in a group role play on cognitive restructuring. Each of the men should also have presented in the group examples of cognitive distortion that they observed in their life between groups.

Estimated Completion Time

This module should take approximately 1½ sessions. The educational portion, the group role plays, and the presentation of individualized scenarios and observational homework should each take approximately half of a session.

Discussion

Although this and the previous two modules present cognitive-behavioral techniques, the education and awareness that occur here are significant. Power and control, discussed in other modules, become reality here. Root expectations and the male emotional funnel system are directly challenged. The men learn new communication skills at the same time they question their own distortions.

MODULE 13: RELAXATION

Rationale

Most men in our groups have very little awareness of their own tension levels, the amount of stress they experience, or what it feels like to be relaxed. Relaxation is incompatible with anxiety (Wolpe, 1973) and can effectively lower levels of anger (Bernstein & Borkevec, 1973; Rosen, 1977). Novaco (1977, 1978) has found that relaxation training and cognitive restructuring are more effective in reducing anger when used together than when either is used alone.

Learning relaxation techniques is also important in learning self-awareness of emotional states. Focusing on body tension and relaxation are introspective exercises, and introspection is a skill with which most of the men in our groups are unfamiliar. Relaxation is also an important adjunct to the behavioral programs discussed above.

Although we place this module at the end of the behavioral section, we often introduce it earlier. Some programs will begin relaxation training immediately after the development of Control Plans. We have placed it here only because of the logical connection of this group of material, rather than temporal sequence.

Relaxation Training

The easiest, and probably most effective, relaxation training program to teach this population is Jacobson's (1938) progressive relaxation. This is a fairly straightforward exercise involving intentionally tensing and then relaxing individual muscle groups. We tend to start with the hand, asking the men to make a fist and tense the muscles in one hand, directing them to hold that tense state for a number of seconds, then telling them to let go of the tension and relax. We then progress from the hand to the forearm to the biceps to the shoulders, and then do the other arm. We then have the men do the same progression with their legs, starting with their feet, their calves, then their thighs. We then have the men tighten and relax their stomach muscles, then their chests, then their necks and shoulders. Finally we have them tighten and relax their necks, jaws, eyes, and foreheads.

Because this relaxation exercise progresses slowly, the men tend to feel less panic about relaxing their constant controls than with guided imagery or semihypnotic techniques. Some men will still have a difficult time as a result of their attachment to tension. They feel safe and defended when they are tense. We warn the men that they may feel more anxious as they begin to relax and direct them to focus on regulating their breathing. This tends to minimize the risk of panic attacks during the exercise.

We ask the men to evaluate their levels of tension on a scale of 1 to 10 at the beginning and end of the exercise. This increases their awareness of the effects of relaxation and of how much tension they live with on a daily basis. Once the men have been able to complete the exercise in group, we ask them to practice three times a week. A tape can be made by the facilitators of the progressive relaxation directions, duplicated, and issued to the men to use as part of their homework.

Completion Criteria

Relaxation training is accomplished when the men report that they are able to achieve a moderate state of relaxation using the techniques at home and have practiced relaxation three times per week.

Estimated Completion Time

Relaxation training should take no more than one session, with some follow-up discussion of homework in other sessions.

Discussion

Although relaxation will not stop battering, it is an important skill upon which the men can build. It is an introduction to a method of examining oneself and what one is feeling, rather than simply acting impulsively. It increases the value of a time-out. Once the men are familiar with relaxation and able to achieve a moderate state of relaxation without going through the exercise, they can use this in conflict management to refocus themselves and defuse their impulsive angry responses. Finally, it is an accomplishment and a new ability that most men will feel some sense of pride in doing.

PART 2

This final group of modules provides the educational components that the men will need to continue their journey toward nonviolence. In this section, the men will learn about men's use of power and control to dominate women and how their own violence is a part of a continuum of abusive behaviors directed at women in our culture. They will examine how they learned this way of being with others through their early childhood experiences and through their socialization as males in our culture.

The focus of the group on violence will be expanded in this section to include emotional abuse, psychological abuse, and sexual abuse and marital rape. As in the module dealing with the most violent incident, shame will be a continuing factor throughout this portion of the group. The men will be challenged to share their secrets and to relinquish what they considered to be their "traditional male rights." If the men are successful in this section, they may have a good start on the road to peace.

MODULE 14: PSYCHOLOGICAL ABUSE

Rationale

As a society, we pay less attention to psychological abuse than to more dramatic physical displays of cruelty. Women are disabled and even killed by physical assaults, thus making this behavior more worrisome. Bruises to the psyche and spirit are largely hidden. Walker (1979) discovered, however, in her interviews with battered women, that attacks on self-esteem—humiliation and put-downs— were the most hurtful, debilitating aspects of their ordeals.

We describe an approach in this book that gives intervention in physical abuse the highest priority above other interventions. This is based in the recognition that physical abuse is life threatening. Such a priority can be the only responsible and ethical first step in ending men's abuse of women in relationships. Despite this necessity, other forms of abuse are rampant. An abuser's growing sensitization to violence and abuse must include sensitization to the nonphysical, yet cruel ways in which he treats his partner. Sonkin, Martin, and Walker (1985) state that psychological abuse may be the most difficult behavior to change in counseling batterers. This has been our experience as well. Nevertheless, we believe all attempts to counsel abusers should underscore this form of abuse and require the same level of accountability from perpetrators.

We should also comment on the intentional placement of this module in the Middle Phase. While some readers may think it is late, we believe that members have more than enough to deal with in the Beginning Phase in their attempts to cease physical abuse. Sensitization to abuse is a gradual process that we believe should begin by attending to the most identifiable form. While we must define the spectrum of abuse at the beginning of the group (as was done in the prior phase), we believe batterers are ready to examine this behavior in detail in the Middle Phase. To do so earlier is to risk overwhelming clients with a seemingly impossible agenda for change.

Power and Control

This module begins with a short lecture on power and control in relationships. We find the "power and control wheel" a helpful model in discussing this issue (see Figure 2). Its value is most apparent in its ability to highlight the need for power and control as the underlying motivation in directing abuse at others. Physical abuse, which occupies the narrow rim of the wheel, is merely the most extreme method for maintaining power over another.

When used in group, the model accomplishes two things. It reveals a more complete perspective on physical abuse by illuminating its source—namely, need for power and control. This, by the way, is congruent with and supports the notion that the male sex-role prescription for dominance and control over women is a root cause of wife abuse. Second, it stresses a continuum model of abuse according to which increasingly coercive methods are used until control is established. This continuum notion makes it increasingly difficult to minimize the seriousness of psychological and emotional coercion.

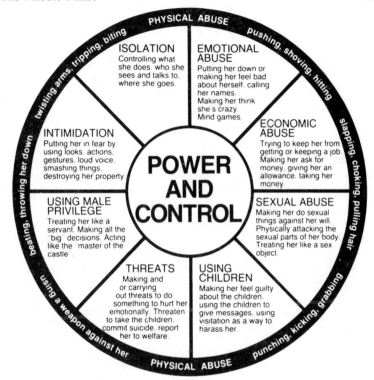

Figure 2. Power and Control Wheel
SOURCE: Reprinted with permission from Minnesota Program Development, Inc.; (218) 722-2781.

If available, the video recording titled *Power and Control: Tactics of Men Who Batter* (Pence, Paymar, & Duff, 1985) is an excellent accompaniment to the lecture. It presents a series of vignettes, each of which acts out one form of control. Counselors can describe one form of control, play the corresponding vignette, and invite discussion.

Effects of Abuse on Victims

Counselors can educate men on the effects of abuse through various methods. One informal method is to show a videotape of battered women who talk about their experiences. Though there are numerous tapes of this kind available, *Power and Control*, mentioned above, organizes battered women's stories according to the types of abuse reflected in the power and control wheel.

When we have had two men conducting a group, we have invited experienced counselors of battered women's groups to speak to the group about the effects reported by women in group counseling. Visiting women speakers relating women's experiences may add both seriousness and credibility to the material. In arranging this, therapists should be certain that the speakers are as comfortable as possible coming into a group of batterers. Both guest speakers and the group's leaders should define and agree on their respective roles for this setting. Guests may find it helpful to define in advance any boundaries for their participation. Such definition often means having answered a number of questions prior to entering the group: Is the guest responsible for defending the content of her presentation? Will she respond to redundant questions? Will she state how she feels being present in an abusers' group? Is it her job to deal with men's anger? As the group's counselors, we assume responsibility for altering any negative process.

A third method of conveying the effects of abuse is simply to deliver a lecture that relies on the counselors' knowledge or written resources. Useful written material can be found in Walker (1979) or Walker's chapter in Sonkin et al. (1985). This method, while quick, seems less effective than the first two.

Brainwashing and Psychological Abuse

We have instituted a particularly powerful consciousness-raising exercise on psychological abuse. NiCarthy, Merriam, and Coffman (1984) write about an activity used in battered women's groups that reframes psychological abuse as a torture or brainwashing technique. We have adapted this for use with abusers. Both NiCarthy et al. and Russell (1982) have reprinted Biderman's Chart of Coercion. Presented originally in an Amnesty International publication, this chart outlines the commonalities in brainwashing methods used with prisoners of war and political prisoners in various countries. The similarity of these documented techniques to the psychological abuse of batterers is striking.

At the beginning of this activity, we do not tell the men about the source of this chart. Instead, an adapted version of Biderman's chart is displayed in the group and is referred to simply as another list of categories of controlling behavior. The adapted list is presented below.

(1) isolation
(2) forcing the woman's awareness of the abuser, his anger, or the threat of anger
(3) creating exhaustion, dependency, and feelings of incompetence
(4) making threats
(5) giving occasional rewards for obedience
(6) demonstrating superior power
(7) degrading and humiliating
(8) enforcing trivial demands

Under each category, we offer one or two examples of this behavior and ask the men to give further examples by relating their own behavior toward their partners. While this can be a free-flowing discussion, with any man offering examples, a preferable method is to have each man take a turn. In this respect it is similar to the format used in the most violent incident module. The latter method is preferable because it helps reduce denial by requiring all men to participate; it results in a more complete, group composite list. It is advisable to allow an ample amount of time for this activity—perhaps up to 5 minutes per man. When the group's list is complete, we tell the men the source of the chart.

Completion Criteria

Each man should demonstrate an understanding of the concepts, recognize the relationship of these to his behavior, and identify his own patterns of psychological abuse.

Estimated Completion Time

This module consumes two group sessions.

Discussion

Abuse definitions presented in the first module and the ongoing identification of men's psychological abuse by counselors when men report violence communicate that this behavior is regarded seriously by the program. Nevertheless, prior to this module, most members have minimized the seriousness of psychological abuse. At first glance, it seems inconsequential in comparison to physical assaults. This module has the power to change that opinion.

In our experience, this module has a powerful effect on most batterers. Redefinition of their behavior in terms of torture techniques can be shattering. The tyranny they innocently thought existed only in totalitarian regimes is something they practice in their homes. Along with the reframing of this behavior, men hear about the effects of this behavior on their victims. During these activities, most members' facial expressions are telling; they look thoughtful, serious, and ashamed. Most are silent. Some express shock and wish it were not true. However, most reluctantly accept it as inescapable truth.

Occasionally, one or two men will argue energetically with the therapists. They deny the similarities between torture techniques and their behavior or accuse the program of overstating the issue. Often those adopting this stance have assumed the role of group rebel. They are a subgroup that has been consistent in opposing the counselors on many issues. Those most vehement in their opposition might also be those who have been most psychologically abusive or for whom this module has elicited the most shameful feelings. In either case, a group in the Middle Phase should be maturing to a point where it is unnecessary and even unwise for counselors always to accept the burden of defense. Instead, the group can often be trusted to be responsible for resolving these issues. More often than not, in the later Middle Phase and the Ending Phase, we deflect choice questions and issues back to the group with comments such as, "What do all of you think?" If the majority support the program's stance, it will have much more impact than if a subgroup and the therapists become locked in dispute. A subgroup opposing blatantly obvious material usually retreats when fellow batterers support an idea on the basis of their own experiences as abusers.

We urge therapists to maintain awareness of group mood and affect. While the intention of the program is not to punish, or to induce shame or self-loathing, the approach we present rapidly reflects the real horror of batterers' behavior. Consequently, members occasionally do feel punished, ashamed, and demoralized. If these feelings become too intense, there is risk of dropouts or generalized hopelessness concerning change. Such intense feelings are counterproductive.

We recommend that therapists not allow a demoralized, shameful group to continue without attempting to relieve the intensity of these feelings. This module and the next are particularly hazardous in this regard. They constitute four consecutive sessions, each of which elicits dramatic, powerful realizations and feelings. One relatively easy countermeasure is to structure an exercise at the end of each session that will accentuate positive aspects of individual men, the group, and the overall positive meaning of the work in which the group is engaged. For instance, we have addressed each group member in turn and told him of positive aspects of his personality or his struggle as we have seen this expressed in the group. We have reminded the group that most men who batter refuse to ask for help and work to change; since they represent the few who have, they should be proud of their courage and strength. Finally, we have felt free to insert a process session between this module and the next. That session can consist of Sharing Time alone, or a portion of it can be devoted to an activity or discussion designed to reduce the intensity of negative feelings.

MODULE 15: FAMILY OF ORIGIN[1]

Rationale

Many assaultive men grew up in families where they were direct victims of abuse or witnessed abuse directed against others. According to social learning theory, modeling of abuse by parents or other influential people increases the likelihood that children witnessing this will reenact this abuse in adulthood. In our experience, many batterers are reluctant to label these family of origin events as abusive or violent. For a variety of reasons, they employ euphemisms such as "discipline," "strict child rearing," and other terms that minimize or deny the reality of their childhood environments.

There is value in requiring men to talk in detail about these formative experiences. Talking aloud about their own experiences and hearing other men speak of theirs often elicits powerful emotional responses. The power of these responses essentially contradicts their denial and readies them to redefine these events as what they really were—abuse and violence. Additionally, men can begin to understand the intergenerational cycle of violence and the part they are playing in keeping it alive and transmitting it to their children. Furthermore, if used effectively, the emotional content unearthed by this activity helps men learn to experience empathy for the victims of their abuse.

There are other, perhaps less apparent, benefits to this experience. When men endure powerful and confusing emotional reactions and are successful in not responding to this arousal by being abusive, they learn of their capacity to tolerate pain without the need for an abusive outlet. They also attain some degree of liberation from the secrecy so often maintained by abuse victims. Finally, this event allows them to test (and reinforces) their abilities to use other people for support during distress.

Family of Origin

The structure of this activity is simple. Each man in turn talks about the family or families in which he grew up. He relates this information to the group by answering a standard set of questions. As during the module dealing with the most violent incident, some men may attempt to give sketchy information or otherwise hurry through these questions. Counselors should slow down the process and strive for thoroughness. We allow 10-15 minutes for each man to tell his story.

We insist that every member undergo this activity. Unfortunately, this sometimes means that a member who has been absent for this module must answer these questions during a later session. Though it is difficult to do this alone, this module is a group milestone and we regard the benefits as indispensable.

There are two lists of questions; Part I is covered in the first session and Part II in the second. Part I is listed below:

(1) How were emotions expressed in your family?
(2) How did individuals in your family handle anger?
(3) How did people solve conflicts?
(4) What methods of discipline were used?
(5) How did you react to this discipline?
(6) How did individuals in your family express love and affection?

After every man has addressed these questions, counselors tell the group that any negative feelings they are now experiencing are the same that their partners feel in reaction to being abused.

The items in Part II, covered in the second session, are as follows:

(1) As a child, what was the one phrase you remember hearing most often from your parents?
(2) How were you praised? Criticized?
(3) How is your present behavior affected by your family of origin? What emotions, thoughts, and behaviors come from growing up in that family?
(4) In what ways are you similar to your dad? Your mom?
(5) What parallels are there between the way children were treated in your family of origin and the way you now treat children?

Because this module is among the most stressful experiences in an abusers' group, therapists should caution men to be extremely vigilant in watching for cues to anger and violence during the next two weeks. It is not uncommon for men to escalate in response to arousal stemming from the family of origin module.

Completion Criteria

Each man must undergo the process of talking about his family of origin.

Estimated Completion Time

This module consumes two sessions.

Discussion

In our experience, at least 70% of men in any group grew up in families where they were directly or indirectly maltreated. Those subject to indirect maltreatment witnessed the abuse of others. Informally, we have also observed that many men who report no abuse nevertheless describe a family characterized by low warmth and lack of nurturing. On average, only one or two men from each group describe nonabusive and caring families of origin.

There are some common responses to many of these questions. Interestingly, many men respond to the first question by answering the second. When counselors say "emotions," these men hear "anger." Often anger was the only explicit emotion in these families. In many families, conflicts were always resolved through aggression, resulting in the strongest winning through either violence or intimidation. The only person with any rights was the strongest. Many members do not remember expressions of affection. To some, this question is startling, as if the concept of expressing affection in a family is totally alien. Others respond with cynical sneers that seem to mask considerable anger and sadness. Phrases most remembered by men are usually negative: "You're no good," "You'll never amount to anything," and "You're just like your father" are common. Most commonly, praise was absent but criticism abounded.

Some men relate truly horrible accounts of wife and child assault. They tell of receiving injuries while trying to protect their mothers by standing between the adults during the violence. In some cases, the assaults stopped when the man reached a physical size allowing him to beat up his father. Most men promised themselves never to be like their fathers but realize painfully at some point in the group that they are very much like them. We have noticed that almost all men coming from violent families identify the father or male father figure as the perpetrator of violence. The role of mothers in this context varies. In many cases, the mothers alone were the targets. In other families where children were at risk, some mothers attempted to protect their children when fathers were about to strike out. In some cases, mothers seemed to divert his violence and take the blows intended for the children. In other families, mothers seemed so broken by long-term abuse that they were powerless to protect the children. Though quite uncommon, we occasionally hear of mothers who were either equally violent by teaming up with fathers against the children or who were the sole perpetrators in a home where child abuse was rampant.

The effects of this module are deep and far-reaching. Many men are forced to redefine their childhoods radically as abusive. With this realization comes a variety of feelings. Lingering anger is very common. A profound sense of grief and sadness can emerge as a man faces past realities and mourns the loss of a protected, healthy childhood. As recommended in certain previous modules, counselors should end these painful sessions with something positive. If the group is especially demoralized, a process session between this module and the next may help heal the wounds.

Counselors also are deeply affected. It is impossible to listen to these stories and witness members' pain without leaving these sessions feelings raw, sad, and perhaps incredibly fortunate if these stories are in contrast to the counselor's family of origin. In the interest of self-care, counselors should structure time for debriefing at the end of these sessions.

MODULE 16: MALE SOCIALIZATION

Rationale

In the family of origin module, the men in the group focused on emotional experiences and learning from growing up in their individual families. This module expands this awareness to the experience and learning process of growing up as a male in our culture. In addition, we examine the current pressures of our society that make remaining nonviolent difficult.

Male socialization has both obvious and subtle effects on men's lives. Some of the effects can be recognized only if one understands the overall impact of this socialization on every aspect of men's experience and behavior. For example, until men understand the educational material presented in this module, they are not likely to view their "logical" mode of problem solving as a system they have been trained to rely on by their masculine socialization. They are unlikely to perceive any possible alternative modes of thinking, or, if they do perceive them, they are likely to devalue them.

On a more overt level, men's beliefs about what it is like to be male and what is "good" or "bad" behavior within that system are more easily recognized by the group. Most men can refer to or joke about the "John Wayne," "macho" image that men are supposed to live up to, although they rarely personalize this information.

The purpose of this module is not only to educate the men to both overt and subtle effects of socialization, but also to work with them to personalize their own indoctrination into the male system. Once men have permission to examine their experience of growing up around other men and boys honestly, especially the ways in which shame and embarrassment are used to keep one "in the system," they may begin to mourn the loss of opportunities for developing creativity and intimacy that male socialization denies them. They also need to look honestly at the benefits they gain by being part of the system at the expense of others, particularly women and children.

We are not willing to support the men in the group in feeling as though they are victims when going through this material. For this reason, we often spend a short period of this time focusing on what growing up female is like in this culture and what it means to be denied power as a human being by another class of human beings. We believe that it is acceptable to mourn lost opportunities, as long as that mourning is accompanied by a change in real behavior and attitudes toward others.

Male Socialization

We begin the module on male socialization with a brainstorming exercise. We ask the men to list attributes of men versus women—in other words, how they would describe men as compared to women. We then list all of these attributes on a chalkboard. Often the resulting list will look like this:

men	*women*
strong	weak
possessive	accepting
unemotional, stoic	emotional
competent	incompetent
aggressive	gentle
in control	nurturing
achievement oriented	relationship oriented
dominant over women	passive

We next challenge the men to rephrase the women's attributes in positive language and the men's attributes in less positive language. Strong becomes rigid, emotional becomes caring, aggressive becomes violent, passive becomes patient, achievement oriented becomes anxious and driven, and so on. Then we ask the men to examine the restrictions of being male and what they lose in being afraid to behave in ways that might be perceived as "feminine."

At this point we introduce some educational material regarding male socialization so that the men can understand what is being discussed in a broader context. We explain how men are socialized as children, not only by their parents but by the school system, other children, and every other aspect of their lives. We then discuss the ways in which they are pressured as adults by organizations and by other men to support the system and continue in their abusive behaviors.

We then share some of our own experiences of socialization with the men and ask each of the men to talk about his personal experiences. As the men talk about their lives, we offer them a great deal of support and encouragement for "breaking the rules." At the same time, we challenge their beliefs about shared values and ideals about being men.

As mentioned above, a short educational section is presented here on what it means to grow up as a female in our culture. By presenting both sides, men can see how sex roles are damaging to both genders and how their participation in supporting these stereotypes is a way of continuing their abusive behavior.

Male Sexual Socialization

Although we talk about sexual abuse and marital rape in the next module, sexual socialization is a powerful factor that contributes to gender socialization. We talk about sexual socialization at the end of this module as a transition to sexual abuse in the next section. Therefore, we use a structure that introduces the topic, leaving a further expansion of the subject to the next section.

The men are asked to remember their adolescence and how sex influenced their opinions of others and their feelings about themselves. We ask the men what they thought in high school about other men who were thought to be having sexual relations and what they thought about women who they thought were also having sexual relations. These opinions are usually quite diverse and quite revealing. We then ask how many of the men still hold these same values today.

We introduce some lecture material about how men sexualize women in our society through their language, attitudes, and behaviors and through the media and other means. We discuss how this demeans women and we point out how damaging it is to objectify someone in this way. Most of the men will admit to talking with other men about sex as though it were a sport, and we attempt to show the group what this means in terms of men's ability to be intimate with others. In this same vein, we examine the effects of pornography on their lives as well as on women.

We generally do a group exercise/discussion at this point. First, we ask the men what they could do to interrupt, intervene, or interfere with jokes or conversations with other men where women are sexualized and/or demeaned. This is difficult for the men to deal with, as socialization and fear of humiliation and inadequacy as males frightens them away from confronting or disagreeing with other men about their abusiveness. We remind them of the assertiveness training material and set up role-play situations where they nonaggressively confront another male regarding sexist language or sexualizing women.

Completion Criteria

Each of the men should have contributed to the brainstorming and group discussions. In addition, each should have been involved in a role-play situation.

Estimated Completion Time

This module generally runs from 1½ to 2 group sessions. The men usually come back to the second session with questions, concerns, and challenges, and counselors should plan for time to address these concerns.

Discussion

This is one of the most difficult sections for the men to understand and their resistance to hearing this material is generally high. Although much of this material strikes at the roots of men's assaultive behavior toward their partners, it is placed late in the program so that the men in the group will have more investment in the group process and will be more willing to address these issues.

Teaching this material is difficult, and a dry, polemic argument is likely to meet with resistance. When men are resistant in this module, they generally act confused. While some men may be genuinely confused, counselors should explore the possibility of resistance as a cause of men not understanding the material. Some men will act as though this material is a revelation to them and will seem to be "too compliant" in the exercise. There is little that can be done with this more subtle form of resistance, other than to address it in the evaluation module.

To teach this material, counselors should have some personal experience exploring the effects of sex-role socialization and the sexualizing of relationships in their own lives. If a male counselor has not had this opportunity through his own therapy or through a men's group, we recommend that program staff meet and discuss these issues on a personal level with each other prior to this module. Not only will it help to clarify the material for the counselor, the counselor can also use this personal opportunity to develop a number of his own experiences to share with the men. This will add a breath of life to this section and can help counteract the group's resistance.

MODULE 17: SEXUAL ABUSE AND MARITAL RAPE

Rationale

As mentioned in the first chapter, sexual assault and marital rape are closely associated with physical violence in marriage and cohabitation (Bowker, 1983; Frieze, 1983; Hanneke & Shields, 1985; Sommers & Check, 1987). Attitudes that support physical violence toward partners are similar to attitudes that justify rape (Briere, 1987). In addition, male socialization, which advocates men's dominance and control over all aspects of their partners' and children's lives, also gives men "rights" to their sexual lives, as well.

Because it is difficult for men to distinguish between sexuality and intimacy, often they do not see their inappropriate sexual behaviors as abusive. They also normalize sexually abusive behavior because they see it on television or they see their friends doing it. Often men reframe their behavior to avoid seeing themselves as abusive. In a study of college males, Stille, Malamuth, and Schallow (1987) found that 22.7% of the men said they would "rape" a woman if they were sure they would not get caught, while 49.1% said they would "force a woman to do something sexual which she did not want to do" under the same circumstances.

Although there are no clear studies that we are aware of regarding the association of child sexual abuse and battering, our experience suggests that the incidence is much higher than most clinicians or non-mental health professionals might suspect. In addition, given the high incidence of sexual abuse of male and female children in our culture, it is likely that many of the men in group, raised in chaotic and violent families, have been victims themselves. This section can not only open up an examination of sexually inappropriate behaviors performed by the men in the group, it can also be an opportunity for them to disclose their own histories of victimization.

Sexual Abuse and Marital Rape

Sexually abusive behavior tends to be cyclical in much the same way as physical abuse. In this module, we lead the men in a group discussion of sexual abuse, show them a film on rape and sexual assault, and then cover the "dysfunctional cycle" and "sexual assault cycle" (Ryan et al., 1987).

Our first discussion is a brainstorming session focusing on how sex might be involved in physical, emotional, or psychological abuse and in power and control behaviors directed at one's partner. We encourage the men to talk about how they use sex to resolve conflicts, how they use sexual terms in their verbal abuse (especially during escalation), how they ignore their partners' feelings in a sexual context, how they use sexual humor to degrade their partners, and how they insist, manipulate, coerce, or force their partners to have sex with them or to perform certain sexual acts they would not have otherwise chosen to do. When men acknowledge the last act in this list, we then talk about this in terms of rape. Although the men may be resistant at first, reframing their behavior as rape has a powerful impact on them.

Following this, we show the men the movie *A Scream from Silence* (Poirier & Gagn, 1980), which is distributed by the National Film Board of Canada. This film is a powerful, realistic rape portrayal that also includes didactic material to generalize the personal drama presented in the movie with women's lives in general. This film has been shown to reduce rape proclivity in a general population (Stille et al., 1987) and has a strong effect on the men in the group. The film should be shown only when there is sufficient time following the film for the men to discuss it, as it can be extremely emotionally upsetting.

In the group following the film, we discuss the dysfunctional cycle and the sexual assault cycle (see Figure 3) (Ryan et al., 1987). Both cycles are circular models, similar to each other, that are used to explain negative, acting-out behavior. The cycles begin with an essential poor self-image and an event that lowers self-esteem or increases

DYSFUNCTIONAL CYCLE

Poor Self-Image
Feeling Bad about Self
"Poor Me"

Expecting Rejection
"They won't like me"
"Everybody is against me"

Promising "never again"

Isolation or Withdrawal
(to avoid rejection)

Being afraid of or feeling
bad about getting caught

Anger: attempts to control
and/or blame others

Negative Behaviors/
"Acting Out"
-Sexual assault, molestation
-Exploitation
-Drug/alcohol abuse
-Vandalism
-Violence
-Suicide
Etc.

Fantasies to make feel better
"I'm bigger, better, stronger,
smarter, sexier, etc."

Planning
-Retaliation
-Something to make feel
better/more powerful

SEXUAL ASSAULT CYCLE

Poor Self-Image
(events that lower self-esteem
or increase helplessness)

*CD - "I won't do again"

*CD - "I'm the victim"

Reconstitution/Suppression

Anticipation of
negative reaction
(rejection, loss, in trouble, etc.)

*CD - "I won't get caught"

*CD - "Maybe it'll go way"

Transitory Guilt
(based on fear
of getting caught)

Withdrawal/Isolation

*CD - Reinforcement:
"Victim liked"

*CD - Externalizing blame

Sexual Assault
*CD - Objectification, decision to act

Anger and/or Power Behaviors

*CD - "I showed them, I'm OK"

Fantasy/Masturbation
(increased sexual activity, planning
and rehearsal, victim selection)

* Cognitive Distortions/irrational thoughts/"thinking errors" which enable progression through the cycle

Figure 3. Dysfunctional and Sexual Assault Cycles

SOURCE: Reprinted with permission from *Child Abuse and Neglect*, Vol. 1, No. 3, G. Ryan, S. Lane, J. Davis, & C. Isaac, "Juvenile Sexual Offenders: Development and Correction." Copyright © 1987, Pergamon Press, Inc.

feelings of helplessness. The cycle then progresses, as a result of cognitive distortions, through a number of stages. The individual expects a negative reaction and expects to be rejected or to be in trouble. The person feels like a victim. This leads to isolation or withdrawal and a hope that "it'll go away."

The person then becomes angry and attempts to control others and blame others for her or his problems (similar to the tension-building phase in the cycle of violence). This tends to bring only temporary satisfaction and usually leads to fantasy behavior about being better, bigger, stronger than one is in reality. In the sexual assault cycle, this usually involves masturbation and planning, while in the dysfunctional cycle, it generally leads to planning about retaliation. As in the cycle of violence, this leads to the violent act (or dysfunctional behavior).

Following this, similar to the remorse phase of the cycle of violence (characterized by contrite, loving behavior), is a period of "transitory" guilt. This is described as transitory because it is based on the fear of getting caught or of having something negative happen as a result of the violence (such as partner leaving) and tends to disappear once the threat is gone. The final stage is reconstitution, where a promise is made to oneself not to do it again. The poor self-image is still there, however, and once a negative event occurs, the cycle begins again.

Following this presentation, we ask the men to personalize each of the cycles around their own dysfunctional physically violent and sexually abusive behavior. Our intention here is to demonstrate to the men how sexual assault and abuse are dynamically similar to their physical violence.

The next section of educational material we present to the men concerns sexually abusive behaviors toward children. Although most of the men will deny any sexually abusive behavior with their children, when we remind them of the forms of sexually abusive behavior, including teasing and name-calling, many will identify some behavior they have performed. Our own experience in working with adolescent sexual offenders suggests that inappropriate sexual boundaries and behaviors in a family can be, at times, as destructive as sexual molestation. Many of our young offenders who deny any history of sexual victimization can identify inappropriate sexualized behaviors between adults and children in their families.

Finally, we provide education to the men on the incidence and the consequences of child sexual abuse. Although many men may not have sexually abused their children, with a higher likelihood of divorce and visitation and a history of interpersonal violence, they represent a high-risk group for perpetrating child sexual abuse. Often we see this educational section as preventive. We encourage the men to talk with us privately if they have feelings or information that they wish to share with us following this module.

The last part of this section is a discussion of "normal" human sexuality and intimacy. We build a continuum of intimate behaviors people share, with sex as the bottom of the continuum. Sexuality is presented as only one form of intimate behavior, rather than the only way to be intimate, and mutual and consensual sexuality as the only form of intimate sexuality.

Completion Criteria

Identification and sharing of individual patterns of coercive sexuality is the first goal. Each man should be able to discuss and share material and emotions from the film. Each man should also be able to personalize the dysfunctional cycle and/or the sexual assault cycle. Finally, each man should participate in the discussion of child sexual abuse and "normal" sexuality.

Estimated Completion Time

This module will take at least two sessions, and possibly a third session, to complete.

Discussion

Men often respond to this section with denial, minimization, projection—in other words, with all of the defenses with which they began the program. They may also respond with some panic (although they are unlikely to admit this feeling) because they have learned no other way of being sexual other than abusively. They often feel as though they can do absolutely nothing and that even their normal sexual feelings are, or could be, abusive.

An important method of delineating normal from abusive sexuality is to refer again to issues of power and control. When men attempt to control others and misuse power to obtain what they want by not respecting the rights, wishes, and dignity of others, they are being abusive. This is true in whatever realm they are misusing power and control, whether it is sexual, physical, or emotional. As men look at their coercive behaviors and measure them against this yardstick, the confusion diminishes. Examining a situation in this way might sound like this:

MAN: I've never forced her to have sex with me, although sometimes she makes me so angry I'd like to. Sometimes she's so unresponsive and uninterested in sex I just don't know what to do.

COUNSELOR: What do you do?

M: Most of the time I feel real hurt and get up and leave the bedroom. I stomp downstairs and smoke a cigarette.

C: What happens then?

M: Well, sometimes she comes down and apologizes to me and tries to make me feel better and sometimes she just sits in bed and cries.

C: What happens after she apologizes to you?

M: Oh, she usually feels bad and we end up making love, although I sometimes feel guilty after, 'cause I know she didn't really want to. Sometimes when she stays in bed and cries I go up and apologize and try to make her feel better and then, sometimes, I can get her into the mood from there.

C: So, what you're saying is that you pout and make your wife feel bad until she gives in and gives you what you want or you pretend to feel sorry for what you've done, hoping to manipulate her feelings until she gives you what you want. It seems like the main thing here is what you want, not what Mary wants. It also seems like you're controlling her to get what you want, no matter what the cost is to her. We call that coercion.

M: Well, I guess when you put it that way I can see what your saying, but what else am I supposed to do? If I didn't do that, we'd never have sex.

C: Do you think it's possible that if you weren't trying to control Mary so much, if you were concerned more about her feelings, that she might feel more tender about you?

This is difficult material for the men to learn and, sadly enough, often demonstrates how reluctant they are to give up their abusive behaviors and the negative aspects of their male socialization. On the other hand, this is probably the first exposure they have had to these ideas; it is our hope that, if they stay on the road to peace, they will consider this information further.

Prior to the evaluation and beginning of the program, the men were warned about the counselors' responsibilities to report child abuse and neglect. We do not generally warn the men again at the beginning of this module. In our experience it has been extremely rare to have a group member disclose that he was or is sexually abusing a child. Should this happen, however, it must be reported immediately. In addition, disclosure is a high-risk situation for suicide, and this should be assessed before the man is allowed to leave the group.

MODULE 18: EVALUATION

Rationale

Arrival at the end of the Middle Phase foreshadows the end of the group. More immediately, it is the end of the group's work phase. What is left can be viewed as a polishing of the rough edges and preparing for the group's end. This is not to suggest that a group member's work is finished. His learning in how to live peaceably continues. Nevertheless, this major, enabling chapter of his journey is ending. Though he will have received feedback at various points in the group, we believe it is valuable to devote one session to a formal evaluation.

Formal evaluation two-thirds of the way through group allows a man to be redirected to work on areas he resisted or denied prior to this moment. It is also a time for him to hear things that are difficult to hear or are negative.

Evaluation

There are, of course, many ways of conducting an evaluation. While readers may have their own methods, we include one method here that works well for us. We want this process to emphasize peer feedback. Consequently, we announce the evaluation to members in the previous session and assign homework. Each man is to think of every other man in the group in terms of a number of questions.

Since the term *evaluation* carries unfortunate connotations, we attempt to lessen the group's anxiety by making several comments about the process. The first notion we convey is that evaluation is meant to be a constructive process. It is not a tearing down of another's self-esteem. It is largely about performance, not about the person. The second point we raise is that evaluation should not be a concentration on the negative aspects of a person's performance. While negative elements enter into it, it is best to look at evaluation not as positive versus negative, but as an appraisal of how a person has performed well in the past, areas in which his performance needs improvement, and a constructive, future-oriented approach in which ways the person might improve his performance are explored. We particularly emphasize the first and last functions. The third major point is that this group evaluation is an opportunity to practice assertiveness. By this we mean that men can give considerable thought to ways of giving feedback that will minimize the recipient's defensiveness and maximize his ability to hear the comments.

When the evaluation session begins, we ask for a volunteer to be evaluated. Then each man takes a turn giving that man feedback. The person being evaluated cannot respond to the comments until he has heard from everyone. One of the counselors always is the first to give feedback to each man. The other counselor always is the last to give feedback. Once the man has heard all comments, he has the option of responding.

One suitable list of questions is offered below.

(1) What was positive about this man's participation in the group? What gains do you think he's made?

(2) What have you learned from him as a result of being in group with him?

(3) In what areas do you see him as having trouble or difficulty? On what areas or issues do you think he should still work?

(4) Name at least one thing about him that you like or admire.

The men are also invited to give feedback to the therapists. Because this session consumes a lot of time, we separate feedback to therapists from the process described above. After all men have been evaluated, we invite the group as a whole to share their evaluative comments with us.

Completion Criteria

Every man must receive and give evaluative comments.

Estimated Completion Time

We attempt to complete this module in a single session. Because it is a lengthy activity, it commonly consumes an entire 2½-hour session.

Discussion

Since evaluation often provokes anxiety, counselors should be aware that this module is difficult for many men. Some expect (and are fearful of) a harsh, judgmental process. There are three major ways in which this process can go wrong. One or more individuals may be overly critical and blaming, despite our comments on evaluation. Second, we may have a group that glosses over all areas of the evaluation by offering inane comments. Third, the group may be exceedingly harsh with someone who has fallen into the role of group scapegoat.

It is because of these possibilities that the counselors reserve the right to go first and last in giving feedback. The counselor going first models giving feedback for the group. The counselor going last can modify her or his input in light of the men's feedback to any individual. For instance, if the group has been too careful in its comments to a certain man by withholding or blunting negative comments, the counselor can emphasize this aspect of the evaluation. If the group has been overly critical and has deemphasized positive information, the counselor can restore balance by emphasizing the positive aspects.

SUMMARY

The Middle Phase constitutes some of the hardest emotional work that most of these men have ever done. They have learned new skills and have been introduced to new ways to look at the world. If they have developed and received support from other men in the group and are serious about being nonviolent, they have been given all the basic tools to accomplish their goal. What they do with these tools is now up to them. Ending Phase work will help to solidify and further personalize the new learning necessary for continued nonviolence.

NOTE

1. The Domestic Abuse Project, Minneapolis, has been influential in our choice to use this module and in the module's general format.

10

THE ENDING PHASE

In this book we refer to the last several sessions of our closed group as the Ending Phase. The general notion of endings in counseling always seems ambiguous, and we find that ambiguity in our model as well. There is a sense of yes and no: Yes, it is over, and no, it is not over for each man. On the one hand, this particular group will soon end. After that last session it will not meet again under the same circumstances, or with the same counselors and members. In reaching a termination point, it is over; the group dies. On the other hand, each man in this group has his own road to follow in his search for peace. Some men leave the program and receive no further help; some continue their work in other agencies; some go on to other kinds of help within the same service. Occasionally a man will repeat the program.

As we did with the Beginning Phase, we want to emphasize the importance of the Ending Phase. From our own experience and from supervising others, we have noticed that counselors are thoughtful and vigilant in approaching the Middle Phase, but are frequently neglectful of Ending Phase issues. Indeed, after 20 sessions with the same men, some therapists seem burdened with boredom and talk about "getting it over with." Such a response to this phase suggests a belief that endings are insignificant and uneventful—a stance with which we disagree. With the help of various group theorists, our experience in batterers' groups, samples of group dialogue, and some anecdotes, we will relate how this phase of the group is a meaningful and important part of the road to peace.

ENDING PHASE THEMES IN GROUPS

The Ending Phase is a time when the group prepares to dissolve. In approaching the moment of ending, the group naturally reflects on its past and, with reference to the issues labored over in the group, looks to the future. A number of themes discussed by several group theorists are salient in this phase.

Denial of the end commonly occurs (Northen, 1969; Shulman, 1979). Members refuse to acknowledge imminent termination by forgetting, changing the subject, or otherwise ignoring the counselors' attempts to discuss endings. A group embracing denial seeks to maintain the normalcy of the Middle Phase by processing issues in its usual manner, as if nothing important were impending.

The group usually views termination with ambivalence (Northen, 1969). Members express this theme by expressing uncertainty over their readiness to leave the group. They recognize achievements made in the group and may be excited about moving on to new activities and relationships, but they are also hesitant to give up the gratification provided by the counselor and the group. Balgopal and Vassil (1983) observe that ambivalence about leaving is fed through members recognizing the stark contrasts between life in the group and life "out there":

> While the group as a microcosm can be viewed as incorporating the stable and diffuse elements of society, the special nature of the protective envelope permits interpersonal sensitivities that make the experience slightly different. Frequently, clients ponder questions such as "can I make it on the outside," or "where will the backup and understanding be if I fail." The right to fail in a protective setting hardly corresponds to consequences in the real world. Who is to say that the members' special and learned sensitivities will be rewarded by others' actions? (p. 209)

Anxiety about termination can also be expressed through a return to maladaptive behavior patterns thought to be extinguished in the

Middle Phase. While the counselor may be alarmed and may worry that the group is entering a spiral of retrogression, Northen (1969) believes this should not be perceived as genuine retrogression. Instead, the group is communicating feelings of anxiety and unreadiness to end. Members may also be seeking reassurance that the counselor is still concerned with their welfare.

Shulman (1979) notes that members usually express anger about termination at the counselor, either directly or indirectly. Lateness, skipped sessions, hostile undertones, and disputes over minor concerns can all be due to unacknowledged anger. Counselors should expect this despite any prior agreement specifying the ending date. While client anger is a response to perceived rejection by the therapist, Shulman (1979) believes sadness is often beneath the anger.

Balgopal and Vassil (1983) emphasize loss and mourning as common ending themes. Clients facing termination grapple with feelings of abandonment. Clients who may be most vulnerable because of past difficulties with separation cope with this feeling by withdrawing affect (Northen, 1969). Shulman (1979) highlights a different response to impending loss by noting a heightening of affect between counselor and client in the Ending Phase. Infusing seemingly minor issues, heightened affect may be due to unexpressed resentment about certain aspects of the counseling relationship.

During this phase, members are likely to talk about what they have learned in the group. Particularly when this occurs in difficult groups, therapists feel rewarded by this review of positive experiences (Balgopal & Vassil, 1983), for it validates their work. A group engaged in this review is often characterized by reminiscence and sentimentality. However, Shulman (1979) reminds the counselor that there are also negative experiences that should be voiced but that are difficult for the group to acknowledge.

Finally, members engage in memorialization (Balgopal & Vassil, 1983) or the farewell party (Shulman, 1979). This manifests as planning a party, taking pictures, exchanging addresses, and so on. Although these activities may also evidence group denial of the end, they can also be seen as symbols of the struggles, the pain, the joy of achievement, and the overall preciousness of the group experience.

In our experience with batterers' groups, all the themes cited above are present in varying degrees.

ENDINGS IN ABUSERS' GROUPS

Ending Phase Structure

We would find it difficult to specify an exact demarcation point between the Middle and Ending Phases of our abuser groups. As with other kinds of groups, instead of sharp, identifiable boundaries, there is a gradual shift or a transition period. At the beginning of this transition period, we detect hints of Ending Phase themes in the form of allusions to remaining time, achievements, unfinished work, resentments, and so on. In a 28-session program, we rarely encounter major expressions of these themes prior to the twentieth session. The exact point at which they emerge differs with each group.

We play a major role in stimulating the emergence of Ending Phase themes by creating a sudden structural change in group sessions. Once we have covered all modules, we choose to conduct the remaining sessions with two kinds of activities. The first activity consists of providing any number of supplementary sessions customized for the special needs of a particular group. The decision to proceed this way depends on two factors. The first factor is basically our accumulated observations about the special needs or interests of a particular group. For instance, we may recognize that one group is characterized by its difficulty with understanding and implementing cognitive restructuring techniques. Based on this, we might design one or two supplementary sessions on this skill. A second factor influencing the decision to supplement is the group's self-identified need. For example, in one of our groups, there were an unusual number of violence reports involving physical discipline of children. When we equated spanking with child abuse, the group challenged the program's perspective. Several members challenged us to provide an effective, nonviolent alternative to hitting children. Consequently, we provided two sessions on nonviolent parenting.

The second activity is Sharing Time. Once the modules have been covered, that last portion of every session in the two prior phases is expanded to consume the entire session. Although supplementary structured sessions may seem necessary for any number of reasons, we attempt to preserve as many Ending Phase sessions as possible for Sharing Time. We treasure Sharing Time for a number of reasons. The module format is so structured and packed with essential material, that the counselors can lose sight of each individual man and his personal issues. When modules have limited Sharing Time to the last third or, at times, the last quarter of a session, as many as five men can need a portion of that time. Consequently, they often receive less time than needed. A number of uninterrupted Sharing Time sessions can help redress the imbalance.

Termination Anxiety

We have noticed that men in the Ending Phase express ambivalence about ending by voicing their fears of recidivism. Members often attribute responsibility for their progress to the counselors, as if magic had been worked upon them. Others wonder if they have been cured of their abusive tendencies. Almost all members have doubts about their readiness to leave the group. The anxiety and the perceptions about their abuse implied in these concerns is vaguely reminiscent of behavior in the Beginning Phase; the counselors and the program are again elevated to key positions. Some of the questions in this phase are infused with worry and urgency, and convey disbelief in the individual man's power to live peaceably. Although this resembles the externalizing of responsibility for abuse so characteristic of the Beginning Phase, it is not the same thing. Instead, it is evidence of each man's dependency on the program, his fear of abandonment, and a temporary lack of confidence in himself.

Even more salient in this phase is each man's dependency on the group and his reluctance to leave it. While Beginning Phase dependency centered on the counselors, that attachment is now much more focused on the group. The group has become a second home. Each man has shared information and feelings with this group of men resulting in an intimacy unknown in his everyday life. In particular, common struggles, mutual aid, disclosing violence, exposing of a deep well of shame, and discovering that he is not punished or otherwise rejected makes the group a very special place.

Because members have grown to treasure the group, therapists should not expect the group to initiate direct discussion of Ending Phase concerns. More often than not, members deny the imminence of ending. We almost always have to remind the group that the end is near. We begin this toward the end of the Middle Phase by sprinkling comments at various points. For instance, we remind men that time is passing quickly and that there is considerable work to accomplish before we end. When helping a man examine alternatives to abuse, we allude to the future, when he will not be able to rely on the group. We often begin each session with a comment about the number of remaining sessions. Usually, men either ignore or give minimal acknowledgment to this message. Our persistence in reminding men plants the seeds of awareness that inevitably sprout. Sooner or later the group will raise this issue either directly or indirectly and will not flee into denial.

The dialogue below illustrates how men might indirectly express some of these concerns to the therapists and one way of addressing them.

GEORGE: Some of us were talking last week after group, and we're a bit worried about ending the group so soon. I don't think there's one of us that's ready to go it alone. We were hoping we could stretch it out a bit. Maybe another month or two.

JIM: Yah, I still have problems with Sheila. I'm still getting angry sometimes and I still need a place to talk about it. The guys in this group have been a great help to me.

DAVE: I feel the same way. I'm still having trouble being assertive. I need this program.

COUNSELOR: I understand what you're saying. All of you still have work to do. I know that nobody changes 100% in a 32-session group. I've never met a man who finished our program who was totally sure he could remain nonabusive. In that way, what you're saying today is normal. Am I hearing some nervousness or fear about ending?

GEORGE: Yah, I'm a little nervous about ending. Maybe we're different from other groups. We might need a little extra help. I'm worried I'm going to lose what I learned here. It's you and this group that's kept me from being violent.

COUNSELOR: It makes a lot of sense to me that you feel that way about ending the group. You've come a long way together and some very special things have happened here. George, maybe you and the others forgot something I told you in the first few sessions. I said that we were here as teachers or guides but that we couldn't make you do anything and we didn't have any magic. I said you would be the one to choose whether or not you'd use the skills you learned here. In the beginning, you made a few mistakes, but you got better at it. The same thing is true from this point forward; your decisions are what count in not being abusive.

DAVE: But I need some support in that. Who am I going to talk to?

COUNSELOR: Are you worried about being isolated again?

DAVE: Yah. One thing I learned here is that keeping things to myself had a lot to do with feeling angry.

COUNSELOR: So if you're isolated, you're going to get angry. Are you worried about being violent again?

DAVE: Yah. [other men nod in agreement]

COUNSELOR: You still have other men in this group. The ending of this group doesn't mean you can't have contact with each other. I want to encourage all of you to keep in touch. You also have the option of entering our self-help group.

JIM: But they're not the same guys. I don't even know them!

COUNSELOR: They're guys just like you. They graduated from a group just like this and they have the same struggles as you. The mood in this room seems to be changing. Are you angry with us for ending this group?

JIM: Yah, I'm a little angry about it. It seems like we don't have any say in this.

COUNSELOR: All right, I'm glad you didn't stuff the anger. Let's talk more about it.

There are several noteworthy aspects of the therapist's response in this example:

(1) The therapist is firm in holding to the contract each man has with the program; ready or not, the group has to end at the ordained time.

(2) The therapist puts the experience of not feeling ready in perspective: No man has ever felt totally ready to leave. This response helps normalize the group's feelings and doubts about ending.

(3) Perhaps most important, the therapist recognizes how the men feel and brings this element into the discussion so as not to discount the gravity they attach to ending. It is important that members be allowed the opportunity to recognize and express uncertainty and anger, and to mourn the group's death.

(4) The therapist reminds them that they have learned things in the group and gives them both credit and responsibility for putting their skills to use.

(5) The therapist reminds the men that there are realistic alternatives to prolonging the group.

The Ending Phase and Other Endings

Ending Phase process frequently sharpens members' awareness of other kinds of endings, both past and present. For instance, one of us led a particularly difficult group in which it was necessary to bar one man from the program after he threatened to assault the counselor. This threat and the consequent termination occurred in the middle of a group meeting halfway through the Middle Phase. Throughout his time in the group, the threatening member, who was consistent in his role as group rebel, stimulated a variety of powerful feelings in group members. However, because members feared this man, those feelings were never expressed in his presence. Not until much later, in the last two sessions, did members reflect on this man and the events leading to his termination. While many men expressed hostile feelings, most members had complex reactions; some recognized parts of themselves in him, some felt sorrow over his failure, some even defended him despite unanimous disapproval of his actions. Most notable was the fact that some men were angry because he sidetracked the group; they held him responsible for their failure to make even more gains. In recognizing two unhelpful processes, the counselors were able to help the group understand how it was inappropriately dealing with ending themes. Members were involved in an evaluation process in which they were projecting responsibility for their progress on one member. Moreover, by choosing the absent man as a safe target for their Ending Phase anger, they were avoiding giving negative feedback to the counselors.

In another situation in which different kinds of endings converged, one of us led a group in which a man killed himself in the final portion of the Ending Phase. This very young, vulnerable man elicited caretaking reactions from the group in the way that big brothers feel compelled to care for a little brother. Unfortunately, the intense arousal surrounding this event was expressed as rage toward the counselors. Members believed we should have foreseen this tragedy and criticized us for not being skilled. The entire group behaved in ways suggesting they felt betrayed by us. While we were never overtly accused of dishonesty, we had a vague but insistent feeling of being accused of lying to the group.

In decoding the group's reaction, we came to understand that normal ending themes converged with this ultimate, tragic ending. Without this tragedy, members would have had the normal responses to ending the group, including abandonment, regret, and anger over not achieving more. Balgopal and Vassil (1983) observe that coming to terms with achieving less than the ideal in the course of the group can result in members perceiving the counselor as having tricked them. In noting how members in this phase feel rejected by the counselor, Northen (1969) observes that clients sometimes regard the counselor as a "big liar." The therapist must be a bad parent, for who but a bad parent could throw a child out of the home? If these are the normal processes, we can imagine how the intensity of feelings over normal endings was magnified by this death. First, suicide ironically occurred in a group having the express purpose of ending violence. That man's suicide was the ultimate failure. Men would naturally ask, "How could that have happened in this kind of group if the counselors did not lie?" Second, almost all men in that group experienced despair at some point in the group. The group could not help but empathize with the man's despair and failure to be helped by the counselors' interventions. We believe men were badly shaken as they realized any of them could have made the same decision. Third, suicide communicates an ultimate and stark message of rejection. Exactly who is rejecting whom, however, is not always clear. Did the man's suicide symbolize his rejection of the group and the counselors, or was it a result of the counselors somehow rejecting him? Finally, the men perceived everyone as having failed in his role, but none more so than the counselors. Though big brothers might fail to protect their little brothers, it is unthinkable for parents to fail in protecting their children.

The most common merging of personal and group endings is that of the man facing separation and divorce. Because battering is so destructive to trust and intimacy, half or more of the members of an abusers' group must cope with failed relationships. Though we repeatedly state that the group is not designed to save their relationships, most men minimize this warning. They embrace a secret agenda according to which successful completion of the group will either convince their partners not to leave or persuade them to return. While some men are successful in this, others are not. Consequently, there are usually a few very sad members during the Ending Phase. Not only must they come to terms with ending the group, they must face their failure to save their relationships through the group. Feelings these men have can be exacerbated by the presence of other, happy men who are reuniting with their partners. In addition, sorting through mixed results of attending the group can be confusing. On the one hand, the divorcing man may have been very successful in avoiding abuse and otherwise changing his behavior. This ought to be cause for celebration. On the other hand, he may perceive the result of this success to be domestic failure.

Examining Attitude Change in the Ending Phase

By the time batterers reach the Ending Phase, some have undergone a rapid consciousness-raising process. When the therapist examines their awareness of issues and contrasts this to the level of sophistication in the Beginning Phase, the change seems miraculous. One specific change is a new readiness to acknowledge the abusiveness of certain behavior that would have seemed acceptable a short time ago. While this extends to all kinds of abuse, it is particularly noticeable when considering nonphysical forms of abuse. For instance, some men are willing to admit the abusiveness of such behavior as controlling women through economic means, emotionally pressuring women for sex, name-calling, and withholding affection to punish. It is common for several members to engage in sophisticated and lively discussion about these issues. Some men even begin to voice very liberal attitudes toward women and sex-role issues. So pronounced is this apparent change that we suspect if we administered a questionnaire measuring attitudes toward women, some men would score much more liberal than the general population of men.

Evidence of the change is found in two kinds of activities. When group discussion centers on theory or hypothetical situations, openness to sophisticated analyses of abuse and liberalism in attitudes can be quite pronounced. Second, if a member is struggling with a therapist over the issue of his behavior in a specific situation, other members may ally themselves with the therapist and pressure that man to change his stance. Counselors may wonder if these remarkable events are signs of program effectiveness.

More careful examination reveals something more complex. The same member who seems open and liberal abandons this stance when his behavior is under scrutiny. Indeed, when that liberal member brings his domestic problem to the group, his resistance to admitting to the abusive or controlling aspects of his behavior can be so pronounced that it resembles the struggles so characteristic of the Beginning Phase. Although some men seem to accomplish drastic attitudinal change in a remarkably short time, this change in thinking has not produced a consistent change in actions. In addition, the liberal attitudes are tentatively held, as if a man were trying them on for size. Evidence of a lack of integrity in this realm can be found in a man's responses to stressful situations; when under stress, the man may return to well-established defensive, angry, or abusive responses.

THE COUNSELOR AND THE ENDING PHASE

Sometimes counselors forget that they are as involved in the group's process as are their clients. Consequently, counselors must not only facilitate successful negotiation of Ending Phase issues for the men, they must also be aware of their own responses to this phase. We will discuss some of these below.

Disengagement

At several points, we mentioned that clients experience an intensity that stems from the difficult work in the group. Therapists are partners in this work; they invest considerable time and energy in an abusers' group. Their experiences, of course, are different. The role of helper demands that they lead others to change. Nevertheless, they become bonded to the group through their work with it and through investing their commitment to ending abuse. The resulting relationships, despite obvious limitations in the role of counselor, are real. When the time comes to help the members say goodbye to the group, counselors must also start disengaging themselves from the group.

Therapists can deny the significance of their relationships with each group member by hiding behind a role. Most of us have probably found ourselves doing this at one time or another. We focus on the functional nature of the relationship, examine our work in terms of our role, and concentrate on measuring the achievement of objectives—all of which are necessary. However, if this kind of objectivity functions to shield us from coming to terms with the very human dimension of our relationships with group members, we risk losing the opportunity to say goodbye. Shulman (1979) reminds us of the very human dimension of endings by comparing the dynamics of the Ending Phase to those of death and dying. Although the latter is clearly a more powerful experience, the analogy reminds us that the ending process in a counseling relationship can trigger deep feelings in clients and counselors.

We do not want to overstate the difficulty of "letting go" of batterers in counseling, for we do not think this task is any more difficult than it is with clients with other problems. Nevertheless, we should mention some elements that are not entirely obvious but that can influence therapists to "hang on" to these men. The first element came as a surprise to us when we began this work. Although we abhorred each man's abusive behavior, we discovered that we had a certain kind of affection for almost all abusers with whom we worked. We entered this work expecting to feel, at minimum, mild disgust with wife abusers. This expectation was based on a stereotyped image of abusers. While there were a few men we found exceedingly difficult to like, we felt a liking and an appreciation for at least a few aspects of almost every man's personality. As the group progressed, our appreciation grew as we watched the courage with which most men struggled with their problems. The extent to which we had a positive relationship with any client affected our feelings about saying goodbye to that man.

A second element influencing the process of letting go stems from utilizing a directive style of counseling. When therapists adopt this style, they are actively involved with and assume responsibility for most aspects of the group. In the Beginning and Middle Phases of the group, despite efforts to foster mutual aid, counselors experience the habit of maintaining control and being responsive as something like a reflex. In the Ending Phase, this style should be gradually abandoned so that men can further experiment with mutual aid and decrease their dependency on counselors. The counselor's high level of involvement in batterers' groups can be such that it requires considerable conscious effort to disengage from the group gradually.

In the Ending Phase of every group, we experience a tension between the knowledge that we must let go and our habit of being active and in control. Typically, this becomes evident when a member presents a problem while looking directly at us. Because we are still in the role of teacher or expert, many men value our input more than that of other members. In this situation, we feel a strain as we hold ourselves back from responding. Instead, we look around the group, perhaps endure a few moments of silence, and invite others to respond.

A third element influencing willingness to let go is fear or uncertainty. In accepting responsibility for teaching and facilitating a batterers' group, therapists naturally are concerned about outcome. They cannot escape knowing that, despite attendance in a counseling program, some men will not stop their abuse. Although therapists may know quite rationally that, if they have acted responsibly, they cannot be held responsible for a man's behavior, there is no certain remedy for the fear that a program graduate will reoffend and perhaps seriously injure or kill his partner. Because the potential cost of negative outcome in abuser counseling is horrendous, uncertainties about outcome may make disengagement more difficult than it is with other populations.

Shulman (1979) emphasizes counselors' guilt feelings as a salient theme in the Ending Phase. Frequently, counselors are overcritical of themselves as they view group members' varying degrees of progress. They wonder if they could have engineered greater progress if they had been more skilled, made a few changes in the program, or read the newest clinical books. Additionally, because of concerns for victims, many counseling programs for batterers are scrutinized by victims' counseling services. The frequency and the rapidity of feedback on men's failures after reoffenses constantly remind men's counselors that group work with batterers is not uniformly successful. Therapists can have difficulty escaping the feelings of personal responsibility and guilt over the behavior of their clients.

In the Ending Phase, if counselors are unaware of their uncertainty and guilt, or are unable to view these within the normal range of a counselor's Ending Phase behavior, they may allow these to affect them in several ways. Despite knowing that they cannot predict future assaults, the first thing they may do is begin to wonder (attempt to predict) who will be successful. If they are not careful, they then act out their fear by becoming hypervigilant with the men about whom they worry the most. With only a few sessions remaining, they redouble their efforts to force change in a particular man. They may be overcautious, recommending that a man repeat the program despite his having met all requirements. They may recommend extending attendance in the program through individual counseling sessions. Periodically, an entire program can be in a state of upheaval as it agonizes over revising and extending the duration of abuser groups to reduce the failure rate. Although caution in abuser counseling is always necessary, and a critical examination of skills and program reduces complacency, counselors may save themselves unnecessary worry if they can understand some of their uncertainty as a normal response to the Ending Phase—particularly their struggle to let go of clients.

Facilitating Endings

There are a number of group process tasks counselors should accomplish in the Ending Phase. We base these tasks on our perceptions of the needs of group members that arise out of normal Ending Phase themes. At this level of analysis, clients' needs in abuser groups will not differ significantly from those of clients in other kinds of groups. However, at certain points in our discussion we will suggest the relationship of these needs to the problem at hand.

The first way counselors facilitate endings is through addressing denial by enforcing the fact of ending. We remind men that time is limited, and that there is still considerable work to accomplish. While there are clearly logistical reasons for ending on time, a side benefit of our system of closed groups, with their definite starting and ending dates, is that our holding to a contract we have with group members forces men to recognize and respect the setting of boundaries. We view violation of boundaries, particularly personal ones, as inherent in the abuser's maltreatment of others. Furthermore, by enforcing those boundaries, we believe we underline each man's responsibility for the progress he makes in counseling.

Gradual disengagement from the group, a second method of facilitating endings, alters the atmosphere or tone of the group. Despite members' negative reactions, counselor disengagement serves a number of purposes. First, it enables the mutual aid process to intensify and provides abusers with a more intense experience in seeking and giving help. As such, it allows men to turn to peers, thereby decreasing dependency on professionals. This skill will be invaluable as men either leave to struggle on their own or enter self-help groups. Second, although disengagement by itself may constitute desertion or abandonment, when the counselor exercises it in a context of other supportive strategies, it is an enabling act and a vote of confidence in clients' abilities. Disengagement, then, addresses members' feelings of ambivalence over ending, self-doubt, and anxiety over independence in the struggle for peace. If the act of disengagement could be expressed in a statement to the group, it might be, "I believe you are ready to go forward."

Counselors should balance disengagement with several other attending or facilitating strategies. One of these occurs when counselors offer statements of faith in men's abilities. This is particularly helpful when members express their fears about leaving the group. Such statements are powerful because they emerge from someone who is seen as experienced and knowledgeable—an authority figure.

Counselors also invite members to express their thoughts and feelings about ending. We see four benefits to this strategy. The first is that it helps to combat minimization and denial. Second, counselors who encourage members to talk about their thoughts and feelings about ending are inviting members to process their mourning openly. When feelings over loss are elicited, it is particularly important on the one hand to accept anger, but on the other hand to invite abusive men to broaden their labeling of emotions. For instance, if men have been funneling a number of emotions into anger, counselors invite them to acknowledge sadness, grief, regret, helplessness, and other feelings appropriate to loss. Third, members are directed to examine self-statements about ending and their futures in terms of their anger-producing potential. For instance, the truthfulness of self-statements such as "I can't make it on my own" or "These counselors don't care about me" needs to be examined and changed to reflect reality. Fourth, counselors model assertive behavior rather than responding passively to members' indirectness or passivity. Moreover, through inviting members to speak openly about their reactions, counselors encourage them to abandon passivity and practice assertiveness.

Finally, we urge therapists to be aware of their personal styles in responding to endings and loss, for they too are losing a relationship. The manner in which they respond to the group through this phase will have some effect on the group's ability to negotiate the end. For instance, counselors who typically respond to endings through rapid disengagement and total withdrawal risk abandoning the group and inadvertently facilitating group denial, passivity, and even hostility when this personal style is transferred to group work. To facilitate endings well, we believe it is important to balance disengagement by continuing to be supportive. The coexistence of these two elements is both possible and necessary.

EVALUATION

The Ambiguity of Success

The termination of the Ending Phase is incomplete without an evaluation of each man's progress. Designing an evaluation at this stage is not a simple matter, for it involves determining a program definition of the term *success*. The term is ambiguous because of the different meanings it may denote. For instance, to one person, a man who has been labeled "successful" in abuser counseling is someone who will never again be physically abusive to his partner. Another person might infer that the "successful" man will also not be abusive toward her in nonphysical ways. Both stances are assumptions about the degree to which problem behaviors have been eradicated. More seriously, both stances assume a guarantee for the future—something no therapist can provide.

Although the therapist's inability to predict the future may seem obvious to the reader, there are others in the community who may not understand this. They may expect definitive statements such as a physician might give after administering antibiotics and finding that an infection has disappeared. In particular, persons within the criminal justice system who are influential in determining case dispositions should know the program's definition of *success*. Since that system is, in a sense, a client of the program, the program should make it aware that successful completion of counseling is not a sure remedy against reoffense.

In a similar but more serious vein, a victim who attributes wondrous powers to therapists may believe that her partner is certifiably nonabusive if he has completed a program. This assumption promotes a false sense of security. We must warn readers that some men who have been unsuccessful in completing a program or have been ejected will lie to their partners by telling them they have been successful or are still attending. To avoid misunderstandings and deception, we support Sonkin, Martin, and Walker's (1985) practice of maintaining frequent contact with the victim. Not only does this provide a reporting mechanism for any current abuse, it provides an opportunity to educate the woman about the program and inform her of realistic expectations for counseling.

We believe it is particularly important to inform a partner when a man has dropped out, been ejected, or otherwise been unsuccessful.

This warning may function to help her remain vigilant in taking any self-protective measures. Again, therapists will find this task less complicated if they have secured releases from the man at intake granting permission to talk to the woman. There are other occasional situations in which the man's danger to others is apparent and, regardless of confidentiality concerns, informing possible victims is required by the therapist's legal duty to warn.

Since counselors cannot predict future violence with any accuracy, they should be clear within the program, with the man, his victim, and any mandating agents that "successful completion of the program" means nothing more than it states. It implies no guarantee of the man's future behavior, nor does it indicate that his potential victims are safe. It indicates only that his performance in counseling was at a level sufficient to meet program requirements.

Criteria for Success

We use three major criteria for determining a man's success in abuser counseling. While we insist that he meet all three criteria, we recognize that the degree to which these criteria are satisfied will vary from one man to the next.

(1) The man must have successfully used a Control Plan as an alternative to violence. Although we anticipate some failures in this regard early in the group, we expect a rapid growth in his proficiency in using this plan as the group proceeds. While an isolated failure in a latter portion of the group is cause for grave concern, it does not necessarily imply failure. We look for increasing consistency in finding alternatives to violence.

(2) The man must have provided evidence of a significant change in attitudes and beliefs that support violence against women. For instance, he must regard as wrong those attitudes that function to blame the victim, shirk personal responsibility, and support a man's right to discipline and control his partner. We look for evidence of this change in the content of his statements in the Ending Phase and contrast this to attitudes he exhibited early in counseling.

(3) The man must have satisfied the completion requirements of each module to a reasonable level. We do not think we should be more exact in stating this requirement, for this would necessitate class-biased evaluations such as formal examinations. Instead, we look for an acceptable, working knowledge of the central themes in each module, competency in the majority of skills, and willingness to partici-

pate in the group. The considerable latitude in this criterion is based on the reality of clients' differing abilities.

Evaluation Sessions

There are two basic frameworks for conducting evaluations with group members. The first is an evaluation in the group much like the one we described in the Middle Phase. The second is evaluation of each man in individual sessions. Admittedly, evaluation in individual sessions is time-consuming, but we favor it because the increased time allows for thoroughness. The session should center on the criteria for success outlined above, with both the counselor and the client stating their views on the man's progress. One key task is a determination of disposition.

DISPOSITION

Determination of a counseling plan at the point of completing an abusers' group will largely depend on the agency's resources and the availability of other community resources. We summarize several alternatives below, many of which require considerable breadth of social services in a community.

(1) The man has successfully completed the group and will terminate his contact with the agency. This decision falls short of the ideal. In most such cases, we believe the man would benefit from some kind of additional help, the nature of which would be determined by examining those personal needs not satisfied in the group. Additionally, many abusers can benefit from a more gradual cessation of dependency such as that provided by an abusers' self-help group.

(2) The man is deemed unsuccessful in completing the group. The counselor may believe that allowing him to repeat the group will be unproductive. Mandating agents are informed of this. If applicable, the counselor recommends other, more appropriate strategies. For instance, if a chemical dependency problem becomes evident at this late stage, the counselor may refer the man to a chemical dependency program. Attending to the violence problem may be resumed after the chemical dependency is resolved.

(3) The man is deemed unsuccessful in completing the group. The counselor has reason to believe the man will benefit from repeating the group and offers him this alternative.

(4) The man has been successful and proceeds to a second level of therapist-facilitated, abuse-oriented group counseling designed to build on the work of the primary abuse group and provide support for continued nonviolence. This service may be either in the program or at another community service.

(5) The man has been successful and is referred to an abusers' self-help group for continued support.

(6) The man and his partner are referred to a parenting skills group within or outside the agency.

(7) The man and his partner have decided to preserve and improve their relationship. After careful consideration and consultation with the man, the woman, and the woman's counselor, the therapist facilitates a referral to couple or family counseling within the agency. Alternatively, they are referred out to another service trusted by the therapist to work well with abuse issues.

Two critical factors should be considered when contemplating the last alternative. The first is that the therapist should have confidence in the man's ability to react nonabusively to the stress created by couple or family counseling. Consequently, if the man has been unsuccessful in the primary abuse group, the therapist should not recommend this option or otherwise aid the couple in entering this kind of counseling. If this is ignored, the woman may be placed at greater risk for being abused.

The second consideration centers on the woman and her general state of mental health. If the man has successfully completed an abuse program and is eager to resume a normal relationship, and the woman has not undertaken counseling or otherwise had the opportunity to heal the effects of violence, each partner will have a different ability to negotiate reconciliation successfully. We believe that attempts to reconcile a relationship and raise it to a new level of wellness will be negatively affected to the extent that a woman has not attained a sense of her personal power, devised methods of protecting herself, come to grips with responsibility issues, and accessed her feelings about the abuse. Although we do not approve of inflexible policies that require that a woman enter counseling prior to helping her reconcile with her partner, we do believe that the gigantic power differential existing between an abuser and his victim must somehow be altered before the victim can be an equal partner in the relationship. Counselors should assess these factors, preferably in consultation with the woman, before agreeing to help a couple reconcile. In most cases, we believe a woman who has not had a chance to heal may be better off completing a group counseling program for battered women prior to working on the relationship.

Recognizing Completion of the Group

Men who successfully complete the group appreciate formal recognition of their achievements. We supply this in the form of a letter resembling a graduation certificate. We advise counselors to be careful in the phrasing of this letter for two reasons. First, in comprehensive programs in which the primary violence group is normally supplemented by other services (e.g., a second-phase group, men's self-help group), completion of the primary group may not signify completion of the program. In this case, letters of recognition should explicitly recognize the degree to which the man has thus far completed the program. Second, letters of recognition should explicitly differentiate satisfactory completion from predictions of future behavior. As we discussed in the section on evaluation, we can state whether a man has fulfilled program requirements, but we cannot predict nonviolence. Consequently, in our letter, we explicitly state the pivotal role of the man's willingness to use what he has learned in the program.

In a group in which all members have been successful, men value a small ritual to mark their achievements. We commonly set aside the last hour for awarding the letters, sharing food, and basking in the glow of a job well done.

CONCLUDING REMARKS

As discussed earlier, the Ending Phase brings a sense of ambiguity. Although this group is ending, the reader should not infer that each man's journey is finished. Twenty or more years of learning will not disappear in a few months. The group model we have described in the last four chapters may be viewed as a core intervention in that it addresses the individual's propensity to use violence to solve conflict and maintain control over women. Although it attends to the violence—a prerequisite of concentration on other problems—its narrow focus neglects other needs of assaultive men.

While each man will have different needs as he strives to give up his abuse, we mention some common ones here. Because non-physical forms of abuse seem the most enduring, further work in this area is usually needed. Men may need instruction in parenting skills, particularly nonabusive child-rearing techniques. Couples and families deciding to stay together usually need to come to terms with the past and find new ways of dealing with power. Some men who were victims of child abuse may require individual therapy. Finally, most abusers will benefit from participation in an advanced therapist-led group, a self-help group, or both. These subsequent groups can consolidate learning that has already occurred, as well as intensify the program's focus on subtle expressions of the need to control and dominate women.

PART IV

COUNSELORS' ISSUES

11

COUNSELORS' ISSUES

At times, our work with assaultive men has been an exhausting endeavor. Working with violence in the family takes a toll on us, for the work touches us and our colleagues, sometimes unexpectedly, in vulnerable places. When we began counseling abusers, there was hardly anyone in our communities who also did this work. Consequently, we were on our own with a only a few colleagues who could relate to the struggles of maintaining the integrity and health of person and program.

While we collected a small pile of literature on clinical skills and program development, we thirsted for something that would speak to the personal and interpersonal dimensions of immersing oneself in men's violence against women. This was something the professional literature had mostly ignored. Yet we found ourselves struggling within ourselves, with our co-workers, and occasionally against our co-workers, as we tried to come to terms with the impact of this work on ourselves and our programs.

This final chapter is of a type not often seen in the professional literature. Rather than being skills oriented, or dealing with a certain base of knowledge, or explaining something in a "how-to" manner, we will look at a few issues straddling the boundary between the professional and the personal realms. These issues have to do with personal vulnerabilities affecting us in our roles, our relationships with others, self-care, and our belief systems.

EMOTIONAL IMPACT OF WORKING WITH VIOLENCE

When we first began working with wife abusers, we realized we were afraid. We know we were not supposed to be afraid; the atmosphere of our professional training prescribed a calm, competent, and objective demeanor as an appropriate mark of professionalism. Nevertheless, we were afraid, and to this day we are periodically visited by fear. A metaphor seems appropriate in describing this fear. In touching the lives of the violent, we imagine ourselves as bomb-disposal specialists defusing time bombs. We too must find a way to deal with fear if we are to be able to do our jobs.

Although readers might accuse us of overdramatizing our work, if we are honest about what we do, we cannot suppress an awareness of the danger to ourselves and to others. In adapting to whatever danger exists, the "just world" hypothesis probably helps us in our daily functioning. We believe that if we do our jobs well and remain blameless, nothing bad will happen to us. In our more honest moments, we must admit that bad things do happen to competent, blameless people. We cannot escape the reality that batterers can injure and kill. Hence the therapist's personal safety ought to be an important issue.

In the beginning, a constellation of events, realizations, and a growing sensitivity to violence prepared the way for fear. Repeated exposure to detailed accounts of violence is exceedingly stressful, for we constantly witness the dark side of humanity. We found it a challenge to leave the job at the office. We ruminated over certain clients and their stories, worried, had difficulty sleeping, and sometimes had nightmares of violence.

We were being sensitized to the prevalence of violence. Because this awareness was not restricted to our work lives, we could not shut it off the way one can close a valve. For example, in passing a man and a woman arguing on the street, we would be uncomfortably aware of his anger, of the look in his eyes, and realize he was escalating into rage. An incident such as this made us fearful in several ways. We were afraid for ourselves in the presence of someone so near to rage. We were afraid for him because of what he might do when his anger peaked. We were most afraid for the woman. Our work had opened our eyes to the reality of male anger and of male violence against women.

Other events fed this fear. Some of them, though seemingly innocent and random, took on new meaning in the context of our work. We would leave group at night and find ourselves checking our rearview mirrors. Occasionally, we would take circuitous routes home just to ensure that the car behind was not really following us. A co-worker received hang-up phone calls at home and received subscriptions he never ordered. Was he being harassed by an angry client or were these events unconnected to his work? We have also been personally threatened by violent men, both subtly and directly.

Other events more clearly were cause for fear. A woman from our agency's battered women's group tried to make her partner jealous by falsely claiming she had gone for a drink with his counselor from the batterers' group. The man threatened to assault this counselor. The entire program was on edge for several days until we could convince this woman to tell the truth. In another incident, an anonymous man telephoned to say he was coming to the agency with a submachine gun. Though nothing came of this, we temporarily evacuated most staff and waited a few tension-filled hours.

There are other occasional incidents in group counseling that engender fear. When we must confront a man on his distortions he can become very angry with us. During his escalation, we notice the presence of his self-reported cues for violence: His face flushes, he glares, his voice level skyrockets, and he begins rapid body movements. As we are very aware of the danger in this moment, we watch him closely, gauge the distance between us, speak in firm but soft voices, and wonder if we can reach the exit if necessary. If we look at other group members, we also see fear in their faces. We notice the signs of fear in our bodies: Breathing changes, muscles tense, adrenalin is released. In the midst of this, we are conscious of speaking firmly but softly as we do what we can to help deescalate this man. Clearly, these are signs of fear.

In this work, we have options for handling fear. One of our options is to keep our fear a secret. We can stuff our fear as batterers hide their emotions. We can deny its existence to everyone including ourselves, but we will pay a price for this decision. If we deny for long periods that we are afraid, the process of denial will drain our energy. The longer we suppress this experience, the more stress we must endure. We risk fatigue and burnout.

When fear thoroughly permeates our work, we pay another price.

We will function less effectively as counselors because we will be so distracted by our internal processes that we will not be paying enough attention to what is occurring in the group. It is possible to incapacitate ourselves by the manner in which we deal with fear.

So far, we have concentrated on the counselors' fears for their personal safety. Counseling batterers also engenders fear for the batterer and for his victims. This kind of fear lingers in a violence counseling program. There is always the risk that a man will severely injure or kill himself, his partner, or his children. We have lost clients to suicide, and threats to kill partners are not rare. Anne Ganley (1981b) predicts that every program will eventually have to come to grips with a death. Similarly, counselors of battered women are not strangers to the despair that leads to suicide. Though family violence counseling has its rewards, it is fraught with danger, fear, and sometimes deep sadness.

One of the effects of fear on counselors that we have seen is the internal conversion of fear to anger. Rather than admitting their fear, counselors may feel and express their anxiety as anger directed either at the client or at "the system." The process by which this takes place is similar to that of the male emotional funnel described in earlier chapters. Since batterers and "the system" provide us with ample irritations, it may be difficult to know when we are responding purely to anger-producing stimuli or when our fear fuels our response. Whenever anger appears to be a long-term response and begins to interfere with our ability to do our work, or when counselors report or we notice in ourselves a tendency to fantasize angry or violent responses, personal self-examination is likely to reveal underlying emotions of fear or pain that we are avoiding.

In addition to fear and anger, sadness may permeate our work. Our experiences of sadness in this work are frequently connected to a sense of loss. We too have learned the usual cultural myths that portray the ideal North American family as a group of individuals who respect and care for one another. We sometimes laugh at the roles of husband and father portrayed in such ideal form in television and books. Our laughter and our black humor help us cope with the pain and sadness born of inescapable contrast between the real and the ideal. We find as much comfort in these myths as the next person, and we hurt as they gradually crumble.

COUNSELOR SELF-CARE

We believe it is important for every program to develop methods for staff to care for themselves and each other. The methods used can be both formal and informal. For instance, one formal way of addressing the effects of this work is to build in debriefing sessions that are held immediately after each group meeting. In our settings, we have met with our cotherapist and with the therapists of other batterers' and victims' groups to talk about events in the group and the effect these events have had on us. These meetings are extremely valuable; if, for some reason, we cannot meet after a group, we invariably take the effects home with us after work.

Another structured method of self-care can be developed through regular meetings of a staff group. Instead of dealing with programmatic, administrative, or clinical issues, such a group is an opportunity for all staff to "check in." This focus on the personal-professional juncture considers factors such as the effects of this work on each staff member, relationships between counselors, and other elements affecting each person's work. Although self-disclosure among staff may initially feel risky, we believe risk taking among staff within a formal structure will develop the trust and respect required to deal well with the variety of issues that can emerge out of stress-laden abuse counseling.

Structured staff development and self-care sessions seem necessary not only because of the stress inherent in abuse counseling; they are necessary because, from our observations, the never-ending demand for service from clients fills a workday. When a special time for group self-care is not set aside, it is difficult to provide such time during periods of high stress or crisis. When a program does institute these sessions, they can create a foundation upon which staff can build informal self-care networks evidenced by uninhibited reliance on co-workers for debriefing, problem solving, consultation, and human warmth.

DESENSITIZATION TO ABUSE

Sensitization to violence and the pervasive fear cited above are aversive experiences. Therapists, of course, should do what they can to reduce the destructive effects of these stressors. At times, we have wanted to insulate or distance ourselves from the violence. We should warn that this coping method can create other difficulties; there is a danger of minimizing violence. This is not to suggest that abuse will be trivialized; instead, when counselors shield themselves from the personal impact of violence, they gradually desensitize themselves and can lose sight of the danger permeating their work and their clients' lives.

We see desensitization commonly demonstrated in the ability to listen to accounts of abuse with unusual emotional detachment. If this results in a loss of empathy for victims, counselors may increasingly regard offenders' behavior and its effect on victims as simply a problem to be overcome. While this survival technique is understandable, we believe therapists noticing this tendency in themselves should be concerned about it. Such a reaction to abuse may be a warning sign of counselor burnout and may suggest a need for better self-care.

Beyond personal considerations, there may also be organizational factors contributing to desensitization. Counselors can be desensitized through working in a setting in which they rarely encounter victims' issues. When removed from the reality of victims' pain, violence becomes an abstract issue. One solution to this serious problem is to increase contact between those serving offenders and those serving battered women. Another solution may be found in broadening the base of therapists' work with violence. For instance, we have discovered that it is impossible to maintain an insensitivity to abuse when we have conducted groups for children who have witnessed battering. In our exposure to these violated children, our hearts ache and our outrage is fueled. We recommend that therapists working with batterers balance their perspectives through exposure to these men's children.

WOUNDS OF THE COUNSELOR

Our clients are not the only people who come from families in which there was abuse. There are survivors of abuse in the helping professions as well, including those who work with violence in the family. Many survivors of abuse bear open wounds. If these wounds have not healed, the effect of working with violence in the family can be like salting the wound. Having to respond to offenders or victims can elicit powerful feelings in counselor-victims that stem from their own experiences.

The emotional turmoil we refer to here is different from the powerful feelings any of us experience when we face our clients' pain. No matter what our personal backgrounds, this work will affect us deeply from time to time with horror, sadness, anger, and even rage. Such a human response to cruelty need not be caused primarily by a personal history of being abused. We believe that some emotional response to the pain of another is simply the human capacity for empathy. When we feel these emotions in our work as counselors, they visit us with an intensity and duration appropriate to our status as witnesses of another's pain. Our empathy can be so affected that we are sometimes even pulled into the pain as participants but do not lose our primary status as witnesses.

We believe there is another kind of response to this work that, on the surface, may resemble the emotional response of the witness. Upon closer examination, the balance between witnessing and participating is upset, so that the therapist is drawn into clients' pain as a participant. In being drawn in too deeply, the counselor loses the stance of the healer and becomes lost alongside the client in pain and confusion. Although imbalance in the counselor's life that affects job performance can be due to a variety of stressors, overidentification with or heightened sensitivity to one or more clients may be a signal that intensive involvement in abuse counseling is triggering unresolved personal issues.

This dynamic may suggest overidentification with the battered woman. However, a similar but complex dynamic may develop when counseling batterers. It is possible for a counselor to lose a balanced perspective when being confronted by the abuser's history as a victim in his family of origin when those formative experiences are similar to his or her own. This could lead to overidentification with the abuser and an inability to balance the supportive and confrontive aspects of counseling. In this case, the counselor might be overly supportive of the client and may defend him inappropriately. Alternatively, personal sensitivity to abuse, because of experiences in the counselor's family of origin, could produce hostility toward the abuser and a desire to punish him for his behavior. For illustration, we offer two scenarios below.

Scenario 1

During an intake appointment with Dave, an older, court-mandated client, the counselor was exploring Dave's abuse. Dave had been abusive toward his wife and his children and described a cycle of violence extremely similar to that experienced by the counselor in his own family of origin. Dave resembled the counselor's father in his looks, mannerisms, the use of certain phrases and defenses, and the issues that triggered his violence. During clinical supervision, the counselor claimed that Dave was seriously minimizing his violence and reported that he had conducted a difficult special session with Dave to deal with this issue. The counselor was still dissatisfied and, instead of concluding that Dave was inappropriate for the program, took the unusual step of scheduling a third session for the same purpose. When the supervisor questioned the plan, the counselor became angry and defensive. Shortly thereafter, Dave called the supervisor to ask for another counselor, claiming he was being harshly interrogated.

Scenario 2

Garth, a trainee conducting a group with a staff counselor, was typically unyielding in his refusal to accept a client's excuses for abusive behavior. During the family of origin module, he was close to tears when listening to Tim's disclosures of being severely abused as a child. His cotherapist was unaware of the many similarities between Tim's and Garth's experiences as children. Although the severity of Tim's experience did not stand out in comparison to those of most other men, Garth quickly developed great empathy for Tim. In a later group session, when Tim reported abusing his partner between sessions, Garth's one-sided, sympathetic response supported Tim's perception that his partner had victimized him. The staff counselor intervened in this dynamic by refocusing on Tim's responsibility for his choices. Garth appeared sullen for the rest of the group. During a debriefing session, Garth angrily accused the counselor of callousness and of misunderstanding Tim's situation.

Although we have not furnished an ending for either scenario, we can suggest two basic kinds. In the first, resolution might be aided if the therapist experiencing strong reactions somehow realizes that the client has touched a raw nerve. Where unresolved personal issues are not too disabling, a realization of the problem and a plan to respond differently to this type of client may be sufficient to address the issue. This is the simplest and perhaps most common solution. In a second kind of ending, strong emotional reactions toward that client may persist, a generalized distress may develop, and clinical judgment may be generally impaired. When violence counseling serves to aggravate the effects of a personal history of victimization, the counselor must face the issue of whether to enter counseling.

We do not suggest that counselors who have been victims are less able to work with violence. In fact, we believe some counselors with such a history may be superbly enabled to work in this area because of a clarity of vision offered by prior resolution of personal issues. We do not believe the general question of whether a certain kind of personal history is or is not suitable for abuse counseling is useful. The key question concerns the individual: Do the effects of victimization interfere with the ability of a particular counselor to provide high-quality service to the clients who depend on him or her?

MALE IDENTIFICATION

We touch on an issue here that may resonate with the experiences of other male therapists working with abusers. We remember entering our first group expecting these men to be radically different from us. Naturally, we had a stereotypical image of the wife batterer that suggested a man anyone could pick out in a crowd. After only a few group sessions, we were shocked to realize that very few of our clients conformed to this stereotype. They were from all classes, occupations, races, and educational levels. Many were articulate and soft-spoken. Most seemed so normal that they could have been our neighbors, our fathers, or our brothers. When these men spoke about their lives and their struggles, it became uncomfortably apparent that there were a lot of similarities between their life struggles and ours. Although we have not been violent with our partners, these men often mirror our own life struggles.

This realization led us to look at our own lives under a microscope to compare their experiences with ours. Most unsettling was our reevaluation of our own male experiences. We know with certainty that we have never been physically abusive in our relationships. However, our new definitions of abuse include psychological and emotional abuse. We can spot those kinds of abuse fairly easily in others, such as our clients. But our experience with these men compelled us to look at our behavior. We carefully examined our lives, looking at the range of our intimate relationships. There is no comfort in asking ourselves some of the same questions we ask batterers in assessments: Do you withdraw affection or sex in order to punish her? Do you manipulate her by threatening to leave the relationship? Have you ever insulted or sworn at her? Have you ever used anger, shouting, criticism, or put-downs as a means to win? Have you ever attempted to exert control over her social life? In the area of sexual abuse: Have you ever tried to pressure your partner in any way to have sex when she did not want to? Have you ever had trouble accepting that no means no? Most of us will have to answer yes to some of these questions.

Although it is possible that some women have had similar experiences and that they resonate to parts of this discussion, there is a special dimension in this self-evaluation for male counselors. There is the burden of realizing that all men are more similar than dissimilar. Despite any positive influences from our formative experiences, we all come from the same cultural mold. As men, we have all learned and incorporated society's recommendations for being adequate men. We all were taught that we have the right and obligation to dominate and control women. The only difference between ourselves and our clients is that the latter have felt free to use physical force toward this end.

One way to follow through with this line of thinking is to admit that male therapists helping violent males is something like the blind leading the blind. Men cannot be trusted in this endeavor as long as they hold the reins of power in our society. It would be like asking the privileged class to lead a revolution. Though this is a fairly radical perspective, there are those who support this position.

We favor an alternative. We believe that men who try to help batterers on the road to peace should be men who have been open to a feminist analysis of violence against women, have been open to accepting the insights of that perspective, and are committed to weeding out sexism in their lives. It is important that counselors understand, for instance, how sex roles and traditional male behavior influence the continuation of wife abuse. In what way does this become an issue in counseling? When a man in group tells us about an argument he had with his partner and refers to her as "that bitch," someone must tell him that he is dehumanizing a woman by using that name and that it is much easier to hit somebody who is not seen as human. When a man who believes he has a right to dictate to his wife tells us he hit her because his supper was cold, we must address more than the act of hitting; we must confront him on his need to control his wife.

A similar issue centers on the manner in which we, as men, relate to each other. We believe that the demands of the male sex role lead to problems in male bonding. Because we do not know how to achieve intimacy with other men, we have distant, superficial relationships. We cannot confide in each other about our pain, confusion, struggles, and hopes. Instead, we talk about sports, cars, politics, work, and women. If the desert land of our relationships extended only this far, it would be less of a problem. But men in groups go further; they reinforce each other in their sexist attitudes toward women. This serious problem becomes grave when we consider batterers. The stakes are raised to life-threatening proportions when the oppression of women is expressed with violence.

If male therapists are unaware of the role that traditional male bonding can play in reinforcing the control and domination of women, there will be danger of joining abusers in supporting the more subtle expressions of violence against women. For instance, if we have not grappled with our own sexism, what will we do at group coffee break when a circle of men tries to engage us in conversation about the "good-looking chick" who just walked by? Will we remind them that a human being just passed and that they just reduced her to a sexual toy? Or will we join them with a knowing smile? We believe counseling batterers not only consists of imparting anger control skills; it consists of teaching and modeling alternatives and of sensitizing our clients to the injustice leading to violence.

Fostering this kind of change is a form of social subversion. In striving for fundamental change, we must help our clients question societal prescriptions for masculinity. These messages about masculinity are the most difficult for batterers to hear, for we ask them to reach beyond the violence; we ask them to question facets of a masculine identity learned as children and now taken for granted. This questioning goes beyond encouraging men to be sensitive; the "liberated" man who has rediscovered crying may still be a tyrant.

Of course, there are many ways to proceed in reeducating men about masculinity. We have known some counselors who, with almost evangelical fervor, deliver their message as if hurling a rock. With this approach, men are exhorted, cajoled, and preached at to change attitudes on masculinity. In its most extreme form, this approach liberally sprinkles abuser counseling groups with philosophically oriented sessions reminiscent of men's liberation groups. We believe this zealous attempt to convert abusers speaks to only a minority of abusers who are receptive to this approach. We propose an alternate approach.

Rather than simply exhorting men to change their attitudes and belief systems in the hope that this will produce changes in overt behavior, we think it is more productive to arrange for a change in behavior from the start. We do this in a variety of ways, some of which are not so apparent because they are part of the structure and process of helping rather than identifiable content. For example, when an abuser asks us for help, we insist he enter a group of his peers. The demand that a man be vulnerable to other men and that he learn to ask for and receive help from men is intended to violate male conditioning. We hope that, as men learn to broaden the range of their supports, they will lessen their oppressive and exclusive dependency on their partners. Second, an abuser in a group of his peers experiences being accountable to men on male abuse of women. This valuable experience is exceptionally rare outside of a counseling program. Third, and also rare outside a counseling milieu, abusers in a group receive rewards and support from other men for nonabusive, healthy behavior.

RELATIONSHIPS BETWEEN VICTIMS' AND BATTERERS' COUNSELORS

We have worked with abusers in settings in which victim and abuser counseling exist in the same program. Although there are definite advantages to this approach, there are some thorny issues rising from their coexistence. In this field, we have learned that relationships between victims' and offenders' counselors should never be taken for granted. Indeed, some of the most intense stressors in this work, and some of the most explosive interactions among staff, seem born of the close proximity of victims' and offenders' services and the frequent need to coordinate counseling plans. We have sometimes strolled, and at other times tread carefully, through this mine field only to trigger an explosion hurtful to therapists and damaging to communication channels.

One peculiar phenomenon is the tendency of men's and women's counselors to assume or adopt their clients' agendas. This drama is played out with remarkable similarity to what we witness occurring between batterers and battered women who are in counseling. Victims in counseling access a lot of anger over past abuse. At some point in counseling they may risk venting this anger at their partners. With great clarity, they begin to see their partners' past and present controlling and oppressive behavior. They become understandably suspicious and skeptical of these men. By learning to trust their own perceptions and opinions, they strengthen their identities separate from their partners. By learning to say no to their partners, they begin to draw limits or personal boundaries. We regard these changes as signs of recovery and health.

Abusers are in a very different position. They want to be forgiven and, most of all, they want to be trusted again. They believe this should be automatic since they are enrolled in or have completed abuse counseling. They have difficulty accepting women's anger and skepticism and are often bewildered by the changes in their partners. Interestingly, there is a noticeable shift in relationship power dynamics; men desperately want something that women are not ready or willing to give.

A remarkably similar dynamic can be played out in the relationships between abusers' and victims' counselors. Victims' counselors (usually women) often share their clients' anger and outrage, support their struggle for independence, encourage them in strengthening personal boundaries and in saying no. Victims regularly inform their counselors of abusers' actions, some of which continue to be controlling and oppressive, even if physical violence has ceased. Victims' counselors can become skeptical of the usefulness of batterers' counseling.

Batterers' counselors often face a difficult predicament. Since effective counseling with any client requires some form of bonding, counselors work hard to view these men as multidimensional human beings, complete with strengths and weaknesses, instead of unidimensional, stereotypical batterers. Observers of these counselor-client relationships may wonder if the counselor is indiscriminate in accepting every facet of the man and in advocating for him. When abuser counselors are male, victims' counselors and battered women may be uncomfortably aware of their gender, and wonder if batterers' groups are nothing more than men's clubs where men (including therapists) excuse each other's behavior, or even encourage abuse and the patriarchal system. Where suspicion of batterers' counselors and their counseling approach is pronounced, abuser counselors may retreat to a defensive, hypersensitive, and hostile stance. Victims' counselors, wondering if this in itself is not evidence of guilt, may increase their suspicion and criticism of batterers' counseling, to which men's counselors may respond with increased irritation. An ever-deepening spiral of recrimination, suspicion, guilt, anger, defensiveness, and impaired communication can develop out of which it is difficult to emerge.

In many of these situations, there is a problematic history preceding these events. What precedes such an event often consists of one or more of the following:

(1) Each party lacks knowledge of the objectives, goals, philosophical underpinnings, and content of the other's approach. This can result in the perception (correct or incorrect) that staff are working against each other. Misunderstandings and stereotyping may abound but may not be expressed.

(2) There is a lack of honest communication in the personal realm. Counselors who hide their personal struggles related to abuse counseling chain themselves to an unhealthy role. The demands of that role are that therapists always appear strong, decisive, and knowledgeable. This caricature of a therapist makes it easy to be angry at and suspicious of those who hide their humanity behind a persona.

(3) Similarly, in a staff that is highly politicized, there may be an unspoken but powerful rule that all counselors be politically correct. Because there are often shades of gray in real-life situations, the reality of some situations will conflict with political dogma. When counselors perceive a prohibition against voicing opinions deviating from a party line, resentment and paranoia will fester.

(4) There has been no real legitimation by staff for the existence of offender counseling in the agency. Though program planners and funders may have legitimized the agency's model, some staff may be covertly ambivalent (or even quite unhappy) about the use of scarce wife abuse funding for abuser services. Battered women's counselors in particular, with their awareness of scarce resources and the ever-present need for more victim's services, can have understandable difficulty with this.

Abuser counseling programs lacking a victims' services element are not immune to these issues and may have less opportunity to resolve them. Since responsible counseling of abusers necessitates that the program initiate and maintain contact with victims, and since case consultation with battered women's counselors is desirable and necessary, we believe that similar dynamics will occur. The difference (and perhaps advantage) is that they then fall under the rubric of interagency relations and provide for a more tolerable interpersonal distance. However, because there may be less recognized need to resolve the issues, there is a disadvantage in that they are more difficult to address.

MEN, WIFE ABUSE, AND WOMEN'S ANGER

While writing this section, we are acutely aware that our perceptions and thoughts are shaped by our white, male life experiences. In having never been women with a keen personal awareness of oppression, we have never experienced women's outrage over the treatment of women in this society. Our attempts to understand women's reality will always be limited by the boundaries of our male existence. Hence we are left trying to understand women's experiences of violence from the perspectives of the observer and the listener. We must rely on women's testimony.

We must admit that, despite our support for liberal or feminist perspectives, we are somewhat anxious and uncomfortable in the presence of women's anger. Anger in general is unpleasant; the testimony of women's anger over abuse and oppression carries a certain hard edge for us. We believe this discomfort is experienced by most men, though how it is expressed will vary from one man to another. We believe the discomfort arises from knowing that we are members of a class that is the object of that anger. When one of our clients abuses his partner and battered women's counselors vent their anger, one part of us wants to profess both our innocence and our estrangement from that man. We would like to say, "I didn't do it! It's not me!" or "I tried my best, but he won't change." Another, more honest part of us knows that we are members of the same class as the perpetrator, that we participate as men in an atrocious social structure, and that there is a measure of validity to the notion of "corporate guilt."

One possible reaction is to become defensive; we can try to shut out the voices of women's anger. If we adopt this stance we may be defending against criticism of the ineffectiveness of abuser counseling. Since we still lack a consensus on the usefulness of our approach, our position just may be indefensible. On a more personal level, we will be trying to avoid our sense of corporate guilt and shame over men's evil deeds. We believe the extent to which these occur is the extent to which victim and abuser counselors will have stormy relationships. What we have learned from women about abuse and women's anger leads us to offer three observations that may be relevant to those counseling abusers. Regardless of our discomfort, women's anger is justified. It has a strong basis in reality. It makes an important statement, it has the potential to spark social change, and it is healthy. Second, we cannot realistically expect that anger will always be focused only on those particular men who commit violence against their partners; because of its immensity, it will spill over. Third, violence is only the most dramatic expression of male domination. There are myriad ways in which this domination is exercised. Consequently, we can expect some level of generalized anger at "maleness" to permeate many female counselors' lives.

To complicate matters somewhat, we also believe that all counselors ought to assume personal responsibility and be held accountable for the manner in which they express their feelings. "Just cause" to be angry is not license to express this emotion in destructive ways. We demand this much from our clients; should we not also expect this of ourselves and our colleagues?

FEEDBACK FROM VICTIMS' SERVICES

In our workshops, we notice an unfortunate tendency of some helpers with paper credentials who work for established community services to ignore, minimize, dismiss, or even denigrate the insights of the "battered women's movement," shelter workers, and feminist thinkers. On occasion, when we have asked counselors about their preparatory work in establishing constructive relationships with, say, the local women's shelter, they have seemed puzzled. Even worse, some have dismissed the shelter workers as an incredible militant fringe and have rejected the notion of cultivating positive relationships with these groups.

We believe that assaultive men's counseling programs that isolate themselves from victims' services pay a price for this isolation: They miss sources of valuable information, abandon chances to build coordinated community responses to the problem, and contribute to the endangerment of victims. There are several potential advantages to cultivating relationships with victims' services:

(1) It provides the opportunity to receive feedback on the short-term outcome of abuser counseling from someone other than the abuser. Is a client's abuse ceasing, decreasing, or escalating?

(2) Over a longer term, feedback from victims' services allows for a rough preliminary measure of the program's effectiveness.

(3) It provides the opportunity for regular feedback on the manner in which abusers use or misuse material they have learned in counseling.

(4) It provides a chance to coordinate counseling plans.

(5) It provides an opportunity to educate other services and thereby avoid misunderstandings about abuser counseling programs. The better the program is understood by victims' counselors, the more chance there is of them basing a decision about whether or not to support such a program on fact rather than misinformation.

Beyond the obvious practical advantages of cultivating relationships and soliciting feedback from victims' services, there is another aspect to this issue. We believe it is patently arrogant and unwise to ignore the experiences, opinions, and contributions of any group who has dealt so long with the victims of men's violence.

CONCLUDING REMARKS

We began our work with wife batterers with the hope that we could make a solid contribution to ending violence against women and children. We entered this work with unbridled optimism. Despite our experience as therapists, we were naive. We thought changing batterers would be easier than it turned out to be. The more seasoned we became, the more distant our goal seemed. Although we witnessed many men make astounding changes, others made more modest gains, and still others failed. In this work we always paddle upstream. Our efforts seem dwarfed by years of learning in the family and in our culture. The gains made by men in a handful of hours in our programs sometimes seem insignificant, for these men leave us to live in a culture rife with misogyny and violence.

We also began our work with the unspoken belief that we could do it with only minimal impact on or change to ourselves personally. We felt, since our ideals were noble, we did not have to face the same issues our clients faced. We also felt that our professional roles might give us some distance from the fear, sadness, and anger that is so much a part of the lives of men and women in violent situations. Again, we were naive. Those of us who are male have had to address and struggle with our own male socialization, our own power and control issues in relationships, and, at times, our own anger. We have had to explore new ways of relating to other men, women, children, and our own partners. There have not been many road maps to lead us, other than our own emotions and the knowledge gained from our interactions with others. We have had to learn to care for ourselves more effectively to deal with the fears and pressures of our work.

Finally, we discovered that change meant more than simply stopping the physical violence. In grappling with abuse we come face to face with the dark need to dominate others. Our work spawns an unsettling question. Is our job complete when a man has stopped physically hurting his partner and children? Whereas we once congratulated ourselves when an abuser ceased his violence, our attention is now drawn to the emotional and psychological methods of control. From our observations and from conversations with our colleagues, we wonder if batterers in counseling give up their physical abuse only to rely exclusively on psychological methods of control. These acts seem least amenable to our interventions. Since psychological and emotional abuse may leave no visible bruises but can be as debilitating to victims as physical assaults, we cannot be complacent. The enormity of our work is apparent. We are only beginners in helping men on the road to peace.

REFERENCES

Adams, D. (1988a). Stages of anti-sexist awareness and change for men who batter. In L. Dickstein & C. Nadelson (Eds.), *Family violence.* Washington, DC: Appi.

Adams, D. (1988b). Treatment models of men who batter: A profeminist analysis. In K. Yllö & M. Bograd (Eds.), *Feminist perspectives on wife abuse.* Newbury Park, CA: Sage.

Adams, D., & McCormick, A. J. (1982). Men unlearning violence: A group approach based on the collective model. In M. Roy (Ed.), *The abusive partner.* New York: Van Nostrand Reinhold.

Adams, D., & Penn, P. (1981). *Men in groups: The socialization and resocialization of men who batter.* Paper presented at the annual meeting of the American Orthopsychiatric Association.

Aguilera, D. C., & Messick, J. M. (1978). *Crisis intervention: Theory and methodology.* Saint Louis, MO: C. V. Mosby.

Alberti, R. E., & Emmons, M. L. (1978). *Your perfect right: A guide to assertive behavior* (3rd ed.). San Luis Obispo, CA: Impact.

Allen, C., & Straus, M. (1980). Resources, power, and husband-wife violence. In M. Straus & G. Hotaling (Eds.), *The social causes of husband-wife violence.* Minneapolis: University of Minnesota Press.

Allgood, R., Butler, B. T., Byers, D., et al. (1978). *The assessment and prediction of dangerous behavior: Factors affecting decision making in an interdisciplinary team* (Working Papers in Forensic Psychiatry, No. 9). Toronto: Metropolitan Toronto Forensic Services.

Averill, J. R. (1979). Anger. In H. Howe & R. Dienstbier (Eds.), *Nebraska Symposium on Motivation, 1978.* Lincoln: University of Nebraska Press.

Bales, J. (1988). New laws limiting duty to protect. *American Psychological Association Monitor, 19*(6), 18.

Balgopal, P. R., & Vassil, T. J. (1983). *Groups in social work: An ecological perspective.* New York: Macmillan.

Ball, M. (1977). Issues of violence in family casework. *Social Casework, 58,* 3-12.

Bandura, A. (1965). Influence of models' reinforcement contingencies on the acquisition of imitative responses. *Journal of Personality and Social Psychology, 1,* 589-595.

Bandura, A. (1973). *Aggression: A social learning analysis.* Englewood Cliffs, NJ: Prentice-Hall.

Bandura, A., Ross, D., & Ross, S. (1963a). Imitation of film-mediated aggressive models. *Journal of Abnormal and Social Psychology, 66,* 3-11.

Bandura, A., Ross, D., & Ross, S. (1963b). A comparative test of the status envy, social power, and secondary reinforcement theories of identificatory learning. *Journal of Abnormal and Social Psychology, 67,* 527-534.

Bandura, A., Ross, D., & Ross, S. (1963c). Vicarious reinforcement and imitative learning. *Journal of Abnormal and Social Psychology, 67,* 601-607.

Beck, A. T. (1976). *Cognitive therapy and the emotional disorders.* New York: International Universities Press.

Beck, A. T., Rush, A. J., Shaw, B. F., & Emery, G. (1978). *Cognitive therapy of depression.* New York: Guilford.

Berkowitz, L. (1973). The case for bottling up rage. *Psychology Today, 7,* 24-31.

Bern, E. H., & Bern, L. L. (1984). A group program for men who commit violence towards their wives. *Social Work with Groups, 7*(1), 63-77.

Bernard, J. L., & Bernard, M. L. (1984). The abusive male seeking treatment: Jekyll and Hyde. *Family Relations, 33,* 543-547.

Bernstein, D. A., & Borkevec, T. D. (1973). *Progressive relaxation training.* Champaign, IL: Research Press.

Biaggio, M. K. (1980). Assessment of anger arousal. *Journal of Personality Assessment, 44,* 289-298.

Biaggio, M. K., & Maiuro, R. D. (1985). Recent advances in anger assessment. In C. D. Spielberger & J. N. Butcher (Eds.), *Advances in personality assessment* (Vol. 5). Hillsdale, NJ: Lawrence Erlbaum.

Biaggio, M. K., Supplee, K., & Curtis, N. (1981). Reliability and validity of four anger scales. *Journal of Personality Assessment, 45*(6), 639-648.

Bograd, M. (1984). Family systems approach to wife battering: A feminist critique. *American Journal of Orthopsychiatry, 54,* 558-568.

Bograd, M. (1986). A feminist examination of family systems models of violence against women in the family. In M. Ault-Riche (Ed.), *Women and family therapy.* Rockville, MD: Aspen Systems.

Bograd, M. (1988). Feminist perspectives on wife abuse: An introduction. In K. Yllö & M. Bograd (Eds.), *Feminist perspectives on wife abuse.* Newbury Park, CA: Sage.

Boudouris, J. (1971). Homicide in the family. *Journal of Marriage and the Family, 33,* 667-676.

Bowker, L. H. (1983). Marital rape: A distinct syndrome. *Social Casework, 64*(6), 347-352.

Breines, W., & Gordon, L. (1983). The new scholarship on family violence. *Signs: Journal of Women in Culture and Society, 8,* 490-531.

Brennan, A. F. (1985). Political and psychosocial issues for spouse abusers: Implications for treatment. *Psychotherapy, 22*(3), 643-654.

Briere, J. (1987). Predicting self-reported likelihood of battering: Attitudes and childhood experiences. *Journal of Research in Personality, 21,* 61-69.

Briere, J., Corne, S., Runtz, M., & Malamuth, N. (1984). *The Rape Arousal Survey: Predicting actual and potential sexual aggression in a university population.* Paper presented at the annual meeting of the American Psychological Association, Toronto.

Browne, A. (1983). *When battered women kill.* Unpublished doctoral dissertation, University of Experimenting Colleges and Universities, Cincinnati, OH.

Browne, A. (1986). Assault and homicide at home: When battered women kill. In M. J. Sakes & L. Saxe (Eds.), *Advances in applied social psychology* (Vol. 3). Hillsdale, NJ: Lawrence Erlbaum.

Browning, J. J. (1983). *Violence against intimates: Toward a profile of the wife assaulter.* Unpublished doctoral dissertation, University of British Columbia, Vancouver.

Browning, J. J., & Dutton, D. (1986). Assessment of wife assault with the Conflict Tactics Scale: Using couple data to quantify the differential reporting effect. *Journal of Marriage and the Family, 48,* 375-379.

Brygger, M. P., & Edelson, J. L. (1987). The domestic abuse project: A multisystems intervention in women battering. *Journal of Interpersonal Violence, 2*(3), 324-336.

Burt, M. (1980). Cultural myths and supports for rape. *Journal of Personality and Social Psychology, 38,* 217-230.

Buss, A. H., & Durkee, A. (1957). An inventory for assessing different kinds of hostility. *Journal of Consulting Psychology, 21,* 343-349.

Caplan, G. (1961). *An approach to community mental health.* New York: Grune & Stratton.

Caplan, G. (1964). *Principles of preventive psychiatry.* New York: Basic Books.

Carlson, B. E. (1984). Causes and maintenance of domestic violence: An ecological analysis. *Social Services Review, 58,* 569-587.

Carroll, J. C. (1977). The intergenerational transmission of family violence: Long-term effect of aggressive behavior. *Aggressive Behavior, 3,* 289-299.

Chapman, J., & Gates, M. (Eds.). (1978). *The victimization of women.* Beverly Hills, CA: Sage.

Check, J.V. P., & Malamuth, N. M. (1983). *The Hostility Toward Women Scale.* Paper presented at the 91st Annual Meeting of the American Psychological Association, Anaheim, CA.

Chimbos, P. D. (1978). *Marital violence: A study of interspousal homicide.* San Francisco: R & E Research Associates.

Coleman, D. H., & Straus, M. (1979, August). *Alcohol abuse and family violence.* Paper presented at the annual meeting of the American Sociological Association, Boston.

Coleman, K. (1980). Conjugal violence: What 33 men report. *Journal of Marital and Family Therapy, 6,* 207-213.

Cook, D. R., & Frantz-Cook, A. (1984). A systemic treatment approach to wife battering. *Journal of Marriage and Family Therapy, 10,* 83-93.

Currie, D. D. (1983). A Toronto model. *Social Work with Groups, 6,* 179-188.

Davidson, T. (1978). *Conjugal crime: Understanding and changing the wife-beating pattern.* New York: Hawthorne.

Deschner, J. P. (1984). *The hitting habit: Anger control for battering couples.* New York: Free Press.

Deschner, J. P., McNeil, J. S., & Moore, M. G. (1986). A treatment model for batterers. *Social Casework, 67*(1), 55-60.

Dobash, R. E., & Dobash, R. (1979). *Violence against wives: A case against the patriarchy.* New York: Free Press.

Dutton, D. G. (1983). A nested ecological theory of male violence towards intimates. In P. Caplan (Ed.), *Feminist psychology in transition*. Montreal: Eden.

Dutton, D. G. (1986). Wife assaulters' explanation for assault: The neutralization of self-punishment. *Canadian Journal of Behavioral Science, 18*(4), 381-390.

Edelson, J. L. (1984). Working with men who batter. *Social Work, 29*, 237-242.

Edelson, J. L., & Brygger, M. P. (1984, August). Gender differences in reporting of battering incidents. Paper presented at the Second National Conference for Family Violence Researchers, University of New Hampshire, Durham.

Edelson, J. L., Miller, D. M., & Stone, G. W. (1983). *Counseling men who batter: Group leaders' handbook*. Albany, NY: Men's Coalition Against Battering.

Edelson, J. L., Miller, D. M., Stone, G. W., & Chapman, D. G. (1985). Group treatment for men who batter. *Social Work Research and Abstracts, 21*(3), 18-21.

Eisenberg, S. E., & Micklow, P. (1979). The assaulted wife: "Catch-22" revisited. *Women's Rights Law Reporter, 3*, 138-161.

Elbow, M. (1977). Theoretical considerations of violent marriages. *Social Casework, 58*, 515-526.

Elliot, F. A. (1976, July). The neurology of explosive rage: The dyscontrol syndrome. *Practitioner*, p. 217.

Ellis, A. (1977). The basic clinical theory of rational-emotive therapy. In A. Ellis & R. Grieger (Eds.), *Handbook of rational-emotive therapy*. New York: Springer.

Evans, D. R., & Stangeland, M. (1971). Development of the Reaction Inventory to measure arousal. *Psychological Reports, 29*, 412-414.

Everstine, D., & Everstine, L. (1983). *People in crisis: Strategic therapeutic interventions*. New York: Brunner/Mazel.

Fagan, J. A., Stewart, D. K., & Hansen, K. Y. (1983). Violent men or violent husbands. In D. Finkelhor, R. J. Gelles, G. T. Hotaling, & M. A. Straus (Eds.), *The dark side of families: Current family violence research*. Beverly Hills, CA: Sage.

Faulk, M. (1974). Men who assault their wives. *Medicine, Science, and the Law, 14*(3), 180-183.

Faulk, M. (1977). Men who assault their wives. In M. Roy (Ed.), *Battered women: A psychosocial study of domestic violence*. New York: Van Nostrand Reinhold.

Feazell, C. S., Mayers, R. S., & Deschner, J. (1984). Services for men who batter: Implications for programs and policies. *Family Relations, 33*, 217-223.

Ferguson, T. J., & Rule, B. G. (1983). An attributional perspective on anger and aggression. In R. G. Gein & E. I. Donnerstein (Eds.), *Aggression: Theoretical and empirical reviews* (Vol. 1). New York: Academic Press.

Ferraro, K. J. (1984, August). *An existential approach to battering*. Paper presented at the Second National Conference for Family Violence Researchers, University of New Hampshire, Durham.

Feshbach, S. (1964). The function of aggression and the regulation of aggressive drive. *Psychological Review, 71*, 257-272.

Finkelhor, D. (1984). *Child sexual abuse: New theory and research*. New York: Free Press.

Finkelhor, D. (1985). Violence: The myth of the stranger, the reality of the family. In E. Aronowitz & R. Sussman (Eds.), *Mental health and violence*. Canton, MA: Prodist.

Finkelhor, D., Gelles, R., Hotaling, G., & Straus, M. (Eds.). (1983). *The dark side of families: Current family violence research.* Beverly Hills, CA: Sage.

Fitch, F. J., & Papantonio, A. (1983). Men who batter: Some pertinent characteristics. *Journal of Nervous and Mental Disorders, 171*(3), 190-192.

Foy, D. W., Eisler, R. M., & Pinkston, S. (1975). Modeled assertion in a case of explosive rage. *Journal of Behaviour Therapy and Experimental Psychiatry, 6*, 135-137.

Frank, P. B., & Houghton, B. D. (1982). *Confronting the batterer: A guide to the Spouse Abuse Workshop.* New City, NY: Volunteer Counseling Service of Rockland County.

Frieze, I. H. (1983). Investigating the causes and consequences of marital rape. *Signs: Journal of Women in Culture and Society, 8*(3), 532-553.

Gaguin, D. (1978). Spouse abuse: Data from the national crime survey. *Victimology: An International Journal, 2*, 635.

Ganley, A. L. (1981a). Counseling programs for men who batter: Elements of effective programs. *Response to Victimization of Women and Children, 4*, 3-4.

Ganley, A. L. (1981b). *Court mandated counseling for men who batter: Participants' and trainers' manuals.* Washington, DC: Center for Women's Policy Studies.

Ganley, A. L., & Harris, L. (1978). *Domestic violence: Issues in designing and implementing programs for male batterers.* Paper presented at the annual meeting of the American Psychological Association, Toronto.

Gayford, J. J. (1975). Wife battering: A preliminary survey of 100 cases. *British Medical Journal, 30*(1), 194-197.

Geller, J. (1982). Conjoint therapy: Staff training and treatment of the abuser and abused. In M. Roy (Ed.), *The abusive partner.* New York: Van Nostrand Reinhold.

Gelles, R. J. (1973). Child abuse as psychopathology: A sociological critique and reformulation. *American Journal of Orthopsychiatry, 43*, 611-621.

Gelles, R. J. (1974). *The violent home.* Beverly Hills, CA: Sage.

Gelles, R. J. (1979). *Family violence.* Beverly Hills, CA: Sage.

Gelles, R. J. (1980). Violence in the family: A review of research in the seventies. *Journal of Marriage and the Family, 42*, 873-885.

Gelles, R. J. (1985). Family violence. *Annual Review of Sociology, 11*, 347-367.

Giles-Sims, J. (1983). *Wife battering: A systems theory approach.* New York: Guilford.

Golan, N. (1978). *Treatment in crisis situations.* New York: Free Press.

Goldenberg, I., & Goldenberg, H. (1985). *Family therapy: An overview* (2nd ed.). Monterey, CA: Brooks/Cole.

Goldstein, D., & Rosenbaum, A. (1985). An evaluation of the self-esteem of maritally violent men. *Family Relations, 34*(3), 425-428.

Gondolf, E. W. (1985a). Anger and oppression in men who batter: Empiricist and feminist perspectives and their implications for research. *Victimology: An International Journal, 10*, 311-324.

Gondolf, E. W. (1985b). Fighting for control: A clinical assessment of men who batter. *Social Casework, 66*(1), 48-54.

Gondolf, E. W. (1985c). *Men who batter: An integrated approach for stopping wife abuse.* Holmes Beach, FL: Learning Publications.

Gondolf, E. W., & Russell, D.E.H. (1986). The case against anger control treatment programs for batterers. *Response to Victimization of Women and Children, 9*(3), 2-5.

Goode, W. J. (1971). Force and violence in the family. *Journal of Marriage and the Family, 33,* 624-636.

Groth, N. A. (1979). *Men who rape: The psychology of the offender.* New York: Plenum.

Halpern, M. (1983). *Treatment of the male batterer: The BWA program.* Paper presented at the 91st Annual Meeting of the American Psychological Association, Anaheim, CA.

Hamilton, J. R., & Freeman, H. (Eds.). (1982). *Dangerousness: Psychiatric assessment and management.* Oxford: Alden.

Hanks, S., & Rosenbaum, P. (1977). Battered women: A study of women who live with violent alcohol-abusing men. *American Journal of Orthopsychiatry, 47,* 291-306.

Hanneke, C. R., & Shields, N. (1981). *Patterns of family and non-family violence: An approach to the study of violent husbands.* Paper presented at the National Conference for Family Violence Researchers, Durham, NH.

Hanneke, C. R., & Shields, N. A. (1985). Marital rape: Implications for the helping professions. *Social Casework, 66*(8), 451-458.

Hathaway, S. R., & McKinley, S. C. (1943). *The Minnesota Multiphasic Personality Inventory.* Minneapolis: University of Minnesota Press.

Hathaway, S. R., & Meehl, P. E. (1951). *An atlas for the clinical use of the MMPI.* Minneapolis: University of Minnesota Press.

Hauck, P. A. (1974). *Overcoming frustration and anger.* Philadelphia: Westminster.

Henley, N. (1986). *Body politics: Power, sex and nonverbal communication.* Englewood Cliffs, NJ: Prentice-Hall.

Hilberman, E., & Munson, K. (1978). Sixty battered women. *Victimology: An International Journal, 3,* 460-471.

Hinton, J. W. (Ed.). (1983). *Dangerousness: Problems of assessment and prediction.* Winchester, MA: Allen & Unwin.

Hoffman, L. (1981). *Foundations of family therapy.* New York: Basic Books.

Holmes, T. H., & Rahe, R. H. (1967). The Social Readjustment Rating Scale. *Journal of Psychosomatic Research, 11,* 213-218.

Hornung, C. A., McCullough, B. C., & Sugimoto, T. (1981). Status relationships in marriage: Risk factors in spouse abuse. *Journal of Marriage and the Family, 43,* 675-692.

Hoshmand, L. T. (1987). Judgment of anger problems by clients and therapists: Study of batterers and nonbatterers. *Journal of Interpersonal Violence, 2*(3), 251-263.

Hudson, W. H., & McIntosh, S. R. (1981). The assessment of spouse abuse: Two quantifiable dimensions. *Journal of Marriage and the Family, 43*(4), 873-885.

Huey, W. C., & Rank, R. C. (1984). Effects of counselor and peer-led group assertive training on black adolescent aggression. *Journal of Counseling Psychology, 31*(1), 95-98.

Jacobson, R. (1938). *Progressive relaxation.* Chicago: University of Chicago Press.

Jouriles, E. N., & O'Leary, K. D. (1985). Interspousal reliability of reports of marital violence. *Journal of Consulting and Clinical Psychology, 53*(3), 419-421.

Kozol, H. (1975). The diagnosis of dangerousness. In S. Pasternak (Ed.), *Violence and victims.* New York: Spectrum.

Lange, A. J., & Jakubowski, P. (1976). *Responsible assertive behavior.* Champaign, IL: Research Press.

LaViolette, A. D., Barnett, O. W., & Miller, C. L. (1984, August). *A classification of wife abusers on the BEM Sex Role Inventory.* Paper presented at the Second National Conference for Family Violence Researchers, University of New Hampshire, Durham.

Law Enforcement Assistance Administration. (1981). *The report from the conference on intervention programs for men who batter.* Washington, DC: U.S. Department of Justice.

Lewis, B. Y. (1987). Psychosocial factors related to wife abuse. *Journal of Family Violence, 2*(1), 1-10.

Lion, J. R. (1977). Clinical aspects of wifebattering. In M. Roy (Ed.), *Battered women: A psychosociological study of domestic violence.* New York: Van Nostrand Reinhold.

Macoby, E. E., & Jacklin, A. N. (1974). *The psychology of sex differences.* Palo Alto, CA: Stanford University Press.

Maiuro, R. D., Cahn, T. S., Vitaliano, P. P., Wagner, B. C., & Zegree, J. B. (1988). Anger, hostility, and depression in domestically violent versus generally assaultive men and nonviolent control subjects. *Journal of Consulting and Clinical Psychology, 56*(1), 17-23.

Maiuro, R. D., Vitaliano, P. P., & Cahn, T. S. (1987). A brief measure for the assessment of anger and aggression. *Journal of Interpersonal Violence, 2*(2), 166-178.

Makman, R. S. (1978). Some clinical aspects of inter-spousal violence. In J. M. Eekelaar & S. N. Katz (Eds.), *Family violence: An international and interdisciplinary study.* Toronto: Butterworths.

Malamuth, N. M. (1984). Aggression against women: Cultural and individual causes. In N. M. Malamuth & E. Donnerstein (Eds.), *Pornography and sexual aggression.* New York: Academic Press.

Margolin, G., John, R. S., & Gleberman, L. (1988). Affective responses to conflictual discussions in violent and nonviolent couples. *Journal of Consulting and Clinical Psychology, 56*(1), 24-33.

Martin, D. (1976). *Battered wives of America.* San Francisco: Glide.

Martin, D. (1981). *Battered wives.* San Francisco: Volcano.

Masamura, W. T. (1979). Wife abuse and other forms of aggression. *Victimology: An International Journal, 4*(1), 46-59.

McClelland, D. C. (1975). *Power: The inner experience.* New York: John Wiley.

McGrath, C. (1979). The crisis of domestic order. *Socialist Review, 9,* 11-30.

McNeely, R. L., & Robinson-Simpson, G. (1987). The truth about domestic violence: A falsely framed issue. *Social Work,* 485-490.

McNeill, M. (1987). Domestic violence: The skeleton in Tarasoff's closet. In D. J. Sonkin (Ed.), *Domestic violence on trial: Psychological and legal dimensions of family violence.* New York: Springer.

Megargee, E. I. (1970). The prediction of violence with psychological tests. In C. D. Spielberger (Ed.), *The control of aggression and violence.* New York: Academic Press.

Meichenbaum, D. H. (1977). *Cognitive-behavior modification.* New York: Plenum.

Monahan, J. (1981). *Predicting violent behavior: An assessment of clinical techniques.* Beverly Hills, CA: Sage.

Money, J., & Ehrhardt, A. A. (1972). *Man and woman, boy and girl: Differentiation and dimorphism of gender identity from conception to maturity.* Baltimore: Johns Hopkins University Press.

Moreno, K. J., Fuhrman, A., Brown, J., & Allred, K. (1987, August). *Hostility in depression.* Paper presented at the annual meeting of the American Psychological Association, New York.

Neidig, P., & Freidman, D. H. (1984). *Spouse abuse: A treatment program for couples.* Champaign, IL: Research Press.

NiCarthy, G., Merriam, K., & Coffman, S. (1984). *Talking it out: A guide to groups for abused women.* Washington, DC: Seal.

Northen, H. (1969). *Social work with groups.* New York: Columbia University Press.

Novaco, R. W. (1975). *Anger control.* Lexington, MA: Lexington.

Novaco, R. W. (1977). Stress inoculation: A cognitive therapy for anger and its application to a case of depression. *Journal of Consulting and Clinical Psychology, 45,* 600-608.

Novaco, R. W. (1978). Anger and coping with stress: Cognitive behavioral interventions. In J. P. Foreyt & D. P. Rathjen (Eds.), *Cognitive behavior therapy: Research and application.* New York: Plenum.

Novak, S., & Galaway, B. (1983). *Domestic Abuse Intervention Project: Final report.* Unpublished manuscript.

Oates, M. (1979). A classification of child abuse and its relation to treatment prognosis. *Child Abuse and Neglect, 3,* 907-915.

O'Brien, J. E. (1971). Violence in divorce prone families. *Journal of Marriage and the Family, 33,* 692-698.

Owens, D., & Straus, M. (1975). Childhood violence and adult approval of violence. *Aggressive Behavior, 1,* 193-211.

Pagelow, M. (1981). *Women battering: Victims and their experiences.* Beverly Hills, CA: Sage.

Patai, F. (1982). Pornography and women battering: Dynamic similarities. In M. Roy (Ed.), *The abusive partner: An analysis of domestic battering.* New York: Van Nostrand Reinhold.

Paymar, M., & Pence, E. (1985). *Facilitator's guide to an educational curriculum for court mandated men who batter.* Duluth, MN: Domestic Abuse Intervention Project.

Pence, E. (1985). *The justice system's response to domestic assault cases: A guide for policy development.* Duluth, MN: Domestic Abuse Intervention Project.

Pence, E., & Paymar, M. (Producers), & Duff, P. (Director). (1985). *Power and control: Tactics of men who batter* [Film]. Duluth: Minnesota Program Development, Inc.

Pence, E., & Shepard, M. (1988). Integrating feminist theory and practice: The challenge of the battered women's movement. In K. Yllö & M. Bograd (Eds.), *Feminist perspectives on wife abuse.* Newbury Park, CA: Sage.

Pesner, J. (1985). *Psychologist as cop.* Paper presented at the 93rd Annual Meeting of the American Psychological Association, Los Angeles.

Pirog-Good, M., & Stets-Kealey, J. (1985). Male batterers and battering prevention programs: A national survey. *Response to Victimization of Women and Children, 8,* 8-12.

Pleck, J. (1981). *The myth of masculinity.* Cambridge: MIT Press.

Poirier, A. C., & Gagn, J. (Producers), & Poirier, A. C. (Director). (1980). *A scream from silence* [Film]. Montreal: National Film Board of Canada.

Prescott, S., & Letko, C. (1977). Battered women: A social psychological perspective. In M. Roy (Ed.), *Battered women: A psychosociological study of domestic violence.* New York: Van Nostrand Reinhold.

Ptacek, J. (1988). Why do men batter their wives? In K. Yllö & M. Bograd (Eds.), *Feminist perspectives on wife abuse.* Newbury Park, CA: Sage.

Purdy, F., & Nickle, N. (1981). Practice principles for working with groups of men who batter. *Social Work with Groups, 4,* 111-112.

Quinsey, V. L., & Ambtman, R. (1978). *Variables affecting psychiatrists' and teachers' assessments of the dangerousness of mentally ill offenders.* Paper presented at the annual meeting of the Canadian Psychological Association, Ottawa, Ontario.

Rapoport, L. (1970). Crisis intervention as a mode of brief treatment. In R. W. Roberts & R. H. Nee (Eds.), *Theories of social casework.* Chicago: University of Chicago Press.

RAVEN. (1980). *A presentation of the RAVEN project goals and objectives.* Unpublished proposal.

Ray, J. J. (1986). Assertiveness as authoritarianism and dominance. *Journal of Social Psychology, 126*(6), 809-810.

Reilly, P., & Grusznski, R. (1984). A structured didactic model for men for controlling family violence. *International Journal of Offender Therapy and Comparative Criminology, 28*(3), 223-235.

Rimm, D., Hill, G., Brown, N., & Stuart, J. (1974). Group-assertive training in treatment of expression of inappropriate anger. *Psychological Reports, 34,* 791-798.

Roberts, A. R. (1984). Intervention with the abusive partner. In A. R. Roberts (Ed.), *Battered women and their families.* New York: Springer.

Rosen, G. (1977) *The relaxation book.* Englewood Cliffs, NJ: Prentice-Hall.

Rosenbaum, A. (1986). Group treatment for abusive men: Process and outcome. *Psychotherapy, 23*(4), 607-612.

Rosenbaum, A., & O'Leary, K. D. (1981a). Children: The unintended victims of marital violence. *American Journal of Orthopsychiatry, 51,* 692-699.

Rosenbaum, A., & O'Leary, K. D. (1981b). Marital violence: Characteristics of abusive couples. *Journal of Consulting and Clinical Psychology, 49,* 63-71.

Rosenberg, M. (1965). *Society and the adolescent self-image.* Princeton, NJ: Princeton University Press.

Rounsaville, B. J. (1978). Theories in marital violence: Evidence from a study of battered women. *Victimology: An International Journal, 3*(1), 11-31.

Roy, M. (1977). A current survey of 150 cases. In M. Roy (Ed.), *Battered women: A psychosociological study of domestic violence.* New York: Van Nostrand Reinhold.

Roy, M. (Ed.). (1982). *The abusing partner: An analysis of domestic battering.* New York: Van Nostrand Reinhold.

Russell, D.E.H. (1982). *Rape in marriage.* New York: Macmillan.

Ryan, G., Lane, S., Davis, J., & Isaac, C. (1987). Juvenile sexual offenders: Development and correction. *Child Abuse and Neglect, 11*(3), 385-395.

San Francisco Family Violence Project. (1982). *Domestic violence is a crime.* San Francisco: Author.

Saunders, D. G. (1982). Counseling the violent husband. In P. A. Keller & L. G. Ritt

(Eds.), *Innovations in clinical practice: A source book.* Sarasota, FL: Professional Resource Exchange.

Saunders, D. G. (1984). Helping husbands who batter. *Social Casework, 65*(6), 347-353.

Saunders, D. G. (1988). Wife abuse, husband abuse, or mutual combat? A feminist perspective on the empirical findings. In K. Yllö & M. Bograd (Eds.), *Feminist perspectives on wife abuse.* Newbury Park, CA: Sage.

Schaef, A. W. (1981). *Women's reality: An emerging female system in a white male society.* San Francisco: Harper & Row.

Schechter, S. (1982). *Women and male violence: The visions and struggles of the battered women's movement.* Boston: South End.

Schuerger, J. M., & Reigle, N. (1988). Personality and biographic data that characterize men who abuse their wives. *Journal of Clinical Psychology, 44*(1), 75-81.

Schultz, L. G. (1960). The wife assaulter. *Corrective Psychiatry and Journal of Social Therapy, 6,* 103-111.

Selby, M. J. (1984). Assessment of violence potential using measures of anger, hostility, and social desirability. *Journal of Personality Assessment, 48*(5), 531-544.

Shainess, N. (1977). Psychological aspects of wifebattering. In M. Roy (Ed.), *Battered women: A psychosociological study of domestic violence.* New York: Van Nostrand Reinhold.

Shipley, W. C. (1940). A self-administering scale for measuring intellectual impairment and deterioration. *Journal of Psychology, 9,* 371-377.

Shotland, R. L., & Straw, N. K. (1976). Bystanders' responses to an assault: When a man attacks a woman. *Journal of Personality and Social Psychology, 34*(5), 990-999.

Shulman, L. (1979). *The skills of helping individuals and groups.* Itasca, IL: F. E. Peacock.

Smith, M. J. (1975). *When I say no, I feel guilty.* New York: Bantam.

Smith, M. J. (1988). *When I say no, I feel guilty* (Cassette Recording). New York.

Snell, J., Rosenwald, R., & Robey, A. (1964). The wifebeater's wife: A study of family interaction. *Archives of General Psychiatry, 11,* 107-112.

Sommers, E. K., & Check, J.V.P. (1987). An empirical investigation of the role of pornography in the verbal and physical abuse of women. *Violence and Victims, 2*(3), 189-209.

Sonkin, D. J. (1986). Clairvoyance vs. common sense: Therapists' duty to warn and protect. *Violence and Victims, 1*(1), 7-22.

Sonkin, D. J. (1987). The assessment of court mandated batterers. In D. J. Sonkin (Ed.), *Domestic violence on trial: Psychological and legal dimensions of family violence.* New York: Springer.

Sonkin, D. J., & Durphy, M. (1982). *Learning to live without violence: A handbook for men.* San Francisco: Volcano.

Sonkin, D. J., Martin, D., & Walker, L. (1985). *The male batterer: A treatment approach.* New York: Springer.

Spence, J., Helmreich, R., & Stapp, J. (1973). A short version of the Attitudes Toward Women Scale (AWS). *Psychonomic Bulletin, 2,* 219-220.

Stacey, W. A., & Shupe, A. (1983). *The family secret: Domestic violence in America.* Boston: Beacon.

Stahly, G. B. (1978). A review of select literature on spousal violence. *Victimology: An International Journal, 2,* 591-607.

Star, B. (1980). Patterns in family violence. *Social Casework, 61*(6), 339-346.

Star, B. (1983). *Helping the abuser: Intervening effectively in family violence.* New York: Family Service Association of America.

Star, B., Clark, C. G., Goetz, K. M., & O'Hara, C. (1979). Psychosocial aspects of wife battering. *Social Casework, 41,* 479-487.

Stark, R., & McEvoy, J. (1970). Middle-class violence. *Psychology Today, 4*(6), 52-54.

Steadman, H. J. (1977). A new look at recidivism among Patuxent inmates. *Bulletin of the American Academy of Psychiatry and the Law, 4,* 200-209.

Steadman, H. J., & Cocozza, J. (1974). *Careers of the criminally insane.* Lexington, MA: Lexington.

Stille, R. G., Malamuth, N., & Schallow, J. (August, 1987). *Prediction of rape proclivity by rape myth attitudes and hostility toward women.* Paper presented at the annual meeting of the American Psychological Association, New York.

Stordeur, R. (1983, November). *A description of the Domestic Abuse Project, Minneapolis.* (Available from Attorney General's Office, Province of Manitoba, Winnipeg, Manitoba, Canada)

Straus, M. (1974). Leveling, civility and violence in the family. *Journal of Marriage and the Family, 36,* 13-39.

Straus, M. (1976). Sexual inequality, cultural norms, and wife beating. *Victimology: An International Journal, 1,* 54-76.

Straus, M. (1978). Wife beating: How common and why. *Victimology: An International Journal, 2,* 443-458.

Straus, M. (1979). Measuring intrafamily conflict and violence: The Conflict Tactics (CT) Scale. *Journal of Marriage and the Family, 41*(1), 75-88.

Straus, M. (1981, July). *A reevaluation of the Conflict Tactics Scale violence measures and some new measures.* Paper presented at the National Conference on Family Violence Research, University of New Hampshire, Durham, NH.

Straus, M., Gelles, R., & Steinmetz, S. (Eds.). (1980). *Behind closed doors: Violence in the American family.* Garden City, NY: Anchor/Doubleday.

Straus, M., & Hotaling, G. (Eds.). (1980). *The social causes of husband-wife violence.* Minneapolis: University of Minnesota Press.

Symonds, A. (1979). Violence against women: The myth of masochism. *American Journal of Psychotherapy, 33*(2), 161-173.

Szinovacz, M. (1983). Using couple data as a methodological tool: The case of marital violence. *Journal of Marriage and the Family, 45,* 633-644.

Tavris, C. (1982). *Anger: The misunderstood emotion.* New York: Simon & Schuster.

Thorman, G. (1980). *Family violence.* New York: Harper & Row.

Thyfault, R. (1980). *Sexual abuse in the battering relationship.* Paper presented at the annual meeting of the Rocky Mountain Psychological Association, Tucson, AZ.

Thyfault, R. (1984). Self defense: Battered women on trial. *California Law Review, 20,* 485-510.

Ulbrich, P., & Huber, J. (1981). Observing parental violence: Distribution and effects. *Journal of Marriage and the Family, 43*(3).

Waldo, M. (1987). Also victims: Understanding and treating men arrested for spouse abuse. *Journal of Counseling and Development, 65*(7), 385-388.

Walker, L. E. (1979). *The battered woman.* New York: Harper & Row.

Walker, L. E. (1983). The battered woman syndrome study. In D. Finkelhor, R. J.

Gelles, G. Hotaling, & M. Straus (Eds.), *The dark side of families: Current family violence research.* Beverly Hills, CA: Sage.

Walker, L. E. (1984). *The battered woman syndrome.* New York: Springer.

Watts, D. L., & Courtois, C. A. (1981). Trends in the treatment of men who commit violence against women. *Personnel and Guidance Journal, 60*(4), 245-249.

Weitzman, J., & Dreen, K. (1982). Wife beating: A view of the marital dyad. *Social Casework, 63,* 259-265.

Werner, P. D., Rose, T. L., & Yesavage, T. A. (1983). Reliability, accuracy and decision-making strategy in clinical prediction of imminent dangerousness. *Journal of Consulting and Clinical Psychology, 51*(6), 815-825.

Wolpe, J. (1973). *The practice of behavior therapy.* New York: Pergamon.

Yalom, I. D. (1975). *The theory and practice of group psychotherapy.* New York: Basic Books.

Zacker, J., & Bard, M. (1977). Further findings on assaultiveness and alcohol use in interpersonal disputes. *American Journal of Community Psychology, 5*(4), 373-383.

INDEX

ABOUT THE AUTHORS

Richard A. Stordeur, M.S.W., was the founding Coordinator of EVOLVE, a Canadian wife assault counseling program in Winnipeg. He has worked in community mental health and as a therapist in private practice, with a special interest in adult survivors of child abuse. He has conducted workshops in the areas of domestic violence and crisis intervention. Most recently, he designed, implemented, and supervised a child sexual abuse treatment program for NEW FACESS, a Winnipeg child welfare agency.

Richard Stille, Ph.D., is a clinical psychologist in private practice in child sexual abuse and domestic violence in Seattle, Washington. Previously, as Clinical Director of North Central Human Services Center in Minot, North Dakota, he was instrumental in developing and coordinating its Domestic Violence Treatment Program and Child Sexual Abuse Treatment Program. He has presented workshops and professional papers nationally in the areas of spouse abuse, child sexual abuse, and forensic psychology.